"Rarely do we get to sit by the side of two spiritual leaders at the height of their powers, to savor their wisdom as they unveil the deep wisdom and compassionate heart in the Book of Psalms. These ancient poems, newly translated, have spoken to seeking souls across the generations. Thanks to Rabbis Riemer and Spitz, they can speak to us now!"

—**Rabbi Bradley Shavit Artson**, Dean of Ziegler School
  of Rabbinic Studies at the American Jewish University

"The readings presented by these two master teachers bring the history and power of the Psalms to life. Prepare to be changed!"

—**Julia Reinhard Lupton**, Distinguished Professor of English,
  The University of California, Irvine

"In DUETS ON PSALMS, two remarkable rabbis breathe new life into the ancient words of The Book of Psalms. Rabbi Elie Spitz and Rabbi Jack Riemer perfectly complement one another offering us close readings, new translations, modern scholarship and timeless wisdom. They give us the tools to allow the words of the Psalms to open our minds and enter our hearts. This illuminating work is a literary journey filled with faith, wisdom, hope, healing, meaning and inspiration."

—**Rabbi Naomi Levy**, author of *Einstein and the Rabbi* and *To Begin Again*

"Not just rabbis and pastors, but everyone who loves the Psalms should own this wonderful book. Rabbi Jack and Rabbi Elie have not only learned the Psalms all their lives, they have lived the Psalms through decades of ministry to people in every possible phase and crisis of life. This book oozes with authentic wisdom that only comes from investing a lifetime in both God's Word and God's world."

—**Pastor Rick Warren**, author of *The Purpose Driven Life*

"In DUETS ON THE PSALMS, Rabbis Riemer and Spitz, two of the master teachers of our times, prove the truth of the rabbinic adage, 'Turn [the Scripture] over and over again, for all is in it,' by providing new readings of familiar texts. Through their multi-layered explorations of and commentaries upon eleven psalms that address the gamut of human emotions and aspirations, they provide the reader with new insights and meanings into the human condition that stimulate the mind but more significantly transform the soul. Theirs is a spiritual masterpiece!"

—**Rabbi David Ellenson**, Chancellor Emeritus of Hebrew Union College-
  Jewish Institute of Religion

"What a brilliant combination. Rabbis Jack Riemer and Elie Spitz, two of Judaism's most inspirational teachers, offer a lifetime of insights on the Bible's most inspired book. A work to read and reread and to return to for inspiration."
—**Rabbi Joseph Telushkin**, author of *Jewish Literacy* and *Words that Hurt Words that Heal*

"The Jewish sages recommend that the Torah not be studied alone but in community, minimally with one other. This injunction has resulted in the tradition of hevrusa—the study partner. Here is a book in which the richness of such study is made visible, and it results in a reading of selected psalms that brings them to life in a dialogical context. There is nothing quite like it in the literature of psalms. The reader is in the presence of minds fruitfully learning from and with one another."
—**Peter Pitzele**, creator of Bibliodrama and author of *Our Father's Wells.*

"An insightful and inspiring modern look at our precious ancient Psalm heritage by two thoughtful rabbis of different generations. Read it and be rewarded."
—**Stuart M. Matlins**, founder & former publisher, Jewish Lights Publishing

"This marvelous dialogue combines poetry and wisdom to make a book that gives both learning and life guidance to any seeking soul."
—**Rabbi David Wolpe**, Rabbi Emeritus of Sinai Temple, Los Angeles, author, *David: The Divided Heart*

"Halleluyah! Take a deep dive into these magnificent poems with two of our most thoughtful teachers of Jewish spirituality, Rabbi Jack Riemer and Rabbi Elie Spitz. You will never read or pray the Psalms the same way again after experiencing these important and uplifting 'duets.' A wonderful 'community read' for an entire congregation and Torah study groups."
—**Dr. Ron Wolfson**, Fingerhut Professor of Education at American Jewish University and author of *Relational Judaism.*

"In this day and age when so many are searching for meaning, spirituality, and connection, Rabbis Spitz and Riemer masterfully distill the psalms in a way that is deep, accessible, and personal at the same time. A true testament to the evergreen wisdom of the Psalms if we see them in the right light and bring our honest selves to them."
—**Rabbi Josh Warshawsky**, composer of music for Psalms

"Two deeply spiritual rabbis explore the Book of Psalms — one of the holiest and most heartfelt books ever composed — and they make it come alive for us today. They draw on the most recent biblical scholarship, but also on their own wisdom, gained from decades in the pulpit and from counseling thousands of struggling human beings. DUETS ON PSALMS is a gift. Open it and you will be uplifted, inspired and surprised."

—**Daniel Matt**, translator of the Zohar, author of *God and the Big Bang*, *The Essential Kabbalah*, and *Becoming Elijah: Prophet of Transformation*

"My experience in reading this inspiring book started as hearing two voices thinking together who were joined by all the sources they brought along and soon after that hearing my own thoughts and ideas spontaneously join theirs. That was a delight. I thought, 'These songs keep singing themselves!'"

—**Sylvia Boorstein, co-founding teacher, Spirit Rock Meditation Center, author,** *That's Funny, You Don't Look Buddhist: On Being a Faithful Jew and a Passionate Buddhist*

"'Sing Unto God a New Song.' Rabbis Jack Riemer and Elie Spitz, who are spiritual guides with the souls of poets, do just that as they bring the poetry of the biblical psalmist-of-old to our modern sensibilities. Their wise, insightful interpretative commentary makes the psalms come alive, and enter into our hearts, touching our deepest yearnings and greatest joy. God is smiling and singing along."

—**Rabbi Wayne Dosick**, author of *Living Judaism* and *The Real Name of God*

"The Psalms are a national, indeed a global, eternal treasure. Rabbi Riemer and Rabbi Spitz have offered us a sweet gift with renewing the Psalms back to life for us through nuanced spiritual interpretation, powerful moral stories and richly woven together applications."

—**Rabbi Shmuly Yanklowitz**, author, *Forty Arguments for the Sake of Heaven: Why the Most Vital Controversies in Jewish Intellectual History Still Matter*

"When great souls come together, there can be sparks. When they unite to find new meaning in the sacred songs and poems of the book of Psalms, a fire burns."

—**Craig Taubman**, singer and composer

Duets on Psalms

Drawing New Meaning From Ancient Words

Jack Riemer and Elie Spitz

Ben Yehuda Press

Teaneck, New Jersey

Published by Ben Yehuda Press
122 Ayers Court #1B
Teaneck, NJ 07666
http://www.BenYehudaPress.com
To subscribe to our monthly book club and support independent Jewish publishing, visit https://www.patreon.com/BenYehudaPress

Ben Yehuda Press books may be purchased at a discount by synagogues, book clubs, and other institutions buying in bulk.
For information, please email markets@BenYehudaPress.com

Cover illustration of lyre by Peter Pitzele.

ISBN13 978-1-953829-62-7

23 24 25 / 10 9 8 7 6 5 4 3 2b   20231104

Dedicated to our wives:

To Sue — *Libavteni*, "You have captured my heart" (Song of Songs 4:9)
— Jack Riemer

To Linda/Rivka Batya — *Vayehehaveiha*, "And he loved her" (Genesis 24:67)
— Elie Kaplan Spitz

And to our children:

Yosef, Vitina, and Adena;

> and to our grandchildren: Nathan, Lisa, and, Naomi;
> and to our great-grandchildren, Caleb and Asher.

> — Jack Riemer

Joey- and Allyson; Jonathan; and Anna- and Lev;

> and to our newly-born grandson, Hudson John (Simcha Haim).

> — Elie Kaplan Spitz

With hopes that you, our descendants, will also love the psalms.

Contents

Introduction:
Falling in Love with Psalms

Rabbi Elie Spitz

Psalms are companions across time. Readers have turned to these spiritual poems to mark celebration, find solace, and seek God's presence. As great songs, psalms give us words to express our deepest feelings and guide us toward greater inner peace and hope. You have probably recited "The Lord is my shepherd" (Psalm 23) at a funeral or chanted multiple psalms at a communal prayer service, whether Jewish or Christian.

These ancient psalms continue to seep into contemporary secular culture as well. Leonard Cohen's "Halleluyah" is among the songs most performed by street musicians and recorded by diverse artists. The title of the 2022 Academy Award-winning film *The Power of the Dog* is taken from the King James translation of Psalm 22:30. New York's Lincoln Center in 2017 hosted "The Psalms Experience," ten days of musical performances of all 150 psalms. A National Public Radio reviewer commented, "The psalms are a portal to a deep introspection. This project is massive and abstract, yet simple to understand. You just need to bring your humanity to get the most out of it."[1]

Our goal is to make these spiritual poems more accessible and inspiring for you, regardless of faith or familiarity with the Bible. For Jews, the psalms are known in Hebrew as *tehillim*, "praises." They are our people's favorite songs, a playlist sung and studied over millennia and encompassing the range of human emotions. And yet, despite the large role that psalms play in liturgy, I only recently began to appreciate their artistry, origins, and richness of content. What I found engaged my heart and mind. I fell in love with psalms and I want to show you why.[2]

You might be surprised that a rabbi who had chanted psalms for decades could do so with such a limited awareness of their literary composition, intended associations, and depth of expression. Such is the nature of even our favorite songs. Have you found yourself humming a song's melody or singing its words but without taking the time to really consider what the memorized words mean to you, let alone to the composer? Such is the nature of prayer, too. I had chanted the psalms and was drawn to their beauty and the familiarity of the melodies and words. I had swayed to the rhythm of the Hebrew or a phrase repeated over and over in mantra-like fashion. But I had never paused to consider what had prompted these heartfelt words, their meaning, and their artistic weave. When I did, I found myself more deeply engaged by the thoughts and feelings that echoed across generations.

To understand and make these spiritual poems my own meant to listen attentively to what the psalmist had to say. Although traditionally largely ascribed to King David, the actual authorship is shrouded in mystery. In reading closely, I heard a priest, a pilgrim, even a king appear across time, and I felt the privilege and perspective of continuity. I wondered about the author's prompt and intended message. Commentaries across generations revealed multiple understandings of the same words, often artfully ambiguous. Ultimately the goal of my close reading was to ask, "How is this psalm meaningful to me today?"

I recall attending my first poetry reading by an author in my freshman year of college. When the reading ended, a student offered an interpretation and asked, "Is this what you meant by the poem?"

"It is not what I intended that matters," the poet responded. "It is what you gain from the words that now have a life of their own."

When I react to a psalm, I am aware that I am not my ancestors' rabbi. I do not see the Creator as a vengeful warrior actively intervening in human affairs. I approach psalms with a modern lens where ideas often have a historical context. Worldview is autobiography: our perspective is filtered through our own experiences of a specific time and place. I know that we are fortunate to live with greater comforts, medical know-how, and communication access than people of the past enjoyed. At the same time, ours is a time of heightened dangers due to the ever-increasing human power to pollute and kill. And yet since the psalms were first written three thousand years ago, people today share the same human longings for relationship, safety, purpose, and justice, as well as a desire to reach beyond our limited selves to an enduring, caring Presence. These ancient words are not artifacts but pulsate with enduring emotional and spiritual resonance.

What I learned in studying psalms is that they display consistent honesty because they were written to a very specific intended audience: God. The words of the psalmist flow unselfconsciously with the assumption that the Creator knows all of us, will not be surprised by our thoughts or emotions, and will accept us caringly. Martin Buber, the twentieth-century Bible scholar and theologian, wrote that theology is the intellectual attempt to describe God, which is like reading a menu. Conversely, prayer, according to Buber, is actually tasting the meal.[3] Psalms are a feast of conversations with or before God that evokes conscience, provides clarity and catharsis, and enlarges our context for saying thank you and expressing wonder at the order and beauty of creation.

Pilgrims to the ancient Temple in Jerusalem are described in psalms as listening to these words sung by a chorus of Levites, accompanied by an orchestra. Many of the psalms begin with an introduction that makes reference to the conductor or refer to the use of specific musical instruments. When we study psalms we are examining lyrics; the words were often put to music. Music interprets and imprints the words and amplifies the emotions. While we lack knowledge of the original melodies, when used in liturgy our psalms are still often sung. Even without music, the words themselves have enormous power.

The song-poems were repeated in many lands. "Like a tree planted alongside flowing waters" (Psalm 1), echoes of the ancient past offered vital spiritual nourishment. The psalms kindled memories of King David's victories and challenges and the priest-led ritual celebrations that evoked a national hope of restoration. Some gave voice to despair and others to hope; some thanked God and others challenged God's absence. Some compositions were used for communal worship and others for personal contemplation. I often wish that we knew more about the original context and setting for each psalm, for they keep a lot of secrets. We do not know how they sounded with their music and whether they struck a chord with their own generation when they were recited. And yet despite the obscurity of their origins and the selection process that included them in the Bible, the psalms collectively convey the essence of Judaism's spiritual life.

The Challenges of Translation and Interpretation

During the COVID-19 pandemic, I found an opportunity to study psalms and make the words more fully my own as spiritual prompts and conduits. With the aid of Zoom, I sought students from my congregation and across the globe to explore the psalms. I began the process not knowing how far I would get in my teaching before normalcy and in-person demands reduced my time for scholarship. I chose to teach three psalms a week with half-hour presentations followed by discussion. I devoted many hours of preparation for each psalm and crafted my own translations. I already knew from Bible study that all translations are interpretations, literally "bridges of language."

To enable the psalms to resonate with a contemporary reader, I chose in my translations to avoid using exclusively male pronouns for God and human subjects. I also sought to cleave as closely as possible to the Hebrew to reveal the literary artistry of wordplay, purposeful repetitions, and intentional ambiguities. What I could not convey in English were the rhythms and Hebrew sounds of the original oral recitations that helped convey the poet's message and a sensory experience.

The project of translation made me keenly aware of the differences between Hebrew and English.[4] A translation never fully reveals the nuance that is before us. For starters, Hebrew words are more ambiguous and subject to wordplay than English words. Hebrew root words are composed of three consonants and lack vowels. To choose a pronunciation to convey the intention of a word depends on context, which is often uncertain. In the original biblical text, there is also no punctuation, lending doubt to the demarcation of phrases and even sentences. Consider the difference a small comma makes: "Let's eat kids" and "Let's eat, kids." In Hebrew, words are not capitalized.[5] "He" or "You" may refer to God, a person, or even an enemy group.

The grammatical tense is also uncertain. The English language has past, present, and future, but biblical Hebrew has just two overlapping tenses.[6] I have found the same sentence interpreted quite differently depending on the tense of the translation. The poet often chooses obscure words or even invents new ones. This intrinsic ambiguity undermines the all-too-common assertions of those who claim the Bible as plainly understood. As in the case with art, the meaning attributed often says more about the viewer's assumptions than the author's intentions.

I used many translations and commentaries to discern the Hebrew roots and usages of words. There was a wide variety of interpretations of the setting, prompts, and goals of a particular psalm. Commentaries described as much about the time and needs of the reader as the text. The rabbis of the Middle Ages, for instance, consistently saw the compositions as written to comfort them in exile, with trajectories that pointed to Messianic redemption. I visited with these diverse interpretations across generations as if participating in a communal conversation with the privilege of pulling up a chair to listen before speaking.

A close reading of the Psalms reveals words repeated and phrases juxtaposed to emphasize a concept. Images are chosen to prompt emotional associations. As those before me, I paid particular attention to each psalm's opening and closing words, which often serve as a frame, and counted them to identify the middle phrase as another indicator of the psalm's central message. Psalms invite personalization because they are personal. As the Spanish poet and philosopher Moses ibn Ezra (10th-11th centuries) stated, "Words from the heart penetrate the heart." My students and I were often surprised by what images or words resonated for us and by our shared insights. We read psalms as if for the first time and questions emerged.

Many of us knew Psalm 23, with the famous King James translation "The Lord is my shepherd; I shall not want. . ." But only with translating did I notice a trajectory from childhood into adulthood, from passivity to responsibility, with roundabouts of justice as the turning point. And in pondering what was the goal of that life journey I found the answer embedded in the psalm.

As students, we expected that psalms would describe gratitude and praise of God, which they do repeatedly. But we also found angry protests over God's failure to act (Psalm 44) and even a frightening, emotional darkness in a psalm that is absent in our traditional prayerbook (Psalm 88). Why was such anguish included in *tehillim*, biblical prayer-poems identified with the repeated word *Halleluyah* (Praise God)?

The opening of Psalm 137, "By the rivers of Babylon," was familiar from reggae music[7] and the mournful chants of Tisha B'Av services,[8] but most of us had never read the closing line: "Happy who will grab and hurl your babies against the rock!" How could such brutality be found in a prayer-poem?

After eighteen months, my Zoom study group and I completed Psalm 150. I was as delighted as if I had reached a mountaintop after a formidable climb. Along the way I found that each psalm is distinctive and that its placement within the book of Psalms has a story to tell. The compositions range in size from two verses (Psalm 117) to 176 (Psalm 119). Some psalms use all the Hebrew letters sequentially as the starting letter of each line to convey a core comprehensive idea, while others present conflicting thoughts as if to acknowledge a seesaw of faith. Some identify a specific moment in David's life, and others transcend any singular moment. Some are deeply personal, while others even call on the entirety of creation to join in song.[9] Like a great symphony, the psalms build to a crescendo of Halleluyah rejoicings. The close readings engaged heart and head, as my students kept me striding forward, psalm after psalm.

The Origins Of This Book As A Partnership

Rabbi Jack Riemer, among the most oft-quoted contemporary rabbis, joined many of my Zoom classes. His presence delighted me and raised the bar for my presentations. Through the years I had regularly cited Rabbi Riemer's sermons, which he had written out each week and shared with colleagues. I read his sermons religiously (pun intended) because of how he applied the insights of the Torah text and current commentators to our own lives: evoking a smile of recognition, and even entertainment, while conveying wisdom.[10] When my wife, Linda, met Jack over thirty years ago, she commented on his curiosity and enthusiasm by saying that "Jack is the oldest teenager that I know." Jack recently celebrated the eightieth anniversary of his bar mitzvah and remains strongly engaged.

Pulpit rabbis are in the business of meaning-making. In our teaching we tend to comment on the weekly Torah reading and apply the lessons to our lives. When I completed my teaching of the 150 psalms, Jack offered to teach some favorite psalms to his congregation in Boca Raton, Florida. I joined his Zoom presentations and found his scholarship and personalization similar to his memorable Torah preaching. After Jack finished his cluster of psalm classes, his wife, Sue, encouraged the two of us to consider a joint writing project on the psalms. I immediately agreed. Jack was initially uncertain and needed some convincing. Yet once he began, he was enthusiastically prolific. The goal was to teach psalms in the same way that we have taught Torah for so many years, reading the sacred text closely to discern what the words mean in context and how the ideas illuminate our lives today.

Our voices are different and complementary. For each of our selected psalms, we take turns analyzing the psalm's artistic composition as a foundation for interpretation. In "Going Deeper," we provide short essays on how those ideas play out in our lives and in our world. While we both explore the flow and word choices, Jack is more associative in linking the ancient words with folk stories, poetry, and lessons for our day. Our shared goal is to identify enduring insights that transcend place and time. As pulpit rabbis, we figuratively wear bifocals: seeking a clear view of *then* while looking closely for what is relevant for our lives *now*.[11]

We have chosen thirteen psalms that are among our favorites, on which we had something creative or insightful to say, and which represent a hearty taste of key themes prevalent in the book of Psalms. These are our subjects:

1. The Nature of Happiness: 1
2. The Grandeur of Creation: 8
3. Faith and Protest: 19
4. Trust and Progress: 23, 27
5. Danger and Gratitude: 30
6. God Fights for Us: 35
7. Inner Light: 36
8. Despondency: 44
9. Mortal Leadership and Divine Guidance: 95
10. Defeat and Hope: 137
11. Praise: 145, 148

What You Will Gain

Secular songs are containers for self-expression. We surprise ourselves with what song gets stuck in our head and how an immediate mood is revealed when a familiar song spontaneously emerges. Such songs enrich our lives by giving voice to love, loss, wonder, and yearning.[12] Psalms include these themes and go beyond them. Psalms invite us to see our lives as part of a larger community and to address questions of ultimate meaning. A psalmist says thank you to the Source of Creation so as to transcend an immediate moment and to view our lives from a far broader perspective. To read psalms is to hear a call to action to actualize goodness in the world. By listening to the psalmists express their deepest feelings, we are given pause to refine our own worldview. It is as much about the questions evoked as the answers obtained. In many cases, it is not a whole psalm but an image or a phrase that will serve as a source of spiritual nourishment.

Rabbi Riemer and I will guide you through the psalms by telling you their history, artistic structure, and the multiple ways they have been understood. We also want more personally to point out verses or ideas that have touched us and to tell you why. The goal is to serve as your tour guides, opening up the terrain of psalms. We seek to empower you to find your own resonance in the words treasured across generations. For those who do not believe in a supernatural God, we advise when reading a psalm to substitute the word *Good* for the word *God*. Psalms offer insight into that ultimate goodness while acknowledging the reality of pain caused by enemies from without and within. You may choose to read this book sequentially or select a particular psalm or even a resonant phrase.

As you will see, the first words of the book of Psalms are "Happy is the person." This opening phrase identifies what you will gain from reading onward, beginning with defining what happiness is and how to attain it. Later psalms will address pain and unfulfilled longing and even question God's care. This range of emotions addresses the reality of life as deeply felt, along with the possibility of living with greater faith and purpose and less fear. We hope that you find the journey through psalms enriching by engaging with voices across generations and drawing wisdom and connection from deep within you as you react and sing.

Three Warnings Before We Begin
Rabbi Jack Riemer

Let me begin by asking you what you know about the Psalms. What comes to your mind first when you think about the Psalms?

Dr. Lawrence Hoffman, who is a distinguished teacher of Jewish liturgy, says there are three things we do not have that would help us understand the psalms better than we do. First, we don't have the names of the authors or the dates of when the psalms were written. Sometimes we have a reference to the literary school the authors belonged to, but we do not have their names or any knowledge of when and where they lived.

How can this be? One of the wonders of the ancient world was the ability of writers to work anonymously. Nobody does that nowadays. Today, if you want to give a talk about the importance of humility, you have to elbow your way to the microphone first so that you can be heard. There is one contemporary rabbi of whom I have heard that if he goes a whole week without being mentioned in the *New York Times*, he becomes depressed. Some rabbis have a full-time public relations person on their staff whose task is to make sure that their sermons are quoted in the newspapers frequently.

The Sages of antiquity, however, evidently cultivated the art of anonymity. Who wrote the Haggadah? Who wrote the *Nishmat* prayer? Who wrote the *Amidah*? The answer is that we do not know. These are each superb works of literature, but whoever wrote them somehow never signed their name.

We do not have the dates on which these psalms were written either. It would be good if we had these dates. It would help us understand some of the psalms better if we knew the circumstances under which they were written. But for some reason, the psalmists never recorded the dates.

Second, we do not have the musical notes. We know that many of these psalms were set to music, sung by the choir in the Temple and accompanied by musical instruments, but we do not know the musical notes anymore. We have a few of them, such as *laminatseach, mizmor,* and *selah,* but we don't know how to read them anymore, and that is a loss. It is like reading a libretto without having the score.

But there is one more loss — and this is perhaps the greatest loss. We can somehow manage without knowing the names and dates of the authors and without knowing the musical notes. But what makes the psalms so difficult for us to understand is that they were written by people who felt a deep and a personal relationship to God, and we do not have this awareness.

The psalms were composed by people who poured out their hearts to God and who believed that God heard their words. We do not have that awareness — or at least not very often. For us, reading a psalm is just that: reading. We read the psalms the way we read the newspaper. We do not feel the same joy or anger or exaltation or sense of wonder that the psalmists did. We do not feel the presence of God when we recite the psalms. And that is the main difficulty that confronts us.

Compare the difference between the way we sing "America (My Country 'Tis of Thee)" at a ballgame and the way we would sing it if we were welcoming our children home, safe and sound, from a long and bloody war. In the first case, we would recite the words pro forma. In the second, we would recite them with overwhelming gratitude and joy, and even with tears.

It is not always true that we recite the psalms pro forma. All of us can recall moments when we have said these words with all our hearts and souls and minds. If nowhere else, then surely in hospital waiting rooms we have said these words with fervor. There have been moments when we said them with awe or with anguish or with anger.

Let me share with you two examples of how the psalms have had the power to change lives in recent times. The first comes from Rabbi Paul Plotkin, a retired rabbi who lives in Florida, and the second comes from Natan Sharansky, who is one of the great heroes of our time.

Rabbi Plotkin's story begins this way:

> There was a time in my life when I felt that everything was falling apart. My wife was divorcing me. I had no idea how my congregation would feel about having a divorced rabbi or whether I could find another position if this one let me go. And then — the last straw — while riding on a subway, someone picked my pocket and stole my money, my passport, and my credit cards.
>
> I felt an overwhelming sense of despair as I thought about the shambles of my life. I was mired in self-pity. I couldn't eat. I couldn't sleep. I kept thinking: How could this be happening to me? Other people get divorced — not me. I will never love or be loved again. And who will ever hire a divorced rabbi? And what will happen to my kids? How will I be able to provide for their education if I have no job? And how will I be able to hold on to them if I can only see them at certain prescribed times?[13]

He was wallowing in self-pity as he thought about all these things. And then he woke up one morning and prepared to begin his morning prayers. As he put on his tallit and his tefillin, as he did every day, he says that he felt a special message coming into himself:

"Okay, Paul," he said to himself, "it's put-up or shut-up time. All these years you have preached to others about the power of prayer. You have told other people who were in crisis to reach out to God for solace and strength. Now it is your turn.

"Don't pray as you always have. This time pray as if it can really help."

He began the morning prayers, the same prayers that he had said for more than three decades, but this time he said them in a different spirit. The words were the same but the speaker was different.

A few pages into the service, he got to Psalm 30 and the line: "At night you go to sleep crying; in the morning there is joy." When he encountered these words, something changed inside him. "This psalmist and I are kindred spirits," he said to himself. "He understands me as no one else does." Rabbi Plotkin felt for the first time that he was no longer alone. Hope had entered his life for the first time in many months and it was illuminating him. He said to himself, "I can get through this!" And so, in order to make sure that he would remember this verse, he took out his pen and underlined it.

And he did survive. Today, he is remarried and content once again.

There is a footnote to this story. Several months later, he was driving in a car with a close friend, and he mentioned this experience to him. His friend told him that he, too, had had such an experience once at a time when he was in great distress. "Really?" said Rabbi Plotkin. "What line was it that gave you strength?" His friend told him which verse it was. When he heard the answer, Paul pulled over to the side of the road, reached into his briefcase, and pulled out his siddur. Sure enough, they had both underlined the same verse!

This is an example of how a verse in the Psalms, if you read it as addressed to you and not just as a task to recite, has the power to transform your life.

Let me now tell you the story of Natan Sharansky and his book of Psalms.

Natan Sharansky is one of the great heroes of Jewish life in our time. He fought not only for his own freedom and the rights of Soviet Jews but also for the rights of all freedom-seeking Russians. He and his fiancée, Avital, both applied for visas so they could go to Israel. They both received their answers on the same day. Hers said that she could leave the country — but only if she left in twenty-four hours. His said that his request to leave was being turned down and that he must report to the court for sentencing in twenty-four hours.

What should they do with their few remaining hours together?

They had never been to a synagogue before in their lives, but they raced around Moscow until they found a rabbi who would marry them. In the morning, she gave him a farewell gift before they parted. She gave him a book of Psalms with a Russian translation, and then they went their separate ways. She went to Israel and from there to Washington, New York, London, Paris, and many other cities in order to rouse public support on behalf of her husband. He went to prison, where he was immediately put into solitary confinement.

What do you do when you are alone with yourself day after day after day, week after week, month after month, in a Soviet prison?

Sharansky did three things. The first was that he entertained himself by telling anti-Soviet jokes to the guards who passed by. The guards knew that the cameras were on them as well as on him, and that if they laughed, they might be imprisoned too, so they had to try their best to keep from laughing.

Second, he had been a world-class chess player in the world outside and so he entertained himself by playing chess against himself, even though he had no board or chess pieces!

Can you imagine playing chess against yourself without a board? Only a chess player with an incredible memory could do that.

The third thing that he did during the seven years he was in prison was learn the book of Psalms. He learned it first in Russian, and then by means of the Russian he figured out what the Hebrew words meant.

At one point the guards took away his book of Psalms as punishment for maintaining his spirit so courageously. But eventually the pressure of world opinion affected even the Soviet Union. Hundreds of thousands of Jews protested outside the White House to demand Sharansky's release when Soviet leader Mikhail Gorbachev was visiting there. The Russians realized it was time to let Sharansky go. And so, one day they came into his cell and told him that he was going to be set free.

They flew him to Berlin and took him to a bridge where the media was waiting to see him go free. Avital and many Jewish leaders were waiting on the other side. But Sharansky refused to go until and unless they gave him back his book of Psalms. And since they had no choice, the Soviets gave in and gave him back his Psalms.

They told him to walk straight across the bridge. But in order to demonstrate that he was a free man, he zigzagged across — to the delight of the photographers and to the annoyance of his captors.

When he arrived at the other side of the bridge, he hugged Avital and greeted those who had come to welcome him. From Berlin, he flew to Israel. When he got there, he traveled from Tel Aviv to Jerusalem, with crowds singing and clapping on both sides of the road to welcome him to Israel.

When they got to Jerusalem, Sharansky's supporters put him on their shoulders and carried him to the Wall; he was still carrying his book of Psalms in his hands. At the Wall, he triumphantly recited passages from the Psalms in order to express his joy.

There is a footnote to this story, too. I have a cousin in Israel who was once standing in line in a cafeteria when she looked around and found Natan Sharansky standing in line behind her. She told him what a great honor it was to meet him, and she asked if he still had his book of Psalms. He reached into his pocket and pulled it out, worn and frayed from many years of use, and he told her that he never goes anywhere without it.

So here we have two examples from two different continents of how the Psalms still have the power to speak to people in our time, just as they did in days of old.

We invite you to join us on a journey together on which we will meet some of these psalms and see what they say to us.

More than a century ago, Israel Zangwill reflected on the worship experience that he witnessed in a synagogue that he visited. He wrote:

The worshippers prayed metaphysics, acrostics,
angelology, Kabbalah, history, Talmudic controversies, menus, recipes, psalms, love poems, an
undigested mixture of exalted and questionable
sentiments and of communal and personal aspirations of the highest order. It was a wonderful
liturgy, as grotesque as it was beautiful; like an old
cathedral in all styles of architecture, stored with
shabby antiquities and sideshows, and overgrown
with moss and lichen — a blend of historical
strata of all periods, in which gems of poetry and
pathos and spiritual fervor glittered, and painful
records of ancient persecution lay petrified. All
this was known and loved.... And if the worshippers didn't always know what they were saying,
they always meant it.[14]

I love that last sentence. If it describes the prayerbook in the traditional synagogue of the last century in general, it applies even more to the psalms that were recited: "If the worshippers didn't always know what they were saying, they always meant it."

The psalms are no longer recited in our synagogues with the same piety and passion that they were said in the one that Zangwill visited. They are recited politely but with very little responsiveness and without much emotional involvement.

And that is an enormous spiritual loss, for the psalms were meant to — and still have — the capacity to lift the hearts of those who recite them. They express every emotion: gratitude at being alive, wonder at the beauty of the universe, loneliness, pain, anger, and more.

Therefore, these are the two tasks that we have set out to do in this book. Rabbi Spitz will probe the nuances in the words of the psalms.

He will hold these words up to the light, the way a jeweler holds up diamonds, so that we can see the many different refractions they throw off. He will compare and contrast the spirit of the psalms with those of the communities that lived around the Israelites in days of old so that we can gain an understanding of the differences between the worldview of the pagans and the worldview of those who wrote the Psalms. And he will provide us with some of the insights that have been read into and out of these words by Jewish and Christian commentators, and by medieval and modern commentators as well.

My part in this enterprise will be a little bit different from his, although I am sure that there will be some overlap. I love stories, and so I will try to gather some of the legends and stories that have been told in the past and in our own time that echo or challenge what the psalmists say.

I will not be as focused as Rabbi Spitz will be on determining the literal meaning of each passage in the psalms, although I do some of that, too. My concern will mostly be with probing the ways in which the words of the psalms have prompted poets and thinkers down through the centuries and in our time to respond to their words.

We invite you to come along with us on this journey. We believe that you will find hidden treasures of the soul awaiting you and that you will be able to deny Israel Zangwill's quip and become people who know what you say and who mean it.

So come join us . . .

Psalm 1

"Happy Is the Person"

Rabbi Elie Spitz

The door to Psalms opens. The initial words are addressed to us, the readers, offering guidance on how to grow toward happiness. The key message of Psalm 1 is that happiness is possible, but there is danger. For the company that we choose and where we apply our minds will determine our path and our fate. God watches expectantly, seeking our loyalty and goodness.

אַשְׁרֵי הָאִישׁ אֲשֶׁר א
לֹא הָלַךְ בַּעֲצַת רְשָׁעִים,
וּבְדֶרֶךְ חַטָּאִים לֹא עָמָד
וּבְמוֹשַׁב לֵצִים לֹא יָשָׁב.

1 Happy is the person who has not walked in the counsel of the wicked, and in the way of sinners has not stood, or in the seat of the scornful has not sat.

כִּי אִם בְּתוֹרַת יְהֹוָה חֶפְצוֹ ב
וּבְתוֹרָתוֹ יֶהְגֶּה יוֹמָם וָלָיְלָה.

2 But rather in the Torah of *Adonai* is their[15] delight and in [God's] Torah do they meditate day and night.

וְהָיָה כְּעֵץ שָׁתוּל עַל פַּלְגֵי מָיִם, ג
אֲשֶׁר פִּרְיוֹ יִתֵּן בְּעִתּוֹ,
וְעָלֵהוּ לֹא יִבּוֹל,
וְכֹל אֲשֶׁר יַעֲשֶׂה, יַצְלִיחַ.

3 And they shall be like a tree planted by streams of water, which brings forth its fruit in its season, and whose leaf does not wither, and in all that they do, they will succeed.

ד לֹא כֵן הָרְשָׁעִים; **4** Not so the wicked;
כִּי אִם כַּמֹּץ אֲשֶׁר תִּדְּפֶנּוּ רוּחַ. rather they are like the chaff
that the wind drives away.

ה עַל כֵּן, לֹא יָקֻמוּ רְשָׁעִים בַּמִּשְׁפָּט **5** Therefore, the wicked shall not
וְחַטָּאִים בַּעֲדַת צַדִּיקִים. stand in judgment and sinners in the
congregation of the righteous.

ו כִּי יוֹדֵעַ יְהוָה דֶּרֶךְ צַדִּיקִים **6** For *Adonai* knows the way of the
וְדֶרֶךְ רְשָׁעִים תֹּאבֵד. righteous and the way of the wicked
will perish.

READING CLOSELY

Let us linger on the opening two words: *Ashrei ha'ish*, "Happy is the person." Most choose to translate *ashrei* as "happiness," but others have used related words: "fortunate," "blessed," or "praiseworthy."[16] In drawing attention to the opening words, I am reminded of the teaching of Alfred Adler, the early Viennese psychotherapist. He said that if you want to know people quickly, ask for their earliest memory, for such is a distillation of core identity. I have found that the same is true for sacred texts: the opening words often indicate what will unfold. Psalms begins with happiness as the essential quest of the poem-prayers ahead.

Many years ago, I attended a talk by the Dalai Lama, the Nobel Peace Prize-winning Tibetan monk. When he stated that the goal of religion is happiness, I was initially taken aback.[17] Happiness sounded too self-oriented, even superficial. Then I paused, because I admire the Dalai Lama as a profound thinker with a ready laugh and an exemplar of genuine compassion. I reflected on the nature of happiness and recognized that this is indeed the case for Judaism. The substantiveness of happiness comes down to how we define it. Like the biblical word *lev*, which means both "heart" and "mind," happiness is more than an emotion. Happiness as a worthy spiritual goal combines the various translations of *ashrei*: an abiding awareness that one is fortunate and blessed, leading to deeds worthy of praise.

To delve deeper into defining happiness, let us look at the opening letter, which will reveal that happiness is an inner quality. In Hebrew, *ashrei* begins with an *alef* (א), the first letter of the alphabet. One other Hebrew consonant, *ayin* (ע), is silent, taking its sound from the vowel attached. These two letters at the start of a word repeatedly signify inner versus outer. When beginning with an *ayin*, "or" spells "skin"; with an *aleph*, it means "light"; *asher* with an *ayin* means "wealth"; with an *aleph*, it means "happiness."[18] This opening word, therefore, teaches that happiness is an inner experience, distinguished from externals such as wealth. Happiness is a lingering quiet mind and an open heart, a cultivated tendency.

Psalm 1 guides us toward happiness. Thematically, the six verses are organized as three pairs of sentences. The format and chosen words are purposeful.

Verse 1 is like white writing on a black background. The happy person is contrasted with those who are wicked. Three verbs convey increasing familiarity with evildoers: walk, stand, and sit. The sitting suggests joining the scornful, *leitzim*, in a social circle. The medieval philosopher Moses Maimonides (1135-1204) identifies these evildoers with a lack of accountability: their words begin with social gossip, then scorn of the righteous and God's prophets, and ultimately a denial of God's authority.[19] *Leitzim* is related in modern Hebrew to the word for "clown" (*laitzan*). We are cautioned against frivolous personalities and their followers who disorient us. We are told that the company that we keep will shape us. Avoiding those who scorn what truly matters will allow us to proceed on the path of goodness.

Verse 2 shifts our attention to Torah as a steadfast companion. The word *Torah* literally means "teaching." Jewish commentators apply it to the Torah scroll specifically, or more broadly to Hebrew scripture, Jewish law, or even the pursuit of spiritual wisdom. The Torah in this verse is explicitly linked to God and is called *hafetz*, either an "object" or a "desire." The righteous person meditates (*hegeh*) on these sacred teachings with constancy, morning and night. *Hegeh* may also mean "mumble,"[20] contrasting uplifting speech with the words of scorners. Sacred study is not just intellectual contemplation but the internalization of text, including memorization by saying the words aloud. The practice of reading and discussing aloud became normative in rabbinic Judaism. The Hebrew word *krah*, "to read," has the shared meaning "to call out." Talmud study will commonly take place with a *havrutah*, a study partner, as text is read aloud and its meaning debated. Where we place our attention determines our thoughts, serving as a filter for what we notice and value. Sacred text, Torah, is a conversation of a higher order directing us to notice God's presence and realize our accountability.

Bible scholar Benjamin Sommer posits that the redactor placed this psalm at the start of the book of Psalms due to verse 2.[21] The goal, he holds, is to convey the centrality of the study of Torah as life's guiding text. He points out that much of the same vocabulary — Torah, study (*hegeh*), and the need for constancy — is present in the opening chapter of Joshua, where the teaching is directly linked to Moses:

> But you must be very strong and resolute to observe faithfully all the Torah that My servant Moses enjoined upon you. Do not deviate from it to the right of to the left, that you may be successful wherever you go.
>
> Let not this Book of Torah cease from your lips, but recite it day and night, so that you may observe faithfully all that is written in it. Only then will you prosper in

your undertakings and only then will you be successful.
(Joshua 1:7-8)

Although Psalms is identified with King David and prayer, Sommer says that the redactor sought to prioritize sacred study and Moses. He surmises that the very redactor who added the lines to Joshua, which marked the opening of the book of the Prophets, also placed this psalm as the opening of the book of the Latter Writings. While most of Psalms is heart oriented, the mind of study is presented first; in religious terms, study and prayer would provide two balancing poles of religious engagement.

While I find Sommer's presentation illuminating, I also find his focus incomplete. I prefer to see verse 1 as the very reason to start the anthology here — namely, acknowledging our natural desire for happiness. Study becomes an essential vehicle for that happy life. For internalizing the Torah as given to Moses enables acting properly, which offers the roots and natural benefits of righteousness. Sommer notes that the opening three words of the biblical tale of the *Akeidah*, the binding of Isaac, provide the essential lens for reading the story: "And God tested Abraham" (Genesis 22:1). Likewise, when Psalm 1 begins "Happy is the person," we may anticipate that what will follow will be personally useful.

Verses 3 and 4 present images of nature to convey reward and punishment. The righteous are like a fruit-bearing tree planted by flowing waters, suggesting deep roots that are actively nurtured. The wicked of verse 4 are like chaff, the lightweight husk of a grain stalk: valueless and blown away by the wind. The prophet Jeremiah uses a similar image (17:6-8), except the wicked for Jeremiah are tumbleweed, a desert plant with shallow, easily dried-up roots. Rabbi Harold Kushner in his book *Who Needs God?* comments that as a tree draws sustenance from a source underground, people draw spiritual strength from God who is unseen and present.[22]

Verses 5 and 6 begin with "Therefore" and focus on consequences. In judgment, the wicked will not have a leg to stand on. As the psalm opened with a warning to avoid the counsel of the wicked, now the word "counsel" (*eidah*) is repeated but applied to the righteous who will shun the wicked. Judgment is both divine and human and decisive: "The way of the wicked will perish."

A key motif of Psalm 1 is *derech*, "the way." The word appears in the opening verse and is repeated twice in the closing verse, framing the psalm. The message is that we choose a path of goodness or evil, which will determine if we are righteous or not, living with contentment and compassion or not. A way generates momentum, and momentum is a powerful force. The Hebrew phrase at the very center of the psalm, "brings forth its fruit in its season," promises a flourishing life when good choices are made and sustained.

DIGGING DEEPER

The Path of Happiness
Rabbi Spitz

Life up close is incomplete. Amid such gaps anxiety resides. Happiness is elusive. In the words of Helen Telushkin, the mother of the well-known Jewish author Joseph Telushkin, "The only people I know who are happy are people that I do not know well."[23]

Yet we seek happiness. I do. And I want my study of sacred text to offer enhanced stability and joy. My moods rise and fall in the course of a day. At times I feel like a surfer, trying the best I can to willfully maneuver forward despite the power of the waves and the undertow. I pause regularly to appreciate what I might otherwise have taken for granted. In that pause I am keenly aware that as Psalm 1 instructs me, the quality of my life is due to the company I keep and the books I read and what I watch on the screen — okay, that part is not in the psalm, but it's implied — that shape my worldview and motivate good actions.

I was fortunate as a child to have rabbis who inspired me to value the Torah as a book of depth. My synagogue rabbi, Moshe Tutnauer, linked the biblical stories with the Bible's teaching that all people were created in the image of God and each deserved our respect and care. He modeled living Torah by social activism and genuine curiosity for the well-being of others. My day-school educator, Rabbi David Rebibo, introduced me to rabbinic commentaries of Torah and Talmud and challenged me to identify the question that was being debated and to join the family conversation concerning the details of what it meant to live in relationship with God.

To study the Torah is to engage those who came before us — a conversation that has endured because it has something valuable to say. Torah is the Jewish people's account of our history and what God wants from us. Psalm 1 does not yet address God directly, but it describes a God who cares about the choices of our company and promises that if we act responsibly, we will have control over that surfboard during the rise and fall of life, and we will ride with the abiding happiness that comes from a life well lived.

What Influences Our Happiness?
Rabbi Spitz

Rabbi Abraham Twerski was a psychiatrist who wrote over sixty books, including *Happiness and the Human Spirit*.[24] Much of his writing dealt with addiction, his professional focus. He repeatedly said that his sixty books could be distilled into one sentence: "You are worthy of love and are loved." Most people have a hidden doubt about their lovability, which rises and falls. Addictions, he taught, were largely acts of self-medication to overcome the anxiety of feeling unlovable. Rabbi Twerski emphasized that a belief in God as Parent aided us in seeing ourselves as infinitely valuable and beloved, serving to steady us.

Our parents play a vital role in our foundational identity, and yet our peers are active motivators of action and determiners of worth, too. I recall a story shared with me by Professor Robert Cialdini, a leading social psychologist. He had repeatedly tried to help his son overcome a fear of water and had made little progress. One day he came to the pool and his son was swimming.

> "How did you learn to swim?" the delighted father asked.
> Pointing to another child, the six-year-old replied, "Oh, my friend showed me."
> "If you want to enable a change," my mentor concluded, "enlist a peer."[25]

Judith Rich Harris challenged many of her colleagues with her book *The Nurture Assumption*. As the mother of a biologic and an adopted child, she was curious about the source of their differences. She examined data from twin and adoption studies, persuasively arguing that the strongest contributors to personality were genes and peers. Children of immigrants, she pointed out, imitate the accents, dress, and values of their peers. Among the most impactful influence of a parent is directing the choice of peers for their children. Her research explained that the greater propensity of behavioral problems among children of single mothers compared to married couples was linked to living in poorer neighborhoods with a greater likelihood of troubled peers.[26] While I see much wisdom concerning the power of peers, I would also add that growing up with two loving parents provides a sense of self-worth and a model of stability that are key factors in choosing and maintaining healthy friendships.[27]

Psalm 1 conveys that God, too, has a vital role in our happiness, like flowing waters offering spiritual nourishment. Much depends on our ability to reach beneath the surface toward the unseen and simultaneously to accept that our actions matter before a caring Presence. With Psalm 1, God is present even though not addressed directly. In reading the psalm, we look outwardly to those who are our companions, inwardly to reflect on what makes for happiness, and upwardly to God as the source of love and values and to whom we are accountable.

But Is It True?
Rabbi Jack Riemer

I hate to be a killjoy, especially at the very beginning of this book, but there is one question that the first psalm raises that must be challenged.

The psalm is brief and simple — it makes its point in just six verses. The Hebrew is clear and its description of the way the world feels to the author seems accurate. The advice that it offers — that we should study Torah as often as we can — and the warning that we should avoid associating with bad people and with cynics is undeniably good counsel. But the central thesis of the psalm is one that many generations, including our own, have struggled with and have found no easy answer to. It declares that God rewards good people and punishes bad people. And the question it raises is: Is this true?

Moses and the prophets, the sages of the Talmud, the best minds of the Middle Ages — and, for that matter, anyone and everyone who has ever experienced pain that they felt was unjustified — have wrestled with this question.

The last line of Psalm 1 feels glib to anyone who has known suffering that they felt was undeserved or who has seen prosperity and happiness among those who do not seem to merit them. You do not have to have especially good eyesight in order to see people whom you think are bad and yet who seem to prosper or to see people whom you think are good and yet who suffer.

Everyone who reads this psalm knows examples that make this last verse seem like a pious wish and not a description of reality. But let me focus on just one poet to whom the last words of Psalm 1 taste like gall.

David Curzon was born in Poland, raised in Australia, and now lives in New York. His parents sent him from Poland to Australia on the eve of the Second World War because they foresaw the conquest of Poland by the Nazis. After the war, his father, who somehow survived the Holocaust in which the rest of his family were murdered, arrived in Australia and rejoined his son.

Curzon's "Psalm One," which expresses the anger that he feels toward the faith that is found in the first psalm, responds to every line in that psalm with bitter sarcasm. He begins by citing the words of Psalm 1, then he juxtaposes its words with his own responses to it. In order to make clear which lines come from the psalm and which lines are his, he puts the words from the psalm into italics.

Blessed is the man not born
In Lodz in the wrong decade,
Who walks not in tree-lined shade
Like my father's father in this photo, nor
Stands in the way of sinners waiting for
His yellow star,
Nor sits, if he could sit, in their cattle car,

But *his delight is* being born
As I was, in Australia, far away,
And in God's law he meditates night and day.

He is like a tree that's granted
The land where it is planted,
That yields its fruit by reason
Of sun and rain in season.

The wicked are not so they
Burn their uniforms and go their way.

Therefore the wicked are like Cain
Who offered fruit that God chose to disdain,
And *the way of the righteous* is Abel's, whose
Sacrifice God chose to choose
And who was murdered anyway.[28]

Notice that he begins by recalling a time when a Jew like his grandfather could stroll on a boulevard in Lodz, his hometown, and enjoy the lovely shade, and he mourns that this is no longer possible. Then in just three short lines, he moves from Jews not being allowed to stroll on the streets to Jews being forced to wear yellow stars, then from there to Jews being put on railroad cars and shipped to the concentration camps. It is his way of saying how quickly this all happened.

In the third stanza he expresses his sense of frustration and anger that people who have lived in a land for such a long time and who have helped to cultivate it should not be entitled to feel that they belong.

Psalm 1 says that the wicked will be judged for their misdeeds in the end, but Curzon knows that this is not so. As we see in the fourth stanza, he thinks of the Nazis who burned their uniforms and destroyed their identity cards when the war ended and were able to get away and begin new lives — contrary to what the psalm says will happen to the wicked.

The last line is especially painful. You read it and you wince. Curzon is saying that the promise that all works well in the world is not only not true in the world but not even true in the Bible! Abel and many other pious ones whom God loved have met the same end that he did, so how can we accept the claim of Psalm 1?

Psalm 1 and Curzon's poem are at the two edges of the spectrum on which all people can be found. It may be hard for many of us to accept the innocence of Psalm 1, but we are repelled by the cynicism and the bitterness of Curzon's challenge to it. Most of us find ourselves somewhere in the middle between these two positions. We yearn to believe that the psalmist is right, and there are many occasions in our lives when we feel the truth of what he says. There are moments when we feel that the blessings that we possess — the joy of having a loving family and the joy of living a meaningful life — are worth more than what the rich person who loses their health, friends, and family in their drive for success may have.

My father had a saying about such people: "These are such foolish people. They spend the first half of their lives sacrificing their health in order to make money, and then they spend the second half of their lives sacrificing their money in order to get back their health — and they end up with neither."

My father would have respected David Curzon's anger, for he too lost many of his loved ones in the Holocaust. But he treasured the hope and the vision in Psalm 1, and he recited it faithfully many times.

Perhaps we should, too. For hope and faith are better ways to live than in bitterness. And so the editor of the Psalms may have been right in starting off his book with this psalm. Further on, we will find songs of praise and anger, awe and doubt, wonder and pain, but he chose to begin the book with this one that affirms the meaningfulness of our lives. And rightly so.

Hope and Faith — as It Should Be, Not as It Is
Rabbi Riemer

Before we leave this first psalm, let me share two insights that come from the educator Rabbi Benjamin Segal's commentary on it. The first point he makes is that *ashrei* is the key word of the psalm and that it does not mean "prosperous" or "successful." It means "happy," "content," "blessed," or "satisfied with life." The claim of this psalm is not that the righteous will be rich but that they will be able to live contented and meaningful lives.

The second point he makes is that to think that this psalm claims that the good guys always win and the bad guys always lose is to misunderstand it. Notice that the wicked, the cynical, and the sinful are always described in the plural, whereas the righteous person is always described in the singular. That is the poet's way of saying that the righteous person feels terribly alone. They feel that they are like the one good tree that is planted by the water, which means that they may grow beautifully, and they may have fruit and foliage, but there is no other tree anywhere around them. The righteous person of this psalm feels isolated. The world is in the hands of the wicked and they are all alone. This is why they call on God to rescue them and to judge the wicked who surround them. The call to God in the last line of this psalm should be read as a hope and as a vision and not a description of the way that the world is.

If Rabbi Segal's comment is right in this observation, then perhaps all of us — including David Curzon — owe the psalmist an apology, for he may not have been as naïve as we thought he was when we first read this psalm. He may be a person who has known harsh realities but who still keeps his faith in the future. If this is so, then we who live in an uncertain world, as he did, should learn from him.

Judaism is a future-oriented faith. Our golden age is in the future, not in the past, as the Greeks thought it was. The middle prayers of the Amidah, the central daily prayer, are not a shopping list of requests with which we come before God. They start out that way. We begin by asking for intelligence, health, and livelihood, which are things that we need now. But we soon move to prayers for what the world needs, for things that will only come about at the end of days — such as a restoration of justice, the return of God's presence to Zion, and the reestablishment of lasting peace. These are not personal prayers but affirmations of our faith in the way that the world will someday be.

I read Psalm 1 now and understand it differently than the way I did before. Now I see it as a fitting beginning to the book of Psalms because it affirms the hope that was the key to Jewish life then and has been ever since. And I read David Curzon now with sympathy for all he has gone through and with hope that he may be able to hope again. For without hope, neither a person nor a people can live a meaningful life.

Psalm 8

"The Work of Your Fingers"

Rabbi Elie Spitz

Psalm 8 marvels over God's magnificent creation, the Creator's concern for mere mortals, and the immense power of humans, including the capacity for evil.

א לַמְנַצֵּחַ עַל הַגִּתִּית,
מִזְמוֹר לְדָוִד.

1 For the lead player upon the *gittith*, a hymn of David.

ב יְהֹוָה אֲדֹנֵינוּ,
מָה אַדִּיר שִׁמְךָ בְּכָל הָאָרֶץ;
אֲשֶׁר תְּנָה הוֹדְךָ עַל הַשָּׁמָיִם.

2 *Adonai*, our Supreme, how majestic is Your name in all the earth; whose splendor You set upon the heavens.

ג מִפִּי עוֹלְלִים וְיֹנְקִים יִסַּדְתָּ עֹז;
לְמַעַן צוֹרְרֶיךָ לְהַשְׁבִּית אוֹיֵב וּמִתְנַקֵּם.

3 From out of the mouths of babes and sucklings You have founded strength;
on account of Your foes that You might still the enemy and the avenger.

ד כִּי אֶרְאֶה שָׁמֶיךָ,
מַעֲשֵׂה אֶצְבְּעֹתֶיךָ,
יָרֵחַ וְכוֹכָבִים אֲשֶׁר כּוֹנָנְתָּה.

4 For I behold Your heavens, the work of Your fingers, the moon and the stars that You set in place.

ה מָה אֱנוֹשׁ כִּי תִזְכְּרֶנּוּ **5** What are humans,
וּבֶן אָדָם כִּי תִפְקְדֶנּוּ? that You are mindful of them
and mortals
that You have taken note of them?

ו וַתְּחַסְּרֵהוּ מְּעַט מֵאֱלֹהִים, **6** Yet You have made them
וְכָבוֹד וְהָדָר תְּעַטְּרֵהוּ. but a little less than the divine,
and with honor and glory
You have crowned them.

ז תַּמְשִׁילֵהוּ בְּמַעֲשֵׂי יָדֶיךָ; **7** You have made them masters over
כֹּל שַׁתָּה תַחַת רַגְלָיו. the works of Your hands;
all You have placed under their feet:

ח צֹנֶה וַאֲלָפִים כֻּלָּם **8** Sheep and oxen, all of them and
וְגַם בַּהֲמוֹת שָׂדָי. also the animals of the open field.

ט צִפּוֹר שָׁמַיִם וּדְגֵי הַיָּם— **9** The fowl of the heavens, and the
עֹבֵר אָרְחוֹת יַמִּים. fish of the sea — whatsoever passes
through the currents of the seas.

י יְהֹוָה אֲדֹנֵינוּ, **10** *Adonai*, our Supreme,
מָה אַדִּיר שִׁמְךָ בְּכָל הָאָרֶץ. how majestic is Your name
in all the earth.

READING CLOSELY

Erich Fromm, the psychologist and author of *The Art of Loving*, defined the human dilemma as simultaneously being part of the natural world while possessing a power over nature.[29] In Psalm 8 that tension is celebrated as a wondrous gift: "What are humans, that You are mindful of them and mortals that You have taken note of them? Yet You have made them but a little less than the divine, and with honor and glory You have crowned them" (vv. 5-6).

The biblical creation account provides a context for this psalm. Before the creation of Adam there is a pause in the story as if God is thinking out loud: "'Let us create an earthling in our likeness and in our image.' And in the image of God, [God] created them. 'They shall rule the fish of the sea, the birds of the sky, the cattle, the whole earth and all the living things that creep on earth.' And God created the earthling in [God's] image, in the image of God [God] created; male and female [God] created them" (Genesis 1:26-27).[30]

Our psalmist surely knows this tale, and yet poetry is usually triggered by an immediate event. We are left to guess as to the origins of this song that recognizes God's power and empowerment of those "a little less than the divine." Humans do have a divine-like ability to effect change. The answer to our prayers, some have said regarding the COVID-19 pandemic, is the creation of vaccines. While gratitude is the emotional response to receiving a gift, praise is giving voice to a spontaneous "Wow." This is primarily a psalm of divine praise.

In verse 1, we are unsure of the nature of *gittith*. Most commentators assume that it is one of the many musical instruments cited in Psalms, whose distinctiveness is now unknown. A couple of creative commentaries link the root to a symbolic object. For the Meiri (Catalonia, 1249-1315), the *gittith* is identified with the Holy Ark,[31] with revelation as the key divine act of human elevation. For Rabbi Samson Raphael Hirsch (Germany, 1808-1888), the root is linked to a winepress (Isaiah 66:3), thereby suggesting that the partnership between God and a vintner characterizes all human achievements.

"A hymn of David" could either mean that it was composed by David (widely espoused traditionally), for David as a commissioned work, or in the style of David at a far later date (the view held by most modern scholars).

Verse 2 frames the psalm and begins a journey. At the outset, the words are an overview of what is to come: a description of God's majestic creation coupled with God's attention to mere mortals.

Verse 3 acknowledges the potential of each human being to reflect God's power and mystery. Consider the observation of Rabbi Abraham Joshua Heschel:

> One thing that sets man apart from animals is a boundless, unpredictable capacity for the development of an inner universe. There is more potentiality in his soul than in any other being known to us. Look at the infant and try to imagine the multitude of events it is going to engender. One child named Johann Sebastian Bach was charged with power enough to hold generations of men in his spell. But is there any potentiality to acclaim or any surprise to expect in a calf or a colt? Indeed, the enigma of human being is not in what he is but in what he is able to be.[32]

And yet the second half of the verse acknowledges foes. There is danger in the world, pointing to the gift of human free will and the human capacity for evil.

Verse 4 directs us to look upward to see the intricacy of God's handiwork. The use of "fingers" suggests that the moon and the stars are finely woven like a tapestry.[33] The use of "I" conveys the personal nature of the observation.

Verse 5 marks the center of the psalm, a kind of bull's-eye with the phrase "What are humans, that You are mindful of them?" The contrast between the majesty of creation and God's caring presence is baffling. This is not a rhetorical question; rather, it is an expression of wonder and gratitude. We are given a prompt to consider that for the Creator we are worthy of attention; our prayers are heard.

Verse 6 is a celebration of human capacity. Classic commentators, such as eleventh-century Rashi, identify the divine in this verse with the angels, celestial beings with a quality of purity who are devoted to serving God. Others take the verse as stated — namely, referring to people. *Honor, glory,* and *crowned* are words usually reserved for God; here, they are applied to humanity.

Verses 7 through 9 accentuate the power of humanity over all the creation, moving from land to sky to sea with words of dominion identified in the Near East with a king: "all You have placed under their feet"[34] (v. 7).

In verse 10, words that began the psalm as if a title are now expressed as a personal proclamation, for the psalm has prompted us to survey and reflect on God's beneficence.

Mah ("how" or "what") is a reoccurring word. Verses 2 and 10 both contain "How majestic is Your name in all the earth." The first time the phrase is used just before extolling the wonder of creation; the second time, just after acknowledging human power. Between these two uses of *mah* is verse 5, which begins "What are humans, that You are mindful of them?" The repetition links God's majestic creation, concern for a mortal being, and humanity's power: to choose "what" we see and do with our divine-like gifts of creation, celebration, and caregiving.

DIGGING DEEPER

Human Potential
Rabbi Spitz

Only humans write and read words. When Onkelos composed the Aramaic translation of the Bible (circa 110 CE), he understood the meaning of God breathing into the nostrils "a breath of life" (Genesis 2:7) as a "speaking spirit." This refers to more than language — the very ability for divine-like creativity. For in the creation story, God used words to create: "And God said, 'Let there be light.' And there was light" (Genesis 1:3). Our language is a vessel for retaining knowledge, transmitting it across generations, and planning for the future. Our language reveals and fosters thought, whether applied in science to create formulas to understand and heal the human body or to build on the written wisdom of generations before us, whether in conducting affairs of state or a symphony.

Prayer and ritual transcend instinct to such a degree that we may choose to symbolize contrition by self-restraint: not eating and instead using our mouths to express remorse.[35] A capacity for spirituality or religious tradition does not necessarily make us better. How we choose to act is what will matter more than beliefs. Yet our choices are shaped by values and priorities, which at their best prompt discipline, self-sacrifice, and divine-like concerns. I am moved by this psalm as an anthem of marvel over God's gifts of creation and attentiveness, and of human power.

As I read this psalm, I am also sad, for I am reminded of the enormous human potential for destruction. The war in Ukraine rages on and the Russians have elevated their nuclear readiness. It is a frightening possibility. Nuclear bombs can kill vast numbers of people in a matter of minutes and could lead to a retaliation that spirals out of control. Nuclear war could cause irreparable damage to the planet, as did asteroids hitting the earth so many millions of years ago that caused the extreme heating of the planet and the death of all the dinosaurs.[36] We could be next.

Less immediately but ever increasingly impactful, the constant thrust of methane and carbon dioxide into the air has already changed our planet's climate. The unchecked trajectory is one of utter devastation. Sadly, we are wired to think short-term. I am reminded of the biblical admonition "A bribe blinds the eyes of the wise" (Deuteronomy 16:19).[37] Immediate self-interest often leads to only seeing what we are predisposed to see and discounting the evidence of danger. I am saddened that governments until now have failed to act decisively. To sacrifice is to both give up a possession and to do so for a higher purpose. Short-term profits and ongoing comforts have prevented decisions to make necessary, impactful sacrifices.

Surely the ancient psalmist did not imagine the technologies that we wield today. Yet Psalm 8 is a wake-up call. We are given both power and responsibility. The future of God's wondrous creation is in our hands.

Two Opposing Truths
Rabbi Spitz

Rabbi Simcha Bunim, the Hasidic master of Peshischa, Poland (1765-1827), said that a person needed to keep two pieces of paper, each in a separate pocket. One piece of paper reads "I am but dust and ashes," mirroring the words of Abraham to God (Genesis 18:27), and it should be read when feeling overly powerful. The other is a quote of the sages: "The world was created on my account"; it should be read as an antidote to feeling insignificant.[38]

I am reminded of the image of a musical string that only when pulled in two opposite directions simultaneously produces a melodic sound. The two opposite ideas provide the poles of our lives, and we live in between. Rabbi Abraham Joshua Heschel described this back-and-forth as a pendulum.

> Man is "a little lower than the angels" and a lit-
> tle higher than the beasts. Like a pendulum he
> swings to and fro under the combined action of
> gravity and momentum, of the gravitation of self-
> ishness and the momentum of the divine, of a
> vision beheld by God in the darkness of flesh and
> blood.[39]

We need a check on our human power. The human capacity to wage
nuclear war may cause massive destruction. Sadly, rising increments of
carbon dioxide and methane that we humans put into the atmosphere
have already led to changes in climate and to increasingly severe and recurring natural disasters. This psalm celebrates human power: "You have
made them masters over the works of Your hands" (v. 7), highlighting the
need for humility and self-control before the Creator.

Wonder
Rabbi Spitz

Among the most extraordinary human achievements was sending humans
to the moon and then safely bringing them back to earth. Best-selling
author Rabbi Harold Kushner notes that the whole world breathlessly
watched the initial moon landing: "A small step for a man; a giant leap
for all mankind." On the second landing, we caught the event on the evening news. By the third landing, the astronauts only gained our attention
by putting a golf ball. Once we saw we could meet a goal, our attention
moved on. In contrast, Rabbi Kushner emphasizes, the majesty of God's
creation continues to evoke wonder when we pay attention. Although we
may ignore a sunset or see it as simply the end of a day, when we mind-
fully pause before the kaleidoscopic colors, we marvel. A sunset as God's
creation can take our breath away day after day.

The two quotations of Rabbi Simcha Bunim come back to mind: we live with awareness of both our human power and our limitations. We are all here for just a visit, which sets us apart from God. Our days are more precious when we are aware of our limitation of time and our distinctive capacity for wonder. In the words of Rabbi Abraham Joshua Heschel,

> As civilization advances, the sense of wonder declines. Such decline is an alarming symptom of our state of mind. Mankind will not perish for want of information; but only for want of appreciation. The beginning of our happiness lies in the understanding that life without wonder is not worth living. What we lack is not a will to believe but a will to wonder. Radical amazement has a wider scope than any other act of man. While any act of perception or cognition has as its object a selected segment of reality, radical amazement refers to all of reality; not only to what we see, but also to the very act of seeing.[40]

Psalm 8 — Precious and Needed More Than Ever
Rabbi Riemer

With Psalm 1 we studied the words of a psalmist who said that God rewards the righteous and punishes the wicked. In response, we studied the words of David Curzon, a poet of our time who denies this faith. Curzon not only denies that this claim is true in our experience; he even argues that it is not true in the Bible itself.

And so we were confronted with two poems, one that sings the praises of God and declares that God rewards the righteous and punishes the wicked, and another poem that denies that God operates in this way — not in life and not in the Bible.

In Psalm 8, the psalmist declares the glory of God and the sheer beauty of creation, and thanks God for having made the human being but a little lower than the angels and for having put humans in charge of creation.

In his commentary on this psalm, Rabbi Spitz points out that the psalmist looks at the world and is simply overwhelmed by its beauty. He is amazed; more than that, he is astonished at the sheer beauty of what God has made. And he is awestruck by the awareness that God has made humanity but a little lower than the angels and has put us in charge of this world.

Anyone who reads Psalm 8 must agree that this is its central message. And I believe that anyone who *really* looks at the world — who looks at a tree or a flower or the ocean or a sunrise or a sunset with sensitive eyes — shares the psalmist's sense of awe and humility.

And so here I will not argue with the psalmist. I share his faith that the world is full of the glory of God. And I feel that you, the reader, share this sense of wonder; or else no words — of mine or the psalmist or anyone else — will persuade you.

However, there are two points that I want to make about Psalm 8. The first is that I believe that this psalm contains the greatest compliment to humanity that has ever been given in all of literature. The second is that this tribute to the dignity of humanity is under more attack in our time than ever before, and therefore this psalm is a precious document that our generation needs to hear even more than previous generations did.

The psalmist declares that God has "made [human beings] the masters over the works of Your hands; all You have placed under their feet: sheep and oxen, all of them and also the animals of the open field, the fowl of the heavens, and the fish of the sea" (vv. 7-9).

But in the modern age, this view of humanity has been challenged by many experts. Psychologists see the human being as a creature driven by an urge for power and sex that is almost impossible to control. Economists see humanity as divided between those with power and those without power. Astronomers see the earth on which we live as a miniscule planet that is of no significance in the context of the vast cosmos in which it is located.

Let us consider just a few examples of these claims that challenge the dignity of the human being in modern times and the consequences of these claims. The first comes from biology. In the twentieth century, there were biology textbooks in the classrooms of Germany that calculated the worth of a human being by measuring the price of the chemicals that are found within the human body. A generation later, the Nazis who had been brought up on these books determined precisely which instruments for murdering human beings were the most efficient and the most economical and therefore the best to use in the crematoria.

Economists should remember with embarrassment that in its early years, the government of the Soviet Union instituted what they called a "five-year plan" in which thousands and thousands of human beings were allowed to die of hunger for the sake of a future generation that would benefit from their work.

Psychologists should feel concerned at the rise of a generation that seems to be obsessed with woman as object rather than as person and that regards the commitment to lifelong marriage as a naïve idea whose time has passed.

In such a world, the statement of Psalm 8 that humankind is but a little lower than the angels and that God has entrusted us with responsibility for the world that God has created should be treasured and appreciated. Psalm 8 should be considered an important part of our spiritual legacy and armory.

It is easy for modern astronomers to disparage humanity by pointing out how tiny this earth is and how vast is the cosmic system of which it is a part. But I believe that the response to this assertion that the philosopher and theologian Rabbi Milton Steinberg made years ago is still very much on target.

Rabbi Steinberg responded to the claim of the insignificance of human beings with the observation that the vastness of the universe is indeed intimidating, and the cosmic system does indeed make our planet seem puny, but we should never forget that it is the human being — and *only* the human being — who invented the telescope through which we can see the cosmic system.

Steinberg was right in comforting us with this observation and in teaching us that even though we may be the residents of one tiny planet within a vast cosmic system, we are the only creatures in this system who can think and speak and plan and live and love. So it is not really as naïve as some of these cynics think, even in this technologically advanced time, to appreciate Psalm 8 and to share in the awe and the gratitude that it conveys.

Memories of Holiness
Rabbi Riemer

Bernard Precker owns an art gallery in Brookline, Massachusetts. He says that a customer came into his store recently and bought a few pictures with which to decorate a baby's room. Then, as the customer was about to leave, he turned around and said to Precker, "Can I please tell you a story about something that just happened in our house?" Mr. Precker agreed to listen, and this is what the man told him:

> Something very strange happened in our house this week and I don't begin to understand it. Perhaps you will.
>
> A couple of days ago, I brought my wife and our newborn baby home from the hospital.
>
> The first thing we did was show the baby to our older child, who is about four and a half years old. Then we put the baby in her crib and closed the door.
>
> The older child said, "Would you please do me a favor?"

We asked him what it was that he wanted, and he said, "Would you please let me be alone with the baby for just a few minutes?"

At first the parents were a little bit hesitant. They knew about sibling rivalry, and so they said to themselves, "What if this child is resentful that a new child has arrived to share his parents' love? And what if he wants to hurt the baby?"

But they decided that they would let him have a few minutes alone with the baby. After all, they had video and audio monitors set up in the baby's room and so they felt that it would be safe to let this child have his wish. And they hid behind the door so that they could eavesdrop on what their child would say to his new sibling.

As they spied from behind the door, they saw their four-year-old child bend down and stroke the head of his baby sister. And then they heard this child whisper something to the baby.

He said, "Do you still remember what it was like when you lived with God?"

And then he said, "The reason I am asking you is because I am beginning to forget."

Isn't that an amazing story? This four-year-old child asked his newborn baby sister whether she still remembered what it was like before she was born — because he himself was beginning to forget!

You may dismiss this story if you wish, and I am not sure that I believe it myself, but when I heard it, I was reminded of an old Jewish legend that you may remember too.

An old Jewish legend says that during the nine months that the child is inside its mother's womb, an angel lives there with the child, and during these nine months this angel teaches the child the whole Torah. But when the baby is born, the angel hits the child on the upper lip and the child forgets all the Torah they have learned. And that, at least according to the legend, is why the child cries when they are born, and that is why every child is born with a cleft upon their upper lip.

This idea — that a newborn child is not a tabula rosa but comes into this world bearing memories of having once been surrounded by holiness — is a concept that is found in Psalm 8 and that bobs up in some very unexpected places in modern poetry, as I will now show you.

How Majestic!
Rabbi Riemer

E. E. Cummings is a famous poet and playwright who lived in Boston in the beginning of the twentieth century. He wrote a great many poems and a good number of plays, but he is best remembered for inventing a kind of poetry that paid no attention to punctuation.

This is one of his best-known poems, a poem that has been set to music by several different composers.

> I thank You, God, for most this amazing
> day, for the leaping greenly spirits of trees
> and a blue true dream of sky; and for everything
> which is natural which is infinite which is You.

Notice the wonder with which Cummings describes nature in this first verse. Notice the exuberance in these phrases: "the leaping greenly spirits of the trees" and "a blue true dream of sky." And notice the last line: "which is natural which is infinite which is You."

I think that what Cummings is saying in that line is that the world is not either natural or divine but both at the same time. It is natural — that is why we can define it or measure it. But it is also infinite — it is beyond our ability to measure or define. And it is both of these things because it comes from God.

And now let us listen to the second verse:

> (i who have died am alive again today
> And this is the sun's birthday, this is the birth
> day of life and of love and of wings and of the gay
> great happening illimitably earth)

I don't think that the first line — "I who have died am alive again to-day" — is meant to refer to the resurrection but rather to the wonder of a new day. It reminds me of a prayer that we Jews recite every morning in which we thank God for having awoken us from sleep and for having given us a brand-new day of life. I have no idea how or even whether this Jewish prayer came to this poet, but this is the reference that comes to my mind when I read it.

And then Cummings goes on to say that every day is the sun's birthday and yet it feels to him as if it is shining for the very first time. It is a day of life and love and enchantment and so is every day. And that too echoes a prayer in the Jewish morning service that declares that God did not just create the world once and then retire but that God creates the world anew every single day.

And now comes the third verse:

> how should tasting touching hearing seeing
> breathing — any ing — lifted from the no
> of allnothing — human merely being —
> doubt unimaginable You?
>
> (now the ears of my ears awake and
> now the eyes of my eyes are opened)[41]

At first read, this verse seems to be a kind of a hodgepodge in which words appear in what seems to be random order. But if you read it carefully you will understand that what the poet is saying is that ordinary touching or tasting or hearing or seeing or breathing — or as he puts it, "any ing" — cannot reach God. Human beings cannot comprehend God with their ordinary faculties. But when the ears of my ears are awake ... And the eyes of my eyes are opened ...

I think that what the poet is saying in these last two lines is that we cannot see or hear or touch or weigh or define or measure God with our physical senses but we can find God with our inner eye and our inner ear.

These two expressions, the inner eye and the inner ear, are found frequently in medieval Jewish mystical literature, and they are found in Christian and Muslim mystical literature as well. Our merely human senses are simply not capable of comprehending God. But if we open our inner eye and if we open our inner ear, we can feel the presence of God.

This poem is a love song to God. And it can be understood as a commentary on Psalm 8 for it has the same sense of amazement, the same sense of astonishment at the wonder of creation, that Psalm 8 expresses. In his own way, Cummings is saying what the psalmist declared when he said, *Ma adir shimcha bichol ha-aretz,* "How majestic is Your name in all the earth."

Trailing Clouds of Glory
Rabbi Riemer

William Wordsworth was a distinguished English poet of the nineteenth century. We cite him here because he not only expresses his awe at the wonder of creation, as Cummings and many others have done, but because he brings us back to what was affirmed by that four-year-old in Boston who asked his sibling whether she still remembered what it was like to live with God before she was born, and the Jewish legend about the angel who resides in the womb together with each embryo and teaches it

Torah: we come into this world from divinity. How this tradition came to Wordsworth I have no idea. But listen to what he wrote:

> Our birth is but a sleep and a forgetting:
> The Soul that rises with us, our life's Star,
> Hath had elsewhere its setting,
> And cometh from afar:
> Not in entire forgetfulness,
> And not in utter nakedness,
> But trailing clouds of glory do we come
> From God, who is our home;
> Heaven lies about us in our infancy!
> Shades of the prison-house begin to close
> Upon the growing boy...[42]

Here is William Wordsworth, who we assume never heard the Jewish legend about the angel who teaches Torah to children in the womb and who surely never met the four-year-old child in Boston, giving voice to the very same idea!

He is saying that we come from divinity and we come trailing clouds of glory but that after a while, the "shades of the prison house" — by which I think that he means this real world — begin to close in on us. And as we grow older, he says, we forget the clouds of glory with which we came into this world.

It's Still a Wonder
Rabbi Riemer

Now let me tell you a Hasidic story that deals with the relationship between facts and the sense of wonder. This is the story of the first electric carriage that came to Warsaw and how the Hasidim in a *shtiebel*, a prayer room, reacted to it.

The people in the shtiebel were astonished. They had never seen a carriage that was not pulled by horses before and they just couldn't believe it. So they turned to the one *maskil* in their group — a maskil is a sophisticated person, someone who reads the secular newspapers — and they asked him, "Do you understand this phenomenon?"

The maskil said, "Of course, I do."

They asked, "Can you explain it to us?"

He said, "Of course I can."

So they gathered around him and he explained how the electric streetcar works. He said, "Imagine four large wheels in a vertical position in four corners of a square and then picture these four wheels connected to each other by small wires. Do you get it?"

The Hasidim answered hesitantly, "Yes, we get it."

Then the maskil said, "These wires are tied in a knot in the center of the square, and they are placed within a larger wheel that is placed in a horizontal position. Do you get it?"

The Hasidim answered with a little bit more uncertainty in their voices, "Uh . . . we get it."

The maskil then said, "Above this large wheel there are several other wheels, each one smaller than the one below it. Do you get it?"

The Hasidim answered with a little bit more uncertainty in their voices, "Ye . . . ye . . . yes, we get it."

The maskil continued: "On top of the smallest wheel there is a tiny screw, which is connected by a wire to the center of the car, which lies on top of the wheels. Do you get it?"

The Hasidim answered even more cautiously, "Ye . . . ye . . . yes, we get it."

"Then you see that it is really no wonder," the maskil said. "The machinist inside the car presses a button that moves the screw that causes the horizontal wheels to move, which causes the vertical wheels to move, and that is how the car moves down the street. It is really very simple."

And all the Hasidim nodded their heads when the maskil finished his explanation.

But there was one old Hasid listening who said to himself, "Now I understand — and yet to me it is *still* a wonder."

And that is how the writer of Psalm 8 felt. He was simply enchanted and overwhelmed by the glory of God's creation.

For Many More Years to Come
Rabbi Riemer

Amy Grossblatt Pessah, a friend of mine in Boca Raton, Florida, is a truly spiritual person. She has an imagination that enables her to see all kinds of profound truths that other people do not notice. She is married to a doctor, and he has a very different kind of mind. He is a scientist, and he only cares about facts and data that can be tested and validated.

Some time ago, the two of them visited Chicago, their hometown, for a brief vacation. While they were there, they went for a walk together in the Chicago Arboretum. They came to a certain tree that caught Amy's attention. She said to her husband, "Look at that beautiful tree! Can you feel the energy that is coming from that tree!"

Her husband said, "No. It is just a plain ordinary tree, a part of nature like any other tree."

This went on until they came to an even more beautiful tree. This time Amy ran to the tree and tried to put her arms around it. And as she did, she felt simply radiant. Her husband took out his cellphone and took a picture of her hugging the tree.

And sure enough, when they looked at the picture, they saw that the tree and Amy were both shining. She had a beautiful smile on her face, and the tree had beautiful rays of light shining through its leaves.

Amy turned to her husband and said triumphantly, "See!!! I told you that this tree was radiant." He said, "The reason this tree is shining is because there is some water on one of its branches, and the sun just happened to come out at this moment and caught its reflection."

The two of them looked at each other and they both threw up their hands in exasperation. He was exasperated that she could not see what he saw, and she was exasperated that he could not see what she saw.

And then they both said, "You know what? We have been married to each other for many years now. You look at the world one way, and I look at the world another way. And neither of us can persuade the other one. May that continue for many more years to come."

And they clasped hands and walked out of the arboretum together.

You and I know people who have different ways of looking at the world. But, I believe that the author of Psalm 8, E.E. Cummings, and the old Hasid who saw the first electric streetcar come to his village would have understood Amy's sense of wonder.

Psalm 19

"The Heavens Declare the Glory of God"

Rabbi Elie Spitz

When have you felt close to God? Most who answer initially respond by describing a riveting experience amid nature: witnessing the birth of a child; caught in a great storm; recovering from an illness; mesmerized by the changing colors of sunset. This soaring psalm likewise starts with marveling at the wonders of creation, describing the heavenly bodies as producing an inaudible symphony, and rejoicing over the sun's rising each morning like the beaming face of a groom emerging from the wedding canopy. For the psalmist, the universal is only a part of the story. There is also the communal and the personal. Where nature does not care about us as individuals or how we treat one another, the God of the Bible assuredly does. The psalmist also teaches that after revelation amid community and living God's teachings, an individual may also plead for personal redemption.

א לַמְנַצֵּחַ, מִזְמוֹר לְדָוִד. **1** For the Conductor, a Psalm of David.

ב הַשָּׁמַיִם מְסַפְּרִים כְּבוֹד אֵל וּמַעֲשֵׂה יָדָיו מַגִּיד הָרָקִיעַ. **2** The heavens declare the glory of God and of [God's] handiwork the firmament tells.

ג יוֹם לְיוֹם יַבִּיעַ אֹמֶר וְלַיְלָה לְּלַיְלָה יְחַוֶּה דָּעַת. **3** Day to day utters speech and night to night expresses knowledge;

ד אֵין אֹמֶר וְאֵין דְּבָרִים,
בְּלִי נִשְׁמָע קוֹלָם.

4 There is no speech, and there are no words, never heard is their voice.

ה בְּכָל הָאָרֶץ יָצָא קַוָּם
וּבִקְצֵה תֵבֵל מִלֵּיהֶם;
לַשֶּׁמֶשׁ שָׂם אֹהֶל בָּהֶם.

5 Throughout all the earth their voice extends and to the end of the world their words:
For [God] placed in them a tent for the sun,

ו וְהוּא כְּחָתָן יֹצֵא מֵחֻפָּתוֹ,
יָשִׂישׂ כְּגִבּוֹר לָרוּץ אֹרַח.

6 who is like a groom coming forth from his *huppah*, exulting like a hero running on course.

ז מִקְצֵה הַשָּׁמַיִם מוֹצָאוֹ
וּתְקוּפָתוֹ עַל קְצוֹתָם;
וְאֵין נִסְתָּר מֵחַמָּתוֹ.

7 From the end of the heavens is its rising
and its circuit reaches the other end;
and nothing is hidden from its heat.

ח תּוֹרַת יְהוָה תְּמִימָה,
מְשִׁיבַת נָפֶשׁ;
עֵדוּת יְהוָה נֶאֱמָנָה,
מַחְכִּימַת פֶּתִי.

8 The Torah of *Adonai* is complete, reviving the soul; testimony of *Adonai* is trustworthy, making wise the simple.

ט פִּקּוּדֵי יְהוָה יְשָׁרִים, מְשַׂמְּחֵי-לֵב;
מִצְוַת יְהוָה בָּרָה, מְאִירַת עֵינָיִם.

9 The precepts of *Adonai* are upright, rejoicing the heart; the expectation of *Adonai* is clear, enlightening the eyes.

י יִרְאַת יְהוָה טְהוֹרָה ,עוֹמֶדֶת לָעַד,
מִשְׁפְּטֵי יְהוָה אֱמֶת,
צָדְקוּ יַחְדָּו.

10 The reverence of *Adonai* is pure, abiding forever; the judgments of *Adonai* are truth, altogether just,

הַנֶּחֱמָדִים מִזָּהָב וּמִפַּז רָב; **יא**   **11** more desirable than gold, than
וּמְתוּקִים מִדְּבַשׁ וְנֹפֶת צוּפִים.   much fine gold; sweeter than honey,
than drippings of the honeycomb.

גַּם עַבְדְּךָ נִזְהָר בָּהֶם; **יב**   **12** Indeed Your servant is careful
בְּשָׁמְרָם— עֵקֶב רָב.   with them; with observing them —
great reward.

שְׁגִיאוֹת— מִי יָבִין? **יג**   **13** Unwitting errors —
מִנִּסְתָּרוֹת נַקֵּנִי.   who can discern?
From hidden faults — cleanse me!

גַּם מִזֵּדִים, חֲשֹׁךְ עַבְדֶּךָ; **יד**   **14** Indeed from willful sins, spare
אַל יִמְשְׁלוּ בִי אָז אֵיתָם;   Your servant; let them not rule over
וְנִקֵּיתִי מִפֶּשַׁע רָב.   me, then I will be wholehearted;
and I will be cleansed from great
wrongdoing.

יִהְיוּ לְרָצוֹן אִמְרֵי פִי **טו**   **15** May they be acceptable, the
וְהֶגְיוֹן לִבִּי לְפָנֶיךָ:   speech of my mouth and the
יְהוָה, צוּרִי וְגֹאֲלִי.   meditation of my heart, before You:
Adonai, my Rock and my Redeemer.

READING CLOSELY

Three thematic sections divide this psalm: marveling at the heavens (vv. 2-7); extolling God's communal revelation (vv. 8-11); seeking personal redemption by God (vv. 12-15).

Verses 2-4 draw our attention upward: "The heavens declare the glory of God and of [God's] handiwork the firmament tells.[43] Day to day utters speech and night to night reveals knowledge. There is no speech, there are no words, never heard is their voice." We observe the sun, moon, and stars moving predictably across the sky. For the psalmist, the celestial bodies in motion produce a symphony of unheard music. Just as members of an orchestra play their set part, so the bodies of the heavens move in their ordered paths. Audibly unheard, celestial music is grounded in a widespread belief of ancient times.

In an Ugaritic epic of the ancient Near East, the god Baal sends a love message to the goddess Anath: "I have a word that I would tell . . . a word of the trees and a whisper of the stones . . . a word that humans do not know and that the earthly mass do not comprehend." The Greek mathematician and philosopher Pythagoras (sixth century BCE) taught that the planets revolved in circular orbits, producing differing harmonious sounds according to variations in speed and the size of the orbit. Aristotle (fourth century BCE) wrote that celestial objects were intelligent beings, a teaching that Maimonides would quote 1,600 years later.[44]

In verse 2, the heavens declare the glory of *El*, the generic name for God throughout the ancient Near East. God's glory is universal, and even the whole of creation sings God's praise. The verses' very structure portrays the movement. Verse 2's couplets convey circularity: noun, verb, object; object, verb, noun. Verse 3 shifts us forward with a linear use of repetition: "Day to day . . . night to night." And then verse 4 stops us to consider the silence with three phrases, each starting with a negative: no speech, no words, never heard.

Verses 5-7 put the focus squarely on the sun: "Throughout all the earth their voice extends and to the end of the world their words; [God] places in them a tent for the sun, who is like a groom coming forth from his *huppah* [wedding canopy], exulting like a hero running on course.[45] From the end of the heavens is its rising and its circuit reaches the other end; and nothing is hidden from its heat."[46] As the sun moves across the sky, its voice extends across the expanse of the world, serving as a bridge to the opening verses.[47] And now personification shifts to the sun's tent as if the sun returns to rest after the long journey.

In *On the Book of Psalms: Exploring the Prayers of Ancient Israel*, the Bible scholar Nahum Sarna explains that an ancient Mesopotamian prayer describes sunset in terms of Shamash, the sun god, returning to his chamber.[48] In that pagan mythology, the god himself crafted the dwelling, which he shared with his consort, Aya. In this psalm, by contrast, the sun's chamber belongs to God the Creator. Sarna subtitles his analysis of Psalm 19 "an anti-pagan polemic."[49]

The sun is now described "like a groom coming forth from his *huppah*, exulting like a hero running on course" (v. 6). A groom and a victorious athlete are identified with joy and triumph. This too has roots in ancient mythology. In Mesopotamia, Shamash is both the sun and a warrior god. In Egypt, the sun god is described as "the great runner swift of step" who runs a course each day. The psalmist will extoll the sun, saying that "nothing is hidden from its heat" (v. 7) — a contrast with the true Creator, God, who is hidden. In these verses, the sun is not mentioned by name, another device for relegating the celestial body to subservience to the Creator. For the poet has transformed the commonly held myth into a distinctive message of monotheistic faith. For as the Torah has cautioned, "When you raise your eyes to the sky and see the sun, moon, stars, and other heavenly bodies, do not bow down to them or worship them" (Deuteronomy 4:19).

As the psalm gets ready to shift from the "music of the spheres" to the gift of Torah, one last parallel to ancient mythology is worth noting: the sun god was also identified with administering justice, for the sun from its height shining everywhere led to its identification with penetrating awareness and goodness. King Hammurabi of Babylon (1728-1686 BCE) in his famous code of law will cite Shamash in the prologue and epilogue as his inspiration. In Egyptian mythology, Re, the sun god (also spelled *Ra*), had a daughter, Ma'at, who administered justice. In Greece, the god

Apollo was connected to the sun and called radiant and the supervisor of law and order.

For the psalmist in verses 8-11, Torah is from the Creator, given to humanity to learn and to follow. The word *Torah* has many possible meanings: teaching, law, or more specifically, a revealed text. As we saw in Psalm 1 with the description of the happy person who repeats the Torah day and night, in Torah there is a sacred, discrete written text. In our day, we place the Torah scroll containing the Five Books of Moses in the ark as the primary focus of the synagogue. I tend to think that here, too, the psalmist is describing the Torah scroll, which is linked to the revelation of Mount Sinai.

The adjective used for Torah is *temimah*, which has multiple translations: "complete," "perfect," "possessing integrity," or "unblemished." I have chosen "complete" as well-suited to describe both of God's works: the sacred text and people. Noah is described as *"temim* for his generation" (Genesis 6:9), a qualified compliment by defining his completeness or goodness comparatively. Closer to our time, a popular epitaph on the headstones of pious Jews of Eastern Europe was *tam v'yashar*, "possessing integrity and directness." Torah is complete in its revelation, both as a practical and aspirational teaching. And as we will see, the psalmist of Psalm 19 will circle back to *tam* as a personal longing.

As the sun enables plants to grow, so Torah revives a person's spirit and enlightens the eyes.[50] The sun is linked to Torah but with a shift from the physical plane to the inner life. The phrases that follow are aspects of Torah: testimony (*edut*), precepts (*pekudei*), expectation (*mitzvah*), reverence of God (*yirat-Adonai*), and judgments (*mishpatei*). We can never know the actual thinking of the poet. Perhaps the multiple words are only synonyms to create a pile-on effect for emphasis.[51] Or they may be seen as a progression: *edut* is often identified with the Ten Commandments, "the tablets of testimony"; *pekudim* are identified with memory, precepts tied to historical events such as the going out from Egypt; *mitzvah* is literally a command, referring to all the laws of Torah more broadly as God's expectations of behavior, which lead to and are performed with a mindset of reverence, ultimately enabling a society of just laws, *mishpatim*. Multiple benefits accrue from Torah: reviving the soul, making wise the simple, rejoicing the heart, enlightening the eyes; and more, the mindset of reverence is abiding and the judgments are "altogether just."

This middle section focuses on God's teachings, a celebration of revelation. For the psalmist, the story of Mount Sinai marks a communal covenant between God and the Israelites.[52] A covenant is a commitment to loyalty, akin to a marriage. The Bible will record the people's response to God's invitation as *na'aseh v'neshma*, "We will do and we will listen" (Exodus 24:7). Moses presents the Ten Commandments and later a fuller text, the Torah, which describes the people's relationship with God as the Creator, Teacher, and Redeemer. For the psalmist, study of the Torah leads to doing. This section culminates with extolling God's teachings as precious and even delicious: "More desirable than gold, than much fine gold; sweeter than honey, than drippings of the honeycomb" (v. 11). The colors of the images are yellow, linking again to the sun.

The final section (vv. 12-15) is distinctly personal, opening with the psalmist's self-reference as "Your servant" and expressing obedience to God's teachings while acknowledging the potential of great reward.[53] A wonderful wordplay appears in verse 12 where the word for obedience, *zahar*, may also mean illumination, another nod to the radiant sun.[54] A prayer takes form seeking cleansing from great wrongdoing.[55] The psalmist reveals vulnerability, "Let [willful sins] not rule over me." We are not told any details of the sin.[56] The word *tam*, formerly used to describe God's Torah as "complete," now reappears: "Then I will be wholehearted (*tam*); and I will be cleansed from great wrongdoing." The closing line is well known from traditional Jewish prayer for it is the last line of the thrice-daily standing prayer, the Amidah: "May they be acceptable, the speech of my mouth and the meditation of my heart,[57] before You:

Adonai, my Rock and my Redeemer." In the Amidah, the words are in the plural as a petition for God to take the needed action to redeem the world, closing with this quote as a deeply personal concluding note.

Readers across generations will select individual lines of this psalm. Bach will begin a cantata with the opening verses, "The Heavens are Telling . . ."[58] I have witnessed ecstatic dancing of yeshivah students in Jerusalem while chanting the words of verse 8 over and over.[59] And on the Lincoln Memorial, taken from Abraham Lincoln's second inaugural address, is an inscription of verse 10, "The judgments of the Lord are true and righteous altogether." And yet the psalm as a whole is a purposeful journey: beginning with a celebration of the universal, honoring the communal as a mediator of God's revelation, and closing by expressing the deeply personal — perhaps so personal that the specifics of the psalmist's taint is left between the poet and God.

As is the nature of Psalms, the focus is largely on a relationship with God. God in the second verse is referred to as *El*, the generic name for God. In the final eight verses, the only divine name used is *Adonai*. This covenantal name appears seven times, a number that signifies wholeness. As the psalmist's attention moves from looking upward rhapsodically to extolling the gift of God's teaching, a path is forged for a personal relationship with God. The wondrous Creator who discerns errors and hidden faults also hears personal prayer and cleanses the sinner. With God's forgiveness, the psalmist can become Torah-like: *tam*, whole and complete.

As the psalm opened with the movement of the heavenly bodies, the second to last word describes God as "my Rock," conveying stability and protection. And the last word, "my Redeemer," has a familial ring. Next of kin in the Bible are called *go'el* when conveying the duty for redeeming a hostage or, as in the story of Ruth, taking as a wife a childless widow. God as *go'el*, the final word, has moved our recognition of the transcendent God to the immediacy of God's familial care.

DIGGING DEEPER

Creation and the Sun's Demotion
Rabbi Spitz

Have you wondered why in the Genesis creation story the sun and moon are only put into the sky on the fourth day? Or have you noticed that the sun and moon are referred to as "the little light" and "the big light" rather than by name? Bible scholar Jacob Milgrom explained that the answer to both is that the account seeks to dissuade against worship of the sun.[60] For in Babylonia and Egypt, the sun was widely viewed as a god. The Torah sought to convey that there is only one God and the celestial bodies were subservient to that Creator.

Clarence Darrow in the 1925 Scopes trial defended a high school science teacher who had taught evolution, violating a Tennessee statute. Among the defense counsel's arguments on behalf of evolution was that "a day" was not twenty-four hours but an undetermined timeframe as the sun was only put into the sky on day four. Sadly, Darrow lost the case, but his arguments persisted against claims of creationism.

The goal of the Genesis account is not to convey science or history but a worldview. Milgrom pointed out in his teaching of Genesis chapter 1 that the account has a symmetry, with creation of containers on the first three days, getting filled in subsequently in parallel fashion:

> Day 1: "Let there be light."
> Day 2: Separations of water and light.
> Day 3: Separation of water and land.
> And then the parallel creations:
> Day 4: The large and small lights placed into the sky.
> Day 5: Fowl and fish.
> Day 6: Animals and humans.
> And on day seven, standing alone, the Sabbath.

Among the value lessons of the creation story are the following: the world has a sole Creator, which points toward an ordered plan and purpose; the Creator surveyed creation and said that "it was good," challenging us to look at creation as good despite daily news accounts; humans distinctly are "created in the image of God," eliciting the belief of the essential equality by virtue of the infinite divinelike value of each person.

In Psalm 19, the sun is once again demoted: no name is given and only God has control over the sun's canopy. The polemic against paganism, the viewing of parts of creation as having supreme power, persists. When in the Creation account God displays satisfaction, the Creator is presented in humanlike terms: opening the possibility of God-human relationship. As a relationship, God offers teachings and expectations of goodness and invites an individual to call on God for forgiveness.

God Revealed
Rabbi Spitz

C. S. Lewis, the twentieth-century British author of *The Chronicles of Narnia*, is quoted as saying of Psalm 19, "I take this to be the greatest poem in the Psalter and one of the greatest lyrics in the world."[61] This psalm contains such oft-quoted lines as "the heavens declare the glory of God" (v. 2) and "The Torah of *Adonai* is complete" (v. 8). The wonder evoked by nature and Torah is equated. Rabbi Shai Held in teaching Psalm 19 pointed out that most people, when asked about their spirituality, describe an experience of nature and yet only a God of revelation cares about us individually. He challenged his colleagues to convey a similar excitement in the learning of sacred text.[62] I resonate with his challenge because I too have found inspiration in the study of sacred texts and am unsure how effectively I have conveyed my awe and enthusiasm. At the same time, I would take his teaching of the psalm a couple of steps further, beginning with linking the awe of creation with revelation.

Defining revelation is a tall order as there is mystery to how God's word was conveyed and what it even means to say "God's word." A place to see this uncertainty is in the biblical account of God's proclamation of the Ten Commandments at Mount Sinai. What did the people hear? Most of our sages take the Torah literally and imagine the people hearing God's voice with discrete words conveying the *Aseret Dibrot*, the Ten Sayings. Many say that the people only heard the first two commandments, as colloquially described by Rabbi Lawrence Kushner: "I'm God, and you're not", and our relationship is monogamous. For with the third commandment — You shall treat the name of the Lord Your God intimately — the text shifts to the second person. Some say that the people heard only the first word of the first commandment — *Anochi*, "I am" — and then they were overwhelmed and stepped away.

Finally, there is an eighteenth-century teaching of Rabbi Menahem Mendel of Rymanov[63] that matches my lived experience: all the people heard was the first letter and the law flowed naturally from experiencing the presence of God. Note that the first letter, the *aleph*, is silent. The implication is that when the community experienced God's presence, they collectively intuited a duty to lead a moral life and cultivate a relationship with an expectant, moral Parent. The specifics would emerge over time as the people and their sages combined spiritual intuition and reason to unfold the how-tos, which are presented as expressions of God.[64] What makes "God's teaching" sublime is that it is not just intellectual but a lived, holy existence. Sacred teaching is "altogether just" (v. 10), with the collective achievement of justice as an ultimate goal.

For Jews, revelation at Mount Sinai is distinctly a communal memory. In most of the major religions, spiritual wisdom is only conveyed through a great leader, whether Jesus, Muhammad, or Buddha. And for Jews, too, the Torah scroll is referred to as "The Five Books of Moses." But at Mount Sinai, the Torah records that God addressed the entire people, inviting them into a collective covenant that would include future generations.

Judaism is founded on a community's relationship with God. Community mediates our spirituality, offering the memory, wisdom, and support of generations before us. To actively belong to a people is to know that our potential impact for good is motivated, multiplied, and enhanced by complementary talents and a shared focus. As a rabbi, as much as making Torah alive to my students, I am challenged to convey the centrality of community for spiritual flourishing.

The psalm is in three parts: about God, from God, and to God. In the words of the Bible scholar Michael Fishbane, "Nature reveals God the Creator, the Torah reveals God's will, but the prayer of the lonely soul reveals man's presence and situation."[65] There is a natural progression from universal awe evoked by the mystery and unity of nature to intuiting behind nature's order a caring Being who guides us toward morality and invites our personal prayer. Our most authentic and lyrical voice may emerge, as that of the psalmist, when we identify as "servants" before God, yearning to live up to God's calling for divine-like goodness despite our own human shortcomings.

Cleansed of Guilt
Rabbi Spitz

In *This Is Real and You Are Completely Unprepared: The Days of Awe as a Journey of Transformation*, Rabbi Alan Lew writes concerning forgiveness,

> Self-forgiveness is the essential act of the High Holidays season. That's why we need heaven. That's why we need God. We can forgive others on our own. But we turn to God, Rabbi Elie Spitz reminds us, because we cannot forgive ourselves. We need to feel judged and accepted by a Power who transcends our limited years and who em-

> bodies our highest values. When we wish to wipe
> the slate clean, to finalize self-forgiveness, we need
> heaven — a sense of something or someone larger
> and beyond our self.[66]

Alan Lew was a friend, and I was honored that he cited me in his book, a riveting spiritual account of the journey of the Jewish calendar. Let me share the backdrop for "we cannot forgive ourselves." A woman once came to me with great upset. She had served as the treasurer of her children's school's PTA and other parents had accused her of embezzlement. "I may be a poor bookkeeper," she insisted, "but I did not take anything." She wanted me to vindicate her, but I did not know enough to make a judgment.

"My guidance," I said, "is for you to go into the sanctuary and compose a letter to God describing your situation."

After she completed the letter, I advised, "Return to the sanctuary and write again. This time write a letter as if God is answering you. Allow the words to flow spontaneously."

Fifteen minutes later she knocked. When I opened the door, she appeared relaxed. "I do not care what others say," she explained. "God says that I am honest and that is what really matters."

I wrote about this experience as part of a larger essay on "Letters to and from God" as a tool for rabbinic counseling.[67] What this exchange served to teach me is that seeing ourselves as if through God's eyes has a quality of self-honest reflection that can be liberating from the voices of those who misjudge us, or even our own self-criticism. As Rabbi Lew wrote, "When we wish to wipe the slate clean, to finalize self-forgiveness, we need heaven — a sense of something or someone larger and beyond our self."

The prophet Isaiah describes God's offer: "'Come, let us reach an understanding,' says the Lord. 'Be your sins like crimson, they can turn snow-white; be they red as dyed wool, they can become like fleece'" (Isaiah 1:18).

To sin is to feel stained. Our psalmist feels guilty for wrongdoing and turns to God for redemption: "Let them [wrongdoings] not rule over me, then I will be wholehearted; and I will be cleansed from great wrongdoing" (v. 14). The psalmist seeks what only God can give: fully restorative forgiveness.

In sum, the poet of Psalm 19 has multiple goals: marveling over the songlike grandeur of the heavenly bodies; celebrating the teaching of Torah and the living of its precepts by a people who are its heirs; and yearning for personal redemption in order to more purely serve God.

Some Christians Now Look at the Law in a New Way
Rabbi Riemer

Rabbi Meir Soloveichik is one of the new voices within Modern Orthodoxy. He has a doctorate from Princeton, and he heads the Straus Center for Torah and Western Thought at Yeshiva University. He has a distinguished lineage for he is the great-grandson of Rabbi Chaim Soloveichik, who was the head of the Brisk Yeshivah in Chicago, and he is the great-grandnephew of Rabbi Joseph Soloveitchik, who was the dominant intellectual force at Yeshiva University for many years.

I am not sure what his great-uncle, who warned about the limits of dialogue with Christianity, would say about his descendant who engages in serious discussion with leaders of Christian thought and even invites them to speak to his students.

Rabbi Soloveichik recently wrote an essay in which he described the transformation that is taking place within Christianity in our time in terms of the way in which it understands Jewish Law. His essay begins with a quotation from the English diarist Samuel Pepys, moves on from there to a quotation from C. S. Lewis on Psalm 19, and ends with two quotations that I believe would have startled both Pepys and Lewis.[68]

One evening in 1663, Pepys decided to check out London's latest attraction: the Jews who had been recently allowed back into England. Pepys sought out a synagogue service in order to get some idea of what Judaism was about. By chance, the night on which he chose to visit a synagogue turned out to be Simchat Torah, the holiday on which Jews celebrate the completion of the annual cycle of the Torah reading.

Pepys was bewildered by what he saw in the synagogue that night. "Good God!" he wrote in his diary, "I have never seen such disorder. I have never seen so much laughing and sporting, and so much chaos in a service in my entire life. These people behaved more like brutes than like people worshipping God. I could never have imagined any religion in the whole world so absurdly performed as this one was!" (As quoted in Soloveichik.)

Pepys's visit was ill-timed, but he did witness something remarkable. He did not understand the meaning of what he saw, but this group he watched was demonstrating its love of the Law. They danced and sang in joy because this was the day on which they completed the reading of the scroll of the Law and began it all over again.

He had been taught in church that the Torah was a rigid and complex code consisting of 613 commandments, to which later generations had added a heap of additional prohibitions and obligations. He could not have understood even if someone had explained to him what was going on that night. He could not have understood that for these Jews, this law book was a source of unending joy, that it was the ultimate source of happiness, and that it was God's greatest gift to his people.

We can understand Samuel Pepys's bewilderment. He had probably visited the libraries of law schools and seen students bent over complex and technical law books. But I am sure that he had never seen law students dancing around in a circle, singing the praises of a law book, and so there is no wonder that he could not understand what he saw that night.

Some three hundred and fifty years later, the English don C. S. Lewis, who taught at Oxford and then at Cambridge, wrote a book about the psalms. In it, Lewis made the same mistake that Samuel Pepys did when it came to Psalm 19. When he came to the verse in which the psalmist says that the study of the Torah is for him "sweeter than honey," Lewis was bewildered. He wrote, "One can understand that laws may be important, perhaps even necessary to the religious person, but it is hard to think of them as sweeter than honey. Indeed," Lewis wrote, "for one who studies it out of duty, I should think it should be more aptly compared to the dentist's forceps which one confronts, if one must, but surely not with joy." (As quoted in Soloveichik.)

These two Christians who lived centuries apart shared the same view: the Law of the Jews is a burden and not a delight, as this psalm claims. And they are not alone in holding this view. The apostle Paul started the tradition of looking at the Law as a burden that was too heavy to bear when he taught that God sent a redeemer in order to liberate us from the impossible task of trying to live by the Law. And there were many more among the church fathers who spoke of the Law in these same terms.

But in the last two decades, says Rabbi Soloveichik, "a stunning new type of religious writing has appeared: Christian appreciation of the Jewish love of the Law. It is always good to see how you are perceived by others and we can learn a lot by seeing ourselves through their eyes." And so he devotes the rest of his essay to introducing us to some new Christian theologians who speak about the Jewish love of the Law in a very different manner than Christians have done until now.

Samuel Pepys and C. S. Lewis would have both been equally bewildered if they read the book published in 2006 by Dr. Maria Johnson, a Catholic theologian who teaches at the University of Scranton. Dr. Johnson had heard that the Sabbath is important to Jews and so she got herself invited to the home of an observant Jewish family that she knew for a Sabbath afternoon, so that she could experience the Sabbath firsthand. She expected to find Judaism at its most restrictive, for she had read the Mishnah and she knew that there were a great many kinds of work that an observant Jew is forbidden to do on the Sabbath. She expected to find it to be "a twenty-five-hour prison of petty restrictions," and she expected to find a somber mood in the house as people waited for the grim day to end. Much to her surprise, she experienced the peace that pervades a Jewish home on this day. In a jolt of realization, she began to understand why her Jewish friends spoke of this day with so much love and why they spoke of it not as a prison but as a queen. Dr. Johnson wrote after her visit that

> in an age of almost infinite distractions, the rigidity of the Sabbath laws actually frees people so that they can focus on what is truly important." She wrote, "All the laws, the thirty-nine Sabbath prohibitions that generations have multiplied into hundreds, are an instrument that chisels holiness into the week in a way that cannot be ignored or evaded and must instead be welcomed. Rather than an encumbrance, which is what I thought it was, the law liberates the Jews by ensuring that there is no way to do anything but experience life as creatures made in God's image who are blessed and chosen and called. (As quoted in Soloveichik.)

I am sure that Dr. Johnson would understand the line in Psalm 19 that says that the Law is "sweeter than honey, than drippings of the honeycomb" (v. 11) that so baffled C. S. Lewis, and that she would have appreciated the exuberance with which Jews celebrate Simchat Torah that so offended Samuel Pepys.

In 2012, Rabbi Soloveichik invited the archbishop of Philadelphia, Charles Caput, to speak to his class at the Straus Center. He met him at the entrance to the building and led him to the classroom by way of the Bet Hamidrash, the communal study hall. The prelate stopped in amazement when he saw what was going on there. He saw hundreds of young men sitting in pairs all around the room debating every word of the Talmud with each other, and he was awed by the amount of passion with which these students were studying. "These young people do not merely study God's word, they consume it," he said when he reported back to his church on what he had seen. "Or maybe it would be better to say that God's word consumed them. I saw them form friendships with each other, and more than that, I saw them form a real friendship with God." And then the archbishop said to his congregation,

> I saw in these Jewish students and in the way
> they studied the secret of the durability of God's
> word. Despite centuries of persecution and exile,
> the Jewish people have continued to exist, because
> their covenant with God is alive. God's Word is
> the organizing principle of Jewish identity. It is
> the glue that binds them to each other and to
> God. It is what connects them to their past and
> to their future. The more faithful they are to the
> Law, the more certain they are of their survival.

He ended his homily that day with these surprising words: "I wish that what I saw in that study hall could be seen within our churches. I wish that every Christian would learn to appreciate the Law like these young men do!" (As quoted in Soloveichik.)

Have words like these ever been said before our time by any prelate of the Catholic world? What has brought about this sea change in the attitude toward the Law within the Catholic Church in our time?

Rabbi Soloveitchik offers this guess. He says that we live in an age of libertinism, an age in which the dominant philosophy is that you can do whatever you want as long as you do not interfere with anyone else. In such a world, Christianity now finds itself to be a cultural outsider. It feels itself to be in exile in a way that it has not felt in many centuries. And so some of its brightest young thinkers are looking into Judaism in the hope of finding there some wisdom that will be of help to them. And they are finding it in the Jewish love of the Law.

And then, Rabbi Soloveichik says, may we Jews who have imitated our neighbors in so many ways learn respect for Jewish Law from them too. And may we rejoice together with the psalmist and say, as he did, "Your Torah is sweeter than honey, than drippings of the honeycomb."

The Joy of the Law
Rabbi Riemer

As you may know, there are a great many rules — both positive and negative — that are involved in preparing a home for Passover. Rabbi Meir Margolies, who was one of the early leaders of the Hasidic movement in Galicia, liked to be involved in making these preparations by himself. One of the steps in preparing for Passover is baking the matzah, which requires water. Now in those days, there was no such thing as water from the tap. If you wanted water, you had to bring it from the well. And so one day shortly before Passover, Rabbi Meir Margolies went to the well and filled two big containers with water. He put these two heavy buckets of water on his shoulders and started back for home.

A rich man in a carriage drove by and saw the rabbi walking with these two heavy containers of water on his shoulders, and so he stopped and offered him a lift.

Rabbi Meir Margolies looked at the carriage and at the horses that drew it and he said to the man, "The opportunity of doing this mitzvah comes to me only once a year. *Zol ich evek geben tsu a ferd?* Should I give it away to a horse?"

That is the way our people once felt about the Law. If Rabbi Meir Margolies were to meet Samuel Pepys, C. S. Lewis, or even the new theologians we have learned about in relation to Psalm 19, he would have much that he could teach them. But since he is no longer available, let us show them Psalm 19 and testify to them by the way in which we live that the Torah is "sweeter than honey, than drippings of the honeycomb."

Psalm 23

"The Lord is My Shepherd"

Rabbi Elie Spitz

The power of Psalm 23 is that it contains a storyboard of images that takes us on a journey to answer "How should we live?"[69]

א מִזְמוֹר לְדָוִד. יְהוָה רֹעִי; לֹא אֶחְסָר.	**1** A Psalm of David. *Adonai* is my shepherd; I shall not lack.
ב בִּנְאוֹת דֶּשֶׁא יַרְבִּיצֵנִי; עַל מֵי מְנֻחוֹת יְנַהֲלֵנִי.	**2** In grassy pastures, [God] lets me lie down; alongside tranquil waters, leads me …
ג נַפְשִׁי יְשׁוֹבֵב; יַנְחֵנִי בְמַעְגְּלֵי צֶדֶק לְמַעַן שְׁמוֹ.	**3** My spirit, [God] revives, guiding me on roundabouts of justice for the sake of the [Divine] name.
ד גַּם כִּי אֵלֵךְ בְּגֵיא צַלְמָוֶת, לֹא אִירָא רָע כִּי אַתָּה עִמָּדִי; שִׁבְטְךָ וּמִשְׁעַנְתֶּךָ, הֵמָּה יְנַחֲמֻנִי.	**4** Also, for though I walk through the valley of the shadow of death, I will fear no harm, for You stand with me; Your restraining rod and Your supporting staff, they comfort me.

ה תַּעֲרֹךְ לְפָנַי שֻׁלְחָן נֶגֶד צֹרְרָי; **5** You prepare a table for me opposite

דִּשַּׁנְתָּ בַשֶּׁמֶן רֹאשִׁי; my tormentors;

כּוֹסִי רְוָיָה. You luxuriate my head with oil;

my cup overflows.

ו אַךְ טוֹב וָחֶסֶד יִרְדְּפוּנִי **6** Let only goodness and kindness

כָּל יְמֵי חַיָּי pursue me all the days of my life

וְשַׁבְתִּי בְּבֵית יְהוָה לְאֹרֶךְ יָמִים. and I will find Sabbath in the home

of *Adonai* for unending days.

READING CLOSELY

The opening image of verses 1 and 2, God as our shepherd, conveys constancy of care. A shepherd counts each sheep to make sure that none is missing. Each of us matters to God. We are like infants whose needs are fully met by a caregiver. Shepherds abound in Hebrew Scripture, including Abraham, Isaac, Jacob, Moses, and David. A shepherd is attentive to the physical needs of the sheep. "I shall not lack" also relates to emotional and spiritual needs. As the psalm begins, we are safe and content. God leads us by flowing waters and vegetation-filled pastures. Our senses are soothed by the blues and greens.[70] We are cared for like passive sheep. And then the psalmist glides into adulthood and complexity.[71]

"My spirit, [God] revives, guiding me on roundabouts of justice for the sake of the [Divine] name." With the third verse, we need reviving. The Hebrew word *nefesh* refers to a neck, breath, life, or spirit. There is both a physical and ephemeral dimension to our fatigue. Before us is the challenge of justice. The key words are *ma'gilay tzedek*. In the King James Bible, *ma'gilay* are "paths" and *tzedek* is "straight." Two of the most influential medieval rabbis, Rashi (France, 1140-1205) and Radak (France, 1160-1235), commented that God as shepherd seeks to guide on a straight path so as to limit exertion. And yet the word *ma'gilay* shares the Hebrew root for "circle." *Tzedek* in the Bible consistently means justice or righteousness, as in the oft-quoted line, "Justice, justice, you shall pursue" (Deuteronomy 16:20).[72] To obtain justice means to make choices, just as when we drive on a roundabout with many branching paths. To achieve justice takes effort to discern right and wrong.

We follow the roundabouts of justice, the psalmist emphasizes, for "the sake of the [Divine] name." Pursuit of purpose demands overcoming self-serving interests. Rabbi Harold Kushner comments,

> The struggle against the enslavement of one human being by another, whether in nineteenth-century America or in ancient Egypt, was justified because slavery is wrong. It is wrong in all generations and in all economic circumstances. . . . That is what the Bible is saying when it declares that the Exodus must be seen as God's doing, not Pharoah's, "for the sake of God's great name." Freeing the enslaved must be seen as an aspect of what kind of God He is and what kind of world He demands, not what kind of man and king Pharaoh is.[73]

The third image focuses on trust in God despite mortality. "For though I walk through the valley of the shadow of death, I will fear no harm, for You stand with me; Your restraining rod and Your supportive staff, they comfort me" (v. 4). We naturally fear the unknown, and death is a great unknown, including the anticipated pain and diminishment toward the end of life. In the aftermath of a death, we need to process our loss. We must walk "through" the valley of death when mourning to reach the other side where light shines.[74] We are told not to fear. "Do not fear" is the most repeated command in the entire Hebrew Scripture.[75] If we could live without fear, our lives would be so much freer and purposeful. And the next phrase, the very center of Psalm 23, explains how: "For You stand with me."

To feel God's presence is to feel protected. The word *emadi* is translated in King James as "for you are with me." The Hebrew literally is "stand with me." And now, in my inner ear, I hear soul singer Ben E. King with "Stand by Me" or the country and western singer Tammy Wynette's "Stand by Your Man." To "take a stand" is to identify with and support another. To feel God standing with us is to feel beloved and thereby strengthened to move forward, overcoming fear.

The fourth image is "You prepare a table for me opposite my tormentors; You luxuriate my head with oil; my cup overflows" (v. 5). The table is bountiful and there is gratitude. The oil may describe the act of installing a king or a priest. We may also read the text more broadly as God empowering each of us. The cup may refer to a ritual act with wine, a celebratory meal, or metaphorically the gift of happiness, popularly expressed as "my cup runneth over." And yet there is always danger, even active foes.[76] The tormentors may refer to external threats or inner voices or compulsive behaviors that tear us down. Here, the psalmist describes the capacity to enjoy life's abundant gifts despite these dangers. This is a successful adulthood.

The fifth image is homecoming: "Let only goodness and kindness pursue me all the day of my life and I will find Sabbath in the home of Adonai for unending days" (v. 6). The plain meaning of the verse is that the psalmist longs for communion with God, "to dwell in the House of the Lord forever." Along with the earlier reference to "you luxuriate my head with oil," some modern scholars identify the author as a priest or Levite.[77] Some medieval commentators see this as King David requesting a long life of tranquility — Radak, for example — or as a messianic yearning, marked by the rebuilding of the Temple.[78] Some even see this as referring to the World to Come, an unending time of basking in God's presence.[79] I have chosen to contemporize the translation. The Hebrew word for "to dwell" has the same root as the Sabbath, the day of rest. The yearning expressed is to experience each day as communion with God as identified with the Sabbath day, a time of experiencing the wholeness of self and creation. The path toward inner balance is suggested by the opening phrase "Let only goodness and kindness pursue me."

There is a Hasidic story relating to "pursuit" that I learned from Rabbi Jack Riemer.

> "Where are you rushing?" a startled rabbi asks the passerby.
>
> "I am chasing after a living," the man answers.
>
> "Perhaps your living is running after you. All you need to do is stand still and let it catch up to you."[80]

This final image of Psalm 23 is where we feel valued just for being. Our true identity transcends the externals of income, status, or achievements. When we stop and notice goodness and kindness pursuing us and become fully present, we experience Sabbath. The culmination of Psalm 23 elevates us to a perspective of what really matters: abiding equanimity and inner peace before God.

The power of a storyboard is that it engages our emotions and imagination. Psalm 23 has taken us on a journey. We began as children, cared for by a beneficent shepherd. We were guided to a mature awareness of dangers, choices, and responsibilities: implementing justice for God's sake; living fearlessly for God, who stands steadfastly by; enjoying life's bounty as a gift despite ongoing dangers. And we are elevated to know that we have the capacity to bask in God's presence, to be whole and at peace, to abide in Sabbath.

DIGGING DEEPER

We Will Meet This Together
Rabbi Spitz

Rabbi Ed Feinstein of Encino, California, tells of sitting with his wife, Nina, in his oncologist's office. The physician put up a scan and showed them the white spot. "This is cancer. I think we can get it out."

"What do you mean 'you think'?"

"Well, because of its location there is uncertainty."

And then Ed heard in his mind familiar words, "Yea, though I walk through the valley of the shadow of death."

Nina took his hand in hers and whispered, "I will be with you. We will meet this together."

And the next line of Psalm 23 flowed: "I will fear no evil: for you are with me."

These oft-repeated ancient words, Rabbi Feinstein recounted, were now profoundly real and utterly personal.

We do not necessarily know what prompted the psalmist to compose. But in reading Psalms, we are invited to hold the words closely, to learn them, and to find in these sacred words our own deepest moments. For the psalmist, God is present as a companion amid life's greatest uncertainties and that truly matters.

Life as Journey toward Peace
Rabbi Spitz

My friends' father recently passed away. He was already in his nineties, widowed, and ailing of health when he said that he was done. He marshaled his energy to pull his life together. He apologized to both of his adult children for the ways that he had let them down and expressed his love. He met with his former spouse and asked for her forgiveness. He spoke with genuine gratitude for the gift of his life and those with whom he had shared it. He exuded a quality of newfound peace that was like a light around him and that shined backward over his years. Soon thereafter he went on to hospice. On the one hand, it was sad that he only found such equanimity toward the end of his life, and yet he was a glorious teacher of gratitude, humility, and conscious preparedness for the final homecoming.

Psalm 23 is deeply personal, with the repetition of first-person pronouns. The images beckon us to actively consider our own life's journey, to acknowledge that at all phases of life we have moments of wanting to feel unconditionally loved and taken care of. And yet maturity is marked by also putting our own needs aside for the sake of justice and having the strength and wisdom to make good choices. Adulthood means facing our fears and foes while feeling secure and gifted with abundance; and aspiring to feel God's peaceful presence with each moment, long before we pass.

Compassion
Rabbi Spitz

"Your restraining rod and Your supporting staff, they comfort me." Why does verse 4 include both rod and staff, which are synonyms? And why "they?" The verse could have simply read "Your staff comforts me."

The rabbis will distinguish between the two Hebrew words — שִׁבְטְךָ וּמִשְׁעַנְתֶּךָ — "your staff and your rod." Rashi will say that *shevet* connotes discipline, as in the line from Psalm 89:33: "And I will punish their transgression with the rod."[81] *Sha'an* suggests calm, and Rashi links it to God's mercy in times of affliction. Radak says that the two words refer to one stick used as both a rod to discipline the sheep and as a staff upon which the shepherd leans his weary body. I have translated the two terms as "restraining rod and support staff."

These two types of staff can creatively be understood as a description of two qualities of God. The Jewish mystics posit ten divine attributes. *Hesed*, kindness, is juxtaposed with *gevurah*, restraint. Love needs a container, entailing limitation, so as not to overwhelm a recipient. When the two qualities of kindness and restraint are in balance, they unite as compassion, *tiferet*. The "they" of "they comfort me" is the experience of divine compassion, the combination of divine kindness and restraint that allows us to move forward with confidence.

The Sabbath
Rabbi Spitz

The Sabbath is the only ritual in the Ten Commandments. As the fourth command, it follows three laws that deal exclusively with God, while the fifth command shifts to honoring parents. Sabbath distinctly encompasses both God and other humans: communing with God and appreciating the grandeur of creation; gathering in community; refraining from commerce and creativity; enjoying festive meals with family and friends. When we rest on the seventh day, we are told that we imitate God's final focus during creation. On the seventh day, the work of each day added up to wholeness, and God rested.

Psalm 23's last line can be read, "I will find Sabbath in the home of *Adonai* for unending days" (v. 6). We have come full circle. The psalm began with the simplicity of a child, cared for by God like a shepherd tends a lamb. After taking stock of the challenges and rewards of adulthood, we conclude with a second naivete: life as Sabbath. As a ritual, the Sabbath is an artificial construct. As I walk to synagogue on a Saturday morning and cars speed by, sometimes honking, I smile. They do not know that today is the Sabbath, a day of rest and equanimity. But by setting aside one day a week marked by simply being rather than doing, we taste the core of human dignity and the Sabbath becomes profoundly real. The rabbis describe the future messianic period as a continuous Shabbat, marked by universal peace. By tasting such inner peace on a weekly basis, we aspire to bring that awareness into daily life and more, to live amid Sabbath "for unending days."

Although Psalm 23 presents a journey, its stages do not necessarily move in a straight line. Feeling vulnerable and needy is natural at every phase of life. Part of my strength on any day is the love of family members and close friends. Tasting bounty gratefully while aware of danger defines daily life. Pursuing a living and caring about justice provide purpose and are stressful. As for the Sabbath, the rabbis observe that when the Bible reads "Six days you shall work and on the seventh, you shall rest" (Exodus 20:9), both are commanded: work and rest. On the Sabbath we let go of fixing and doing and celebrate the goodness of our relationships and the beauty of creation. In the course of any one day, each of these images may reflect an immediate mood or need. And yet the inner peace, connection, and joy of the Sabbath accessed more readily and sustained more enduringly is, as Psalm 23 leads us to experience, the ultimate aspiration and a genuine possibility.

The Most Beloved Psalm of All
Rabbi Riemer

Psalm 23 begins by calling God our shepherd, but what does it mean to call God by that name?

The midrash gives three different answers to this question, and all of them are based on two seemingly unnecessary words that appear in the story of how God met Moses at the burning bush. The Torah says that Moses was grazing his sheep *mey'acharey hamidbar*, "at the far end of the desert." The Sages ask: Why do we need to know that the burning bush was located at the far end of the desert? And for that matter, what was Moses doing grazing his sheep at the other end of the desert? Would it not have been easier to graze closer to home?

The first answer is that Moses grazed his sheep at the far end of the desert *kidey liharchik min hagezel*, "in order to distance himself from the possibility of theft."

Moses understood that if his sheep grazed on private property that would be theft. And Moses wanted to be careful that he did not commit the crime of theft directly or indirectly. For him, the law against theft was a central value, even before he brought down the Ten Commandments that proclaim *lo tignov*, "Thou shalt not steal."

And then the Midrash goes on to give a second explanation of why Moses grazed his sheep at the other end of the wilderness. It says that he did it *kidey lihitboded*, "in order to be alone." He wanted to be alone so that he could meditate without any distractions. He understood that you cannot connect with the Holy unless you separate yourself from all the noise around you.

I suspect that if many of us were to go by a burning bush today, we would not even notice it because we would be too busy talking on our cell phones or texting the office or reading the newspaper as we passed by. But Moses was not like that. Moses chose to graze his sheep in a quiet place so that he could meditate without being disturbed.

The third explanation that the midrash gives is that one little lamb ran away from the flock, and so Moses chased after it. He chased after it all the way across the wilderness. When he caught up with it, he gave it some water to drink and then he picked it up in his arms and tenderly carried it back to the other sheep. When God saw Moses do that, He said: "This is the one who is fit to be the pastor of my people."

I believe that what the Sages are giving us in this midrash is a three-part definition of what the Jewish religion is about.

The Jewish religion stands on three principles. The first is respect for law. You must not let your sheep graze on someone else's property, because if you do, it is theft and theft is against the law. Jewish law deals not only with prayer and ritual but with fair advertising and fair pricing and not standing by when your brother or sister is being wronged, because these are essential dimensions of the Jewish religion.

The second pillar of the Jewish religion is that there is a spiritual reality in this world. There is holiness but you can only relate to the Holy if you get away from all the noise and distractions around you. That is why Moses moved to the other side of the wilderness where he would be able to meditate without distraction. This is why many of the great souls in the Jewish tradition went out into the fields in order to pray and then came back and set out to influence the world.

The third pillar of the Torah is compassion for the weak. For the sake of one lamb, Moses was willing to go to the other end of the desert. That story is meant to teach us that at the heart of Judaism there has to be concern for the widow and the orphan, for the poor and the handicapped, for the downtrodden and the neglected. This is what the sages of the Midrash wanted to teach us when they described Moses as a shepherd, and this is what they wanted us to understand when we begin Psalm 23 by calling God our shepherd. They meant by this to think of God as the One who stands for justice, the One who can be found in silence, and the One who cares for the widow and the orphan, the weak and the poor.

"I Have Enough"
Rabbi Riemer

My friend and colleague Rabbi Harold Kushner said he and his wife were once vacationing in a remote section of New England, and they happened to wander into a small village. They noticed a general supply store in the center of the village, and they were about to go inside when they noticed the sign on the door.

The sign said, "If you can't find what you are looking for inside, you probably don't need it." They looked at each other and smiled, and they both said at the same time, "That's probably true."

I believe that the sign that my friends found at the entrance to that store is a modern commentary on two words that appear in the first verse of Psalm 23. The psalm declares that because God is my shepherd, *lo echsar*. The King James Bible translates this phrase as "I shall not want." Here and in other Bibles it is translated as "I shall not lack." Another Bible translates it "I am content with what I have." I even found one that translates it as "What else do I need since I have God?"

Whichever translation you want to use, I think that *lo echsar* are two powerful words, because they challenge the values by which we live more than almost any phrase I can think of.

Ours is a world in which wanting — wanting this year's model, wanting what you have that I don't have, wanting, wanting, wanting — is the great national obsession. We talk about people being addicted to drugs, but I would wager that more people are addicted to what they want and what they think they need than to drugs. We have many rehab centers all around the country whose purpose is to help people recover from addiction to drugs, but I believe that we need at least as many centers to help people recover from wanting. For how many of us, no matter how much we have, are we able to say as this psalmist does, "I have enough"?

There are a great many different names for God in the Jewish tradition. We call God Father and Redeemer, King and Shepherd, Savior and Teacher, and more. But my favorite name for God in the whole collection of names is *Shaddai*. That is the name that the tradition bids us to put upon the doorposts of our houses so that when we enter and when we leave we may contemplate this name. Why did the sages treat this name of God as so central? It is because the sages interpreted this word to be an abbreviation for the words *mi she-omar dai*, "the One who teaches us when and how to say enough."

That is one of the hardest lessons to learn in life. To be able to say "I don't need what you have, and I don't need what I don't have; I have enough" is an enormous test of spiritual strength. And this is what I believe *lo echsar* is meant to teach us every time we say the twenty-third psalm.

Let me tell you about a strange custom that has taken hold in American society in recent years that illustrates the difficulty of living by these two words. We gather together on Thanksgiving Day and give thanks for all the bounty that we possess. Some families go around the room and ask each person to name one of the blessings that they feel especially grateful for. And then what happens as soon as Thanksgiving Day is over? We bolt out of the house as fast as we can in order to go downtown and stand in line so that we can be among the first to get into the department stores in order to buy as much as we can. We buy and buy and buy until we have no more strength, and then we straggle home, loaded down with packages.

What is the Jewish answer to Black Friday? (By the way, I wonder how it got this strange name, don't you?) The Jewish answer to Black Friday is the Sabbath. For twenty-four hours we do not spend any money. We do not even touch money. For twenty-four hours we live by the two words that are at the beginning of Psalm 23: *lo echsar*. For twenty-four hours we give thanks for what we have and express gratitude for the creation instead of brooding about we don't have or thinking about what we would like to have.

Is there a greater antidote to greed, a greater protection against coveting, than these two words of Psalm 23?

To Catch Your Breath
Rabbi Riemer

Nafshi yishovev: I believe this is the most misunderstood phrase in all of Psalm 23. It is usually translated as "He restores my soul." That is how the King James Bible translates it, and many translators since then have followed its example. But that translation is wrong! *Nefesh* here has nothing to do with soul; here it means "breath." *Nafshi yishovev* means "He enables me to catch my breath." The author compares himself to a tired lamb who has gone through a long, hard journey and is now completely exhausted. What does the shepherd do for this lamb? He lets it lie down and rest for a while in a quiet place so that it can catch its breath, and then it wakes up feeling refreshed and able to move again.

Nefesh started out meaning "throat," and then it came to mean "breath." It was centuries later that Jewish and Christian philosophers developed the concept of soul and then that became the meaning of *nefesh*. But here it only means "breath."

The expression "to catch your breath" comes from this psalm. If someone works night and day until they reach the point where they are totally exhausted, we tell them to take some time off to catch their breath. And we do so without realizing that we are paraphrasing a line from a psalm from many centuries ago.

Honoring the Name of God
Rabbi Riemer

I don't think anyone really knows what the phrase *ma'gilay tsedek* means in verse 3 of Psalm 23. Some translate it as "straight paths," and some translate it as "roundabout paths," some translate it as "paths of righteousness." Here Rabbi Spitz translates it as "roundabouts of justice." I don't know what it means either, but let me share one story, told to me by my Israeli cousin Yosef Riemer, that illuminates this phrase for me.

During the Six-Day War, Yosef was in a unit that was on the way to make a surprise attack on an Arab base in the Golan. The commander was leading them on a roundabout way, which was about fifteen kilometers long. Yosef told the commander that he knew a shortcut that would enable them to get to the Arab base in half the time. The commander said, "Yes, I know about this shortcut, but if we went that way, we would have to trample on the fields of the local Arabs and we would end up destroying their harvest, and if we did that, this war will never end."

Is that not an amazing statement? It is alright to attack an Arab military base — that is what you do in a war. But if you ruin a crop on the way, if you destroy the harvest of Arab civilians on the way, then you will cause such hatred that the war will never end.

Sometimes you have to go the long way around because it may end up being the short way. The important thing is that you must travel "on roundabouts of justice for the sake of the [Divine] Name." The important thing is that you do whatever you do in such a way as to bring honor to the name of God and not in such a way as to bring disgrace to the name of God. That was the lesson that this army officer taught his soldiers that day.

We Grow from Challenge
Rabbi Riemer

Up until verse 4 of Psalm 23, the psalmist has been speaking about God in third person. But now, when he is in deepest darkness, now when he is in the valley of the shadow of death, he speaks *to* God and not about God. Now he says, I do not fear for *You* are with me. The Hebrew scholar Robert Alter points out that the first half of this verse, which describes the fearful things that surround him, is a long phrase that has many words but the declaration that he is not afraid consists of only two words. The contrast emphasizes the simple and the total trust that the psalmist feels in the protection of God.

Now we come to a verse that seems very strange: verse 5. The psalmist praises God for setting a table before him in the sight of his enemies. All of a sudden, the speaker is no longer an innocent lamb. Now he is the host who eats a festive meal in front of his enemies. What kind of a religion is this in which a person taunts his enemies by eating a sumptuous feast while they have to look on and get no food? Is this a proper image for a religious psalm to have? Or is this a greedy image that we are embarrassed to find in a psalm?

Let me give you two possible explanations of this passage: one historical and the other spiritual. The first one comes from the Bible scholar Cyrus Gordon; the second comes from Rabbi Zalman Schachter-Shalomi, an influential, spiritual leader of the last century.

Cyrus Gordon knew Ugaritic, Syriac, and many of the other languages of the people who lived before and around the Israelites. He claims that in Ugaritic, *shulchan* means "a shield," not "a table." If that is what it means, this line makes sense: You protect me from my enemies; you set up a shield before me so that my enemy's weapons cannot reach me. This is certainly one way to understand this line. But let me show another way to read this phrase.

This one comes from Rabbi Zalman Schachter-Shalomi. Reb Zalman, as he was called by his disciples, started out in the Chabad movement and went on to create his own movement, Jewish Renewal. He had a fertile imagination that enabled him to find many insights within the words of the siddur and the Torah that no one else would ever have noticed. And this is one of his comments. On the words "You prepare a table for me opposite my tormentors," he says that one of these days he would like to make a festive meal for all of his enemies, for they have taught him so much. He says that if he is a mature person today, it is because of what he learned over the years by struggling with them.

Isn't that a lovely idea — that we all owe a debt of gratitude to our critics, opponents, and enemies because their challenges have helped us grow and become the people we are now?

Those who agree with everything that we say have not really helped us grow, but those who challenged us and who made us defend every point we made are the ones who have really helped us grow.

All the Days of My Life
Rabbi Riemer

And now comes the last line: *Ach tov vachesed yirdifuni kol yimey chayay vishavti biveyt Adonay l'orech yamim*, "Let only goodness and kindness pursue me all the days of my life, and I will find Sabbath in the home of Adonai for unending days" (v. 6). What does it mean to say that goodness and kindness will follow me all the days of my life?

There is a Mexican story that has the same theme. An American tourist hires a fisherman to take him out to sea for a day of fishing. The American tourist offers the fisherman a reasonable rate for his time and for the use of his boat, and they go out to sea. But every few minutes the American tourist's cell phone rings. First, it is his office calling to ask him what stocks or bonds he wants to buy or sell. Then it is one of his agents asking if he wants to join in a big deal or not. This goes on for a while until finally the tourist says to the fisherman, "Take me back. I have too much work to do. I have too many important decisions to make. I am on the edge of a very important deal and so I can't be away from my desk. So please take me back right now."

The fisherman says to the tourist, "I will take you back if you want me to, but do you mind if I ask you just a few questions while we are on the way? My first question is, if you make this big sale that you are going back for, what will you get for it?"

The American tourist says, What do you mean what will I get for it? What kind of a question is that? I'll get a big commission and at the end of the year I may even get a big bonus."

The fisherman says, "That's interesting. Will you please tell me what you will get if you make an even bigger sale?"

The American tourist says, "What kind of a question is that to ask? If I make an even bigger sale, I could get a promotion. They may even make me the chief of a division, and they may even give me a corner office. And at the end of the year, they may give me a big bonus."

The fisherman says, "That would be wonderful, but would you mind if I ask you another question? Do you mind telling me what you will get if you make an even bigger sale than that?"

The American tourist says, "Don't you understand how the business world works at all? If I make an even bigger sale than that, they might make me the CEO of the entire company."

The fisherman says, "That would be wonderful. But can I ask you just one last question? What will you get if you make an even bigger sale than that?"

The man says, "That is such a silly question. You obviously have no idea how the real world operates. If I become the CEO of the whole company, and if we make bigger sales than we ever made before, they will give me such a big bonus that I will be able to retire."

The fisherman says, "Really? And what will you do when you retire?"

The American tourist says, "If they give me such a big bonus that I can retire, I will be able to go down to Mexico and rent a boat and go fishing all day every day for the rest of my life."

And the fisherman says, "Ah, now I understand."

This is what "Let only goodness and kindness pursue me all the days of my life, and I will find Sabbath in the home of Adonai for unending days" means. It teaches us to sanctify each day and not put off the good life until the future.

A Caring God in Modern Psychology and Psalm 23
Rabbi Riemer

Rabbi Michael Samuel is a Chabad rabbi who works as a Hillel director at one of the colleges in upstate New York. Many Chabad rabbis are on college campuses, but I know few who work for Hillel. Even more unusual is that he applied to graduate school. He chose as the topic of his dissertation the concept of a caring God in modern psychology and in Psalm 23.

Now how would you or I do a dissertation? We would go to the library and make a list of all the books that have been written on the subject and we would read them. Isn't that how you do a dissertation?

But that is not what he did. Instead, he went out into the countryside around Cornell with a tape recorder and interviewed shepherds as to how they took care of their sheep and he read the diaries of shepherds of the last generations in order to find out how they cared for their sheep.

You and I would never think of doing that. None of us has probably met a shepherd. But that is what he did. And it turned out that the way the shepherd takes care of his sheep today explains what it means when the twenty-third psalm calls God a shepherd. To illustrate his point, he tells this story.

A shepherd told him the story of what happened when a lamb once ran away from the rest of his flock. The shepherd chased after this lamb and when he found it gave it some water to drink and then picked it up and carried it back to the flock. When he got close to his home, he sounded a note on the horn that he carried with him so that his family would know that he and the lamb were safe.

When he heard this story, the rabbi had a new appreciation for what the psalmist meant when he wrote that "the Lord is my shepherd."

And now a second story from the same dissertation. There was once a rich man who married off his daughter. He arranged a royal wedding for her, and he invited a tremendous crowd in order to honor the bride and groom. When the dinner was over, the father of the bride called upon one of the guests to sing a song in honor of the bride and the groom. This guest was a famous opera singer.

The opera singer chose to sing Psalm 23, and so every one of the guests at the dinner sat back to listen to his performance. As they did, they wondered which version of the psalm would he sing. Would it be the one composed by Beethoven, or the one by Bach, or the one by Dvorak? Or would he sing it as it has been set to music by one of the other great composers?

They sat back to listen to the opera singer's rendition.

It turned out that the opera singer had a superb voice, and he knew the composition that he had chosen very well. He placed every note exactly where it belonged. He was able to reach the highest notes in the composition without any difficulty. And so when he finished, he got a standing ovation. The crowd rose from their seats and cheered him for over five minutes. And they called out, "Encore! Encore!"

The singer bowed and acknowledged the applause and returned to his seat and sat down.

Then an old man came forward and asked if he too could sing a song in honor of the bride and groom.

The father of the bride hesitated. How could this old man follow the famous opera singer? But he was in a good mood and so he gave his consent.

The old man went to the lectern and sang Psalm 23. He sang it, not in one of the versions that had been written by any of the famous composers but to the melody to which Psalm 23 had been sung in his family for many generations. And when he finished, no one clapped, no one cheered, and no one stood and called for an encore. Instead, the audience sat motionless as if they were hypnotized and nobody said a word for almost ten minutes.

Someone who was there asked, "What is going on here? How come, for the famous opera singer, the people stood and clapped and cheered for five minutes, and for this old man, who has a feeble voice and who cannot reach the high notes, no one spoke and no one moved and everyone seemed to be lost in thought for almost ten minutes?"

The man who was standing next to him explained: "For the opera singer we stood and we cheered and called for an encore because we could all see how well he knew the composition. But for this old man we were silent and we were lost in thought because we recognized that he knew the Shepherd. And that made all the difference."

This is our goal in this book. It will be good if we can explain the translation and the grammar and the cultural context of these psalms. But our real goal is to help the reader and to help ourselves to know the Shepherd.

Psalm 27

"*Adonai* Is My Light"

Rabbi Elie Spitz

Psalm 27 opens with "Adonai is my light and my deliverance — Whom shall I fear?" Recited twice a day for the entire fifty-day penitential season,[82] this psalm never mentions repentance.[83] Why did the rabbis select this recitation to prepare for a new year? We will see ahead in this psalm a variety of prompts for reflection or expressions of a feeling before crossing a threshold.

א לְדָוִד.	**1** For David.
יְהוָה אוֹרִי וְיִשְׁעִי— מִמִּי אִירָא?	*Adonai* is my light
יְהוָה מָעוֹז חַיַּי— מִמִּי אֶפְחָד?	and my deliverance —
	Whom shall I fear?
	Adonai is the stronghold of my life —
	Whom shall I dread?
ב בִּקְרֹב עָלַי מְרֵעִים	**2** When evildoers draw near me
לֶאֱכֹל אֶת בְּשָׂרִי,	to devour my flesh,
צָרַי וְאֹיְבַי לִי הֵמָּה, כָּשְׁלוּ וְנָפָלוּ.	my tormentors and my enemies they are to me, they stumble and they fall.
ג אִם תַּחֲנֶה עָלַי מַחֲנֶה...	**3** If a camp encamps against me . . .
לֹא יִירָא לִבִּי;	my heart will not fear;
אִם תָּקוּם עָלַי מִלְחָמָה,	even if war arises against me,
בְּזֹאת אֲנִי בוֹטֵחַ.	in this I do trust.

ד אַחַת שָׁאַלְתִּי מֵאֵת יְהֹוָה,
אוֹתָהּ אֲבַקֵּשׁ:
שִׁבְתִּי בְּבֵית יְהֹוָה כָּל יְמֵי חַיַּי,
לַחֲזוֹת בְּנֹעַם יְהֹוָה
וּלְבַקֵּר בְּהֵיכָלוֹ.

4 One thing I ask of *Adonai*,
of this I seek:
that I may find Sabbath in the house
of *Adonai* all the days of my life,
to behold the pleasantness of *Adonai*,
and to awaken in [God's] palace.

ה כִּי יִצְפְּנֵנִי בְּסֻכֹּה בְּיוֹם רָעָה;
יַסְתִּרֵנִי בְּסֵתֶר אָהֳלוֹ;
בְּצוּר יְרוֹמְמֵנִי.

5 For [God] will shelter me in [the divine] *sukkah* on the day of evil; conceal me in the concealment of [God's] tent; upon a rock will raise me up.

ו וְעַתָּה יָרוּם רֹאשִׁי עַל אֹיְבַי
סְבִיבוֹתַי;
וְאֶזְבְּחָה בְאָהֳלוֹ זִבְחֵי תְרוּעָה;
אָשִׁירָה וַאֲזַמְּרָה לַיהֹוָה.

6 And now raise up my head above my enemies who surround me; and I will sacrifice in [God's] tent, sacrifices of *t'ruah*; I will sing and hymn to *Adonai*.

ז שְׁמַע יְהֹוָה קוֹלִי אֶקְרָא,
וְחָנֵּנִי וַעֲנֵנִי.

7 Hear, *Adonai*, my voice when I call, and grant me grace and answer me.

ח לְךָ אָמַר לִבִּי- בַּקְּשׁוּ פָנָי!
אֶת פָּנֶיךָ יְהֹוָה אֲבַקֵּשׁ.

8 Of You my heart has said —
"Seek my face!"
Your face, *Adonai*, I do seek.

ט אַל תַּסְתֵּר פָּנֶיךָ מִמֶּנִּי—
אַל תַּט בְּאַף עַבְדֶּךָ;
עֶזְרָתִי הָיִיתָ—אַל תִּטְּשֵׁנִי;
וְאַל תַּעַזְבֵנִי, אֱלֹהֵי יִשְׁעִי.

9 Do not hide Your face from me —
do not turn away in anger Your
servant;
You are my help — do not cast me
off; do not leave me, my God of my
deliverance.

י כִּי אָבִי וְאִמִּי עֲזָבוּנִי,
וַיהוָה יַאַסְפֵנִי.

10 For though my father and my
mother leave me, *Adonai* will gather
me in.

יא הוֹרֵנִי יְהוָה דַּרְכֶּךָ
וּנְחֵנִי בְּאֹרַח מִישׁוֹר לְמַעַן שׁוֹרְרָי.

11 Parent me, *Adonai*, of Your way
and lead me on an upright path
despite my watchful foes.

יב אַל תִּתְּנֵנִי בְּנֶפֶשׁ צָרָי:
כִּי קָמוּ בִי עֵדֵי שֶׁקֶר וִיפֵחַ חָמָס.

12 Do not give over my spirit to my
tormentors: for having risen against
me are false witnesses who breathe
out violence.

יג לוּלֵא הֶאֱמַנְתִּי לִרְאוֹת בְּטוּב יְהוָה
בְּאֶרֶץ חַיִּים...

13 If I were not to believe that I will
see the goodness of *Adonai* in the
land of the living...

יד קַוֵּה אֶל הֹוָה;
חֲזַק וְיַאֲמֵץ לִבֶּךָ;
וְקַוֵּה אֶל יְהוָה.

14 Hope for *Adonai*!
Let your heart be strong and
courageous
and hope for *Adonai*.

READING CLOSELY

Psalm 27 opens with strong faith in God's protection but shifts to vulnerability: "Do not cast me off; do not leave me" (v. 9).[84] Some biblical scholars, such as Hermann Gunkel (1862-1912), see two different psalms conjoined, with verse 6 as an initial end point. Most scholars hold that this is one tightly written composition, as evidenced by the many repeated words that lace the two halves together.[85] Why, then, this vacillation in faith? Or is it? And why of all 150 psalms did the Rabbis choose this distinctly as the reading for the period of repentance? Let us begin with examining the psalm as a singular tapestry, woven with clusters of threefold verses and shifting themes.

Absence of fear is the opening focus. The first section builds in confidence by the Hebrew word count of the three verses: five, six, and seven, with seven marking wholeness. Revisit verses 1 through 3 and listen to the psalmist's calm faith in God's protective presence, with "trust" as the final word.[86]

In the second section, verses 4 through 6, the psalmist yearns for closeness to God. Verse 4 asks for "one thing" and then presents three, each subject to alternative interpretations: (1) to sit, rest, or Sabbath; (2) to behold God's pleasantness, *noam*, a Hebrew word identified with relationship; (3) to awaken, which can either refer to deep rest or enhanced spiritual awareness. The three requests equal one — namely, to engage God fully. Verse 4 is popularly chanted by religious Jews, sung as a repeated line to convey longing for God. The word *bekar* in modern Hebrew means "to visit," but in the Bible it implies the taking on of responsibility.[87] The choice of "awaken" is meant to convey enhanced awareness that encompasses service of God.

Verse 5 presents three types of divine dwellings of increasing permanence: "sukkah," the tabernacle of the Israelite during the journey through the desert; "tent," used in the Bible to describe Moses's meeting place with God; and "palace," which can refer to the Temple in Jerusalem (the most likely literal intent), God's heavenly abode, or any place that a person fully experiences God's presence.

Verse 6 begins "And now," marking a shift toward danger and addressing God directly. We are not told the nature or motive of the enemies: whether they are external foes or self-generated woes.[88] The psalmist's insecurity leads to bargaining: "God, if you protect me, I will honor You in a variety of ways: sacrifice, including physical gifts and the broken sounds of the shofar call; and song and hymns," as if praise is the psalmist's ultimate offering to God.

The third section (vv. 7-9) begins with the plea "Hear," initiating doubt as to whether God is paying attention to the psalmist despite his loyalty and longing for God. The psalmist addresses God directly.

Verse 8's first half is uncertain due to Hebrew's lack of capitalizations. Is it God or the psalmist speaking? Consider the following diverse readings:[89]

Robert Alter: "Of You, my heart said, 'Seek my face.' Your face, Lord, I do seek."

Jewish Publication Society: "In Your behalf my heart says, 'Seek My face!' O Lord, I seek Your face."

Martin Cohen: "I heard my heart say, 'Seek me' to You, but surely it is I who need to seek Your face, *Adonai*."

The following possibilities emerge: the psalmist's heart is guided by God[90] or self-initiating; seeking God to pay attention to the psalmist or guided by his heart to pay attention to God. And yet the second half of the verse is clear: "Your face, *Adonai*, I do seek," conveying loyalty that deserves a protective response. As for God's "face," repeated three times in verses 8 and 9,[91] face is a metaphor for divine attention. Repeated use of the human body to describe God, Maimonides would explain, helps make God relatable; and as the philosopher emphasized, the same is true for ascribing human emotions to God. Verse 9 conveys desperate doubt over God's attentiveness with four phrases that begin "do not."

The fourth cluster, verses 10 through 12, emphasizes dependency on God: Verse 10 bothered me in earlier years when my parents were still alive, as if anticipating their death. Now that they have passed, I understand the verse's intent as saying, "Even though the human condition is transient, You, God, are enduring and I can count on You as my guide and nurturer." Robert Alter will say of this verse that it is "perhaps the most extreme declaration of trust in the whole Bible." The nineteenth-century theologian Rabbi Samson Raphael Hirsch understands this line as "Even if I was so depraved that my parents would reject me, God would not."[92] Remarkably, this line is often omitted from translations of this psalm in prayerbooks. I guess I am not the only one who has found the verse troubling.

Verse 11 sees safety in following the upright path of integrity and divine service, suggestive of Psalm 1.[93] The opening word, *horeiney* (הוריני), is often translated as "instruct me" or "teach me" but also "parent me," deliberately picking up on the theme of verse 10. Although our human parents will die, God will parent us always.

Verse 12 states that tormentors are testifying falsely. For some commentators, this line is the prompt for the entire psalm: fear of a court hearing. And yet for psychologically oriented commentators, the false witnesses are the psalmist's inner voice pounding false accusations.[94] The court, moreover, may be the divine tribunal, with God as the judge.

The finale of two verses contains a dramatic pause: a blank to fill in at its very center.

> 13. If I were not to believe that I will see the goodness of *Adonai* in the land of the living…
> 14. Hope for *Adonai!* Let your heart be strong and courageous and hope for *Adonai.*

Verse 13 begins "If," *lulai* (לולא):[95] "If I were not to believe . . ." But the expected "then" is missing. Rashi and Radak, two of the classic commentators, fill in: ". . . then false witnesses would have destroyed me." Leaving the words unsaid suggests that the psalmist cannot even bear to express the outcome of faithlessness in God's goodness. The phrase the "land of the living" is understood by Jewish commentators in a variety of ways: the present world, the World to Come, or the land of Israel.[96]

The final verse repeats the word "hope," combining it with strength and courage.[97] "Let your heart be strong and courageous" echoes the farewell spoken by Moses to the Israelites and to his successor Joshua in anticipation of battles ahead.[98] "Strong and courageous" relates to physical and inner strength. The conclusion reassures that despite enemies, all will be fine. It is unclear who speaks the last line: the psalmist to himself, the psalmist's audience, or even God. And yet the lingering message is "You have reason to hope and to feel strong, because God actively cares."

So, why did the Rabbis choose this psalm, and only this psalm, for the penitential season? They did not explain, so we join generations of commentators in speculation. On a concrete level, an early midrash identifies links to the holidays: "my light" refers to Rosh Hashanah; "my deliverer" to Yom Kippur, plus the mention of the *teruah* is suggestive of the shofar; and there is an explicit reference to the sukkah of Sukkot.[99] Thematically, the psalm's seesaw of faith and doubt aligns with the penitential season. Ahead is an unknown: the new year. For the Rabbis, Rosh Hashanah and Yom Kippur mark a trial before God, whose verdict determines our fate in the coming year. This psalm suggests a court and the danger of false witnesses. We are given pause to consider our true merits and shortcomings. Although uncertain of the outcome, we have reason to hope. God is the parent who knows the truth and with mercy will forgive us. We naturally waver in our confidence before God's judgment and the unknowns of a new year. And yet we return in reading the psalm to the faith that "*Adonai* is my light." Such a trust prompts the courage to live with greater emotional freedom and personal responsibility.

DIGGING DEEPER

The Paradox of Open-Eyed Faith
Rabbi Spitz

Psalm 27 contains opposing themes: confidence in God's presence and uncertainty if God is attentive. I see this as a healthy, open-eyed hope, an understanding informed by the "Stockdale paradox."

Jim Stockdale, a high-ranking naval officer, was held in Vietnam as a prisoner of war for over seven years. He was repeatedly tortured, but he never lost hope that one day he would be freed. Years after the Vietnam War and his release, he reflected on the necessary mindset of survival:

> "Who didn't make it out?" an interviewer asked.
>
> "Oh, that's easy," Stockdale said. "The optimists."
>
> "The optimists. I do not understand," the interviewer responded, now completely confused given what he'd said a hundred meters earlier.
>
> "The optimists. Oh, they were the ones who said, 'We're going to be out by Christmas.' And Christmas would come, and Christmas would go. Then they'd say, 'We're going to be out by Easter.' And Easter would come, and Easter would go. And then Thanksgiving, and then it would be Christmas again. And they died of a broken heart."[100]

This conversation was conducted by the author and business management consultant Jim Collins for his book *From Good to Great*, a guide for companies on how to succeed. The lesson that Collins derived was that a company needs to remain realistic about challenges while retaining hope. As applied to our own lives, pessimism holds us back from the possible and blind optimism — which ignores reality — will demoralize us in time. Although optimism may drive risk-taking and innovation, choices need a reality check to help ensure against tumbling naively into a pit. Greatness emerges from a paradox: seeing reality squarely coupled with a core faith in success. Paradox is logically a contradiction but matches our lived experience. We can simultaneously hold two opposing emotions: when sitting on an airplane, we may feel both happy expectation for what is ahead and sadness in leaving the familiar.

Confidence in life's goodness seesaws with the awareness that life is dangerous. There are enemies who seek to tear us down: whether competitors, frustrating tasks, or our own internal voices challenging our worth. And yet to thrive is to believe that we will prevail, even when the *how* is uncertain. Belief in future success rests on an abiding, intuitive confidence, buttressed by previous positive outcomes. Similarly, lived relationship with God contains an element of doubt. Afterall, we do not see God nor have conversations as with another person. God is Other.

In analyzing this psalm, the Bible scholar Benjamin Sommer writes,

> The direction of the psalm's movement is crucial, because it models the maturing of an authentic relationship with God. A simple faith that asks no questions and admits no anxieties is not the most religious faith. A relationship that can articulate anxiety about the beloved's distance is ultimately stronger.[101]

The arising of doubts is natural, but what keeps a relationship secure is an abiding commitment and the belief that the other person is a trustworthy partner. The same is true with God. We vacillate in faith and yet there is an abiding fulcrum of trust: You shall not fear for I am with you.

The Value of Repetition
Rabbi Spitz

Why the proscription to repeat Psalm 27 over and over during the approach of a new year and for the immediate days afterward?

Like the daily shofar blasts, the repeated words are a wake-up call, asking, "How are you doing? What are the obstacles to contentment in your life? How have you fallen short and how can you improve? How can God help you?" With each recitation, Psalm 27 becomes more familiar. By reading the psalm over and over, we are encouraged to react. Often nothing is elicited but a satisfaction of having met the very goal of twice daily recitation. And then there are those readings when a word, phrase, or image grabs our attention and prompts a strong feeling or reflection. Such is the nature of poetry. The images are prompts. Surprises in rereading emerge as a result of actively and repeatedly engaging with the psalm.

Each year in the pulpit, I had the practice of reading the psalm out loud to my congregants. I invited them to listen as if watching the words flow as images on a screen, and at the end, to choose one image that stuck with them. Once eyes opened and we began to share, I delighted in the range of responses and their explanations of what the images had meant to them. This psalm is a collage of confidence and uncertainty that leads to living with greater faith and hope.

A New Way of Reading Psalm 27
Rabbi Riemer

Rabbi Michael Rosenberg of the Hadar Institute raised a very good question that I had never thought of. He said that there are 150 psalms; why did the sages choose this psalm to be recited twice each day from Rosh Hodesh Elul until Shemini Atseret?

You would think that they would have chosen a psalm that deals with *teshuvah,* "repentance," since that is the theme of this season of the year. And yet if you read Psalm 27 carefully, you will see that there is not a single mention of *teshuvah* in it. It does not mention either sin or forgiveness. So why, then, was it chosen?

Rabbi Rosenberg's answer is that this psalm is about God and about how to reach God. Before we can confess and repent, we have to be able to feel that we are in the presence of God.

This psalmist is terribly afraid of being distant from God. That is why he cries out, "Your face, *Adonai,* I seek. Do not hide Your face from me" (vv. 8-9). He does not want to pray to an abstract impersonal God. He does not want to pour out his heart to a metaphor that inspires us to work for social justice. He does not want to pray to an "unmoved mover" who is the first cause of all that is but who is not involved in our lives. He wants to pray to "The Most Moved Mover," which is how the prophets understood God. He wants to be heard and loved, and he wants to speak to and love the God who cares about him and who listens to his cry.

This is why he cries out near the end of this psalm, "For though my father and my mother leave me, *Adonai* will gather me in" (v. 10). Can there be any more heartrending request than this? I am an orphan. My parents are gone. Will you please be my parent?

Rabbi Rosenberg admits that there are risks in this kind of faith. We run the risk of making God in our image. We run the risk of understanding God as an old white man with a beard who sits on a throne in heaven and judges us by what is written in a book that God examines once a year. We run the risk of committing the sin of idolatry by worshipping this kind of an image of God. And yet he says that all of these risks are worth taking if they enable us to pray, to pour out our hearts in truth, and to plead for a second chance from the One who made us.

I confess that I never understood this way of reading Psalm 27, but now that I do, I will try my best to recite this psalm every day of Elul and then through Rosh Hashanah and Yom Kippur and till the end of Sukkot in this spirit.

A Hundred Times
Rabbi Riemer

Psalm 27 is recited twice a day starting with Rosh Hodesh Elul and ending on Hoshanah Rabbah. If you do the math, you will see that the month of Elul has thirty days, the period from Rosh Hashanah to Yom Kippur is ten days, and the period between Yom Kippur and Hoshanah Rabbah is ten days, which means that if you recite Psalm 27 twice a day during this period, you will recite it a hundred times.

Why is this psalm recited twice a day from the beginning of Elul until almost the end of Sukkot? With the exception of the psalms that are recited every day, I cannot think of any other psalm that is said a hundred times a year.

I think that the simplest explanation is that when we come to the end of a year and the edge of a new year, we are all a little bit apprehensive. On the one hand, when that season arrives we feel a sense of gratitude and perhaps even relief that we have made it through the year that is now ending. There were probably some days during this year that is now ending when we did not think that we would make it. There may have even been some days during the year when we did not want to make it, but thank God we made it and so we feel grateful.

But on the other hand, who knows what the new year will bring? Will it be better than the year that is now ending? Or will it be, God forbid, worse? No one knows, and so everyone enters the new year with a little bit of anxiety.

The period when one year ends and a new one begins is a liminal moment. It is a moment when we stand at the threshold, and threshold moments are always a little bit scary. This is why we have a mezuzah on the doorway of our homes. It marks the border between the home inside and the world outside. It is a liminal place. And this is why we have a bar or a bat mitzvah ceremony at the time when our children have one foot in childhood, the stage of their life that is now ending, and one foot in adolescence, the stage of their life that is now beginning. This is a liminal moment and therefore it is marked with some kind of a ceremony in many different cultures, not just in Judaism.

The moment when we stand between the end of one year and the beginning of another is surely a liminal moment. It is a time when all of us feel a little bit anxious. So we are taught to recite this psalm that is meant to give us the confidence and the wisdom with which to begin a new year.

"Who Need I Fear?"
Rabbi Riemer

Rabbi Richard Levy, who was for many years a Hillel director in Los Angeles and who then became the head of the Hebrew Union College branch in Los Angeles, wrote a very good commentary on the book of Psalms.[102] And when he got to Psalm 27, he told this story:

Back in the 1960s he was a student at the Hebrew Union College in Cincinnati. He says that after a while, the program began to feel a bit boring to him and other students. It was the same routine every day. In the morning there were services and then breakfast and then off to class. Then they had a break for lunch and then it was back to class again. And then it was dinner and time to prepare their homework for the next day.

This went on for about half a year, and by then he and all the other students in his class were beginning to feel a bit restless. Then one day they got a phone call from the office of Rev. Dr. Martin Luther King, Jr. The phone call said that Dr. King was going to lead a demonstration the next day in Birmingham, Alabama, and that he would appreciate it very much if these students would join him in this rally.

A demonstration? In the South? With Rev. Dr. Martin Luther King, Jr.? That sounded like an adventure. And so seventeen students boarded a bus and headed south. Before they did, they sent a telegram to Dr. King telling him that they were on the way and asking him to arrange for someone to meet them when they arrived.

It never occurred to these students that the police in Birmingham would read their telegram — but they did. And so when they arrived, they found Dr. King and his group were there to meet them, and so were the Birmingham police. They were arrested at the bus stop and accused of violating certain local laws that they had never heard of. They were told that, according to the local law, whites and blacks were not allowed to meet at a bus station, and they were told that they were considered outside agitators who had come to disturb the peace of the community. Both groups — the whites and the blacks — were taken to jail.

Even the jails in the South were segregated in those days, and so Dr. King and his people were put into one cell and the students from the Hebrew Union College were put into another cell. Dr. King and his people were used to being arrested by then, but for these college students, this was a very frightening experience; none of them had ever been in jail before in their lives.

The police kept the lights on in their cell all night, and they played loud music into their cell all night as well. And every so often a guard would go by and call out antisemitic insults. It was understandable that the students did not sleep very well that night.

Dr. King understood how they must be feeling, and so he took out a notepad and wrote something on a piece of paper, and he somehow managed to have it smuggled from his cell to theirs. The boys huddled around it to see what it said.

It said, "Remember Psalm 27, verse 1."

Only one of the boys had a Bible with him. The rest of them gathered around him as he looked up the reference. It said, "The Lord is my light and my rescuer; who need I fear? The Lord is my shield and my protector; of whom do I need to be afraid?" That verse gave the students a little bit of confidence and helped them get through that night.

Rabbi Levy says that he has kept that verse in his wallet ever since so that he may have it nearby if he is ever in a situation when he is afraid.

As God Sees Us
Rabbi Riemer

Rabbi Debra Robbins of Houston, Texas decided one year that she was going to recite Psalm 27 a hundred times and she was going to determine what it meant and what it is intended to teach us. And so she decided to meditate on this psalm every day from the beginning of the month of Elul until Hoshanah Rabbah.

This is how she did it: She chose one phrase each day — a phrase that consisted of two words, or three at the most — and she lived with this phrase for a whole day. Instead of just rattling off the phrase, she meditated on what it might mean to her. And she kept a journal at her side in which she wrote down any response to this phrase that came to her mind. When the season for saying Psalm 27 came to an end, she found that she had a journal full of spiritual insights, and she was able to turn them into a book, *Opening Your Heart with Psalm 27*, so that she could help others find meaning in the words of this psalm.

Let me share just two examples from her journal with you. But first, I must explain to you what kind of a year it was in which she undertook this project.

You may remember that Houston was the location some years ago of an enormous flood that covered the city as never before. Hundreds of houses were destroyed. Hundreds of cars floated away and were never retrieved. Several thousand people had to be taken from their homes by boat, and they had to be put up at the convention center until some other kind of housing could be arranged for them. And it was against the background of this event that Debra Robbins wrote her meditations on Psalm 27.

The first comment of hers that I want to share with you is based on the line in Psalm 27 that reads, "One thing I ask of *Adonai*, of this I seek (v. 4); *lachazot binoam Adonai*, "that I will see the goodness of *Adonai* in the land of the living" (v. 13).

Rabbi Robbins looked at that verse for a long time and came to realize that this phrase can be understood in two different ways. It is usually understood as "May I see the sweetness of the Lord," but if that is what it means, why do we have the letter *bet* before the word *noam*? What does this preposition add to the sentence?

Her answer: our goal in life should be to see the world the way God sees the world, to notice and appreciate all the beautiful things around us and within us the way God does. She understands this phrase to mean that her deepest wish should be to see the world and everything in it, including her friends and even her enemies and even herself, the way that God does. She said to herself: Look at how God looked at Adam and Eve after they sinned. You might have thought that He would look at them with anger or contempt. After all, they had been given just one measly commandment — and they had broken it on their very first day in the garden! You might think that God would have disowned them, but He didn't. He saw them as frail and fallible human beings, and so He gave them a second chance. God became a tailor, and made clothing for them so that they would not be cold when they went out into the real world.

What if we could see the people we know who have made mistakes that way?

Or look at how God saw Noah and his family. They were not the most pious family that ever was. You could not compare them with Abraham and Sarah, but God saw that the reason they were not so very pious is that they lived in a wicked generation. God understood that it is hard for anyone to be good when all the people around you are bad. And so God looked upon Noah and his family with kindness and found them worth saving when everyone else was destroyed.

Rabbi Robbins said to herself: Why can't we learn to look at people that way? Why can't we learn to forgive the people we know who sin simply because they live surrounded by evildoers? What if we could learn to look at people who sin the way God looked at Noah? If we could do that, how different the world would be!

Or look at how God saw Naomi. Naomi was a bitter woman, and she had good reason to be bitter. She had left Bethlehem a rich woman with a husband and two sons. She came back a widow who had lost both of her sons and her possessions. Can you blame her for being bitter? And yet God saw the potential in Naomi and helped her rebuild her life. She ended up with a daughter-in-law who loved her and with a grandchild who was destined to become the ancestor of King David.

Can you imagine how different our lives would be if, when we looked at each other, we did not see a competitor but a person who needs us? And can you imagine how different our lives would be if when we saw a handicapped person, we saw someone who is made in the image of God instead of seeing someone who repels us by his or her appearance? If we could ask just one thing of God, would this not be a good thing to ask?

Rabbi Robbins worked as a volunteer at the convention center, helping people who were being sheltered there during the flood. Her job was to run around the room and help in any way she could: to find a toy to bring to a small child who was crying, to bring a pillow to someone who could not sleep, or to supply clean socks for someone who had no socks. And it was in that context that she read Psalm 27 each night. And when she came to the phrase "If I were not to believe that I will see the goodness of *Adonai* in the land of the living . . ." she wondered, what would God look like to the people who were living in that convention center? This is what she wrote:

I saw God, assisted by His angels, turn a convention center into a shelter in less than ten hours.

I saw God and His angels arrange beds all around the room, I saw an angel as a woman who was wearing a red vest with a lanyard around her neck. She had hands and ears and eyes — but no wings, which I was brought up to believe was what angels wore. She had eyes, but her eyes could not see status — not legal status and not social status. She had eyes which could not see the difference between races. All she could see was human beings who needed help, and human beings who held others in their arms.

Do you know what the goodness of God looks like at the convention center? The goodness of God comes in the form of new and clean panties, because when the world is very dark, it is good to have something clean to wear.

The goodness of God comes in the form of clean socks, because when you have been walking through the mud, clean socks refresh you as much as a visit to a spa does.

The goodness of God looks like a bar of soap or a bottle of shampoo or some deodorant because smelling good is essential to self-esteem.

But above all, above all, God looks like a diaper that fits, because in all this mess something should fit right and not irritate your body.

The image of God looks like shampoo, because it is soft and clean, and when it starts to flow, it can flood you with its holiness.

The image of God comes in the form of a blanket that is not completely torn and in the form of a toy that is only half broken and that can still bring a smile to the face of a frightened child.

If you have any of these things at home, bring them to the convention center and you will see the goodness of God manifest as you have never seen it before.[103]

A Call to Trust and Faith
Rabbi Riemer

And now let us look at the last two lines of this psalm.

In the first one, the psalmist says, "If I were not to believe that I will see the goodness of *Adonai* in the land of the living . . ." (v. 13), and he stops in the middle of the sentence. It is as if he is afraid that if he finishes it, what he fears to say would happen.

And the last line is "Let your heart be strong and courageous and hope for *Adonai*" (v. 14). And if you are unable to muster up trust in the Lord? Then find strength and be determined and try again, for without trust you cannot live.

As my parents used to say: *Gelt farloren? Halp farloren. Mut farloren? Alts farloren.* "If you lose your wealth — you have lost half of what you need. But if you have lost your spirit? Then you have lost everything."

Without trust we cannot live. And so this is the last word of Psalm 27. It is unrealistic to have certainty and to think that God will do whatever we want Him to, as the first six verses of this psalm suggest. It is better to have a realistic faith that knows that evil is real and that suffering is an ever-present possibility, as the next six verses declare. But above all, a person must live with hope, for without hope there is no life.

That is why the anthem of the Jewish people is *Hatikvah*, which means "The Hope." And this is why the Five Books of Moses end not with the conquest of Canaan but with Moses dying on the edge of the land. But before he dies, he tells Joshua to have hope and trust and faith in the future.

And this is the way that we must learn to live as well.

Psalm 30

"I Have Recovered: Thank You So Much, O God!"

Rabbi Jack Riemer

I think Psalm 30 was written by a person who was very sick and nearly died and then recovered. And I think that he wrote this psalm in order to give thanks to God for his recovery. Though we recite this psalm on Chanukah, it is actually a reminder to us all, especially in recovery from illness, of the source of our healing and a song of our gratitude.

א מִזְמוֹר—
שִׁיר חֲנֻכַּת הַבַּיִת—
לְדָוִד

1 A psalm — a song for the dedication of the House — for David.

ב אֲרוֹמִמְךָ יְהֹוָה כִּי דִלִּיתָנִי
וְלֹא שִׂמַּחְתָּ אֹיְבַי לִי.

2 I exalt You, *Adonai,* for You scooped me up and did not let my enemies rejoice over me.

ג יְהֹוָה אֱלֹהָי,
שִׁוַּעְתִּי אֵלֶיךָ וַתִּרְפָּאֵנִי.

3 *Adonai,* my God, I cried out to You and You healed me.

ד יְהֹוָה, הֶעֱלִיתָ מִן שְׁאוֹל נַפְשִׁי;
חִיִּיתַנִי! מִיּוֹרְדִי (מִיָּרְדִי) בוֹר.

4 *Adonai,* You brought up my spirit from *Sheol;* You kept me alive! — unlike descenders of the Pit.

ה זַמְּרוּ לַיהֹוָה חֲסִידָיו
וְהוֹדוּ לְזֵכֶר קָדְשׁוֹ.

5 Hymn to *Adonai* [God's] pious and let us praise for remembrance of [Divine] holiness.

ו כִּי רֶגַע בְּאַפּוֹ; חַיִּים בִּרְצוֹנוֹ; **6** For [God's] anger is but for a
בָּעֶרֶב יָלִין בֶּכִי וְלַבֹּקֶר רִנָּה. moment; life is [God's] desire;
in the evening a person lies down
with weeping and in the morning
sings with joy.

ז וַאֲנִי אָמַרְתִּי בְשַׁלְוִי: **7** As for me, I said in my ease:
בַּל אֶמּוֹט לְעוֹלָם. "I shall not stumble ever."

ח יְהוָה בִּרְצוֹנְךָ הֶעֱמַדְתָּה לְהַרְרִי עֹז; **8** *Adonai*, with Your desire You made
הִסְתַּרְתָּ פָנֶיךָ, הָיִיתִי נִבְהָל. me stand strong as a mountain;
when You hid Your face,
I was terrified.

ט אֵלֶיךָ יְהוָה אֶקְרָא **9** To You, *Adonai*, I called,
וְאֶל-אֲדֹנָי, אֶתְחַנָּן. and to my Master,
I pleaded for grace:

י מַה בֶּצַע בְּדָמִי; **10** "What benefit is there in my
בְּרִדְתִּי אֶל שָׁחַת? blood; in my descent to *Shachat*?
הֲיוֹדְךָ עָפָר? הֲיַגִּיד אֲמִתֶּךָ? Shall the dust praise You?
Shall it declare Your truth?"

יא שְׁמַע יְהוָה וְחָנֵּנִי; **11** Listen, *Adonai*, and be gracious to
יְהוָה, הֱיֵה עֹזֵר לִי. me; *Adonai*, be a helper for me."

יב הָפַכְתָּ מִסְפְּדִי לְמָחוֹל לִי: **12** You turned my grief into dancing
פִּתַּחְתָּ שַׂקִּי וַתְּאַזְּרֵנִי שִׂמְחָה. for me; You untied my sackcloth and
wrapped me with joy ...

יג לְמַעַן יְזַמֶּרְךָ כָבוֹד וְלֹא יִדֹּם. **13** in order that my glory shall hymn
יְהֹוָה אֱלֹהַי לְעוֹלָם אוֹדֶךָּ. to You and not be silent.

Adonai, my God, forever I will praise
You."

READING CLOSELY

There is a certain symmetry in the second verse. The psalmist says, "I exalt
You, Adonai." Why? *Ki dilitani* — "for You scooped me up."

The Hebrew word for "bucket" is *dli*. *Dilitani* comes from this same
root. It means I was on the brink of going down into the *Sheol*, into the
pit, and You reached down and scooped me up.

The verse has a certain balance to it. You lifted me up, and so I will lift
You up with my praise.

The second half of this verse says *vilo simachta oyvy li*, "You did not
let my enemies rejoice over me." Who are these enemies? He doesn't say
but this expression appears all over the book of Psalms. You would think
from reading this book that the whole city of Jerusalem was full of vicious
people who roamed the streets looking for psalmists to attack. My guess
is that *oyvy*, "my enemies," is a metaphor. And that it refers to all kinds of
enemies, both external and internal.

I think that for the psalmist, greed is an enemy that can destroy you
if you do not control it. The desire to have what the other person has —
whether it is their car, their house, or their spouse — can destroy you.
There are some people who can never enjoy or be thankful for what they
have because they are obsessed with envy over what someone else has.

Illness and pain can also be enemies. Depression can be an enemy. So
I am guessing that when the psalmist talks about his enemies here, he
means his illness and the depression that it has caused.

I still remember how Dr. Abraham Joshua Heschel explained verse 3: *Karati aylecha vitirpaeni*, "Adonai, my God, I cried out to You, and You healed me." He said that it does not mean that I called out to God and God answered me. It means that I called out to God and the very experience of doing so, *the very experience of praying*, healed me. Have you ever had that experience? Have you ever prayed and as a result of praying come out feeling better, cleaner, more hopeful, and better able to face life's problems than you were before? If you have, then you have experienced the power of prayer.

In verse 5, the psalmist turns to the people in the Temple or perhaps to those outside in the courtyard with him, and he calls out to them to join him in praising God. It is as if we were asking the whole congregation to come to a kiddush that we are sponsoring in honor of our recovery from illness.

Why do we do that? Because a joy is not really a joy until and unless we share it with others, at least not in Judaism. Ours is not an I-Thou religion; it is a We-Thou religion.

Do you know the story about the rabbi who is a fanatic golfer? One year he declares a recess on Yom Kippur afternoon and slips out of the synagogue so he can go golfing. He goes to a golf course where nobody knows him and guess what happens? On the first hole and on the second and on the third hole and on the fourth, he gets a hole in one. He keeps doing this on every hole, and he ends up with a total of eighteen.

The angels in heaven look down and see this and they say to God, "A rabbi who slips out of *shul* on the holiest day of the year in order to play golf, and this is the reward you give him?"

And God says, "You don't understand. This is not his reward. This is his punishment — *because who is he going to be able to tell?*"

A joy is only a joy if you share it. That is why the saddest line in all of Jewish literature is the line in the *Yad Hachazakah* of Maimonides where the great teacher of Jewish law discusses how a Jew makes a seder even if he has no one to share it with. He writes that a Jew in this situation must ask himself the four questions and then he must answer them himself.

Can you imagine a sadder seder than that?

That is why the psalmist in verse 5 calls out to everyone who is within reach of his voice and says, *Zamru la adonoy chassidav vihodu lizecher kodsho,* "Come sing with me to God, let us celebrate His holiness together." By doing this the psalmist turns his personal story about how he was sick and recovered into an event that is shared with the whole community.

In verse 6, we find a double entendre that makes a difference. The text says *Ki rega b'apo chayim birtsono.* There are two ways of understanding the word *rega,* and each of them has a different lesson to teach us.

The simplest way to read it is: when God is angry, there is *roga. Roga* means "to tremble" or "to shake." So, when God is angry, the earth shakes. That could be what the verse means.

But now let me show you another way to read this line. *Rega* means "a moment" or "a short time." Biblical Hebrew has no vowels; in verse 6, this word could be read as *roga* or *rega.* So it may mean God is angry for a brief moment, but his love is constant. Or as the theologian and educator Rabbi Shai Held puts it, "Love is what God is. Anger is what God sometimes gets."[104]

Love is God's normal state. Anger is something that occurs within God on occasion, and when it occurs, all we have to do is wait it out and it will eventually end. We may cry at night, but joy will come in the morning.

Darkness was always a scary time in the ancient world because people had no light. When the sun set, they had nothing to do. They could not read; they could not work. All they could do was sit in the dark and worry. That is why all the stories we heard as children about how the big bad wolf is going to come and get us always took place at night.

Among the greatest accomplishments of the late nineteenth and early twentieth centuries were the harnessing of electricity and the invention of the light bulb. Now night is like day for us. We can work, we can read, we can do whatever we want to. But it was not like that in the ancient world; you can only do so much by firelight.

And so in Psalm 92:3, for example, the psalmist says, *lihagid baboker chasdecho vi emunatecha baleylot*, "I will declare your lovingkindness during the day" (v. 3), because during the day it is easy to feel the presence of God. The world is alive, and the sun is shining. But then the psalmist says *emunatecha baleylot*, "I will speak of your faithfulness at night," because when it is dark, you cannot see the work of God. All you can do is hope and trust that God is with you.

And so here in verse 6, the psalmist says, *ba'erev yalin bechi uvalaboker rina*, "In the evening a person lies down with weeping and in the morning sings with joy" — that is, "At night I may weep and worry but in the morning I feel joy."

Two of my very good friends asked me the same question on this verse. Both said to me, I sometimes go to sleep full of worry and when I wake up — you know what? The worry is still there. So how can I say this psalm without feeling that it is naïve and pollyannish and untrue?

The only answer I could give them was that *boker* does not necessarily mean the very next morning. It may mean someday or eventually there will be joy. It may be an expression of hope, not of glibness or certainty.

Verse 7 can also be read in two ways: as a statement of what the psalmist felt at some time in the past or as a statement of what the psalmist feels now. And which it is makes a very big difference. If it is a statement about the way he felt in the past, then it is a confession. It explains why God has been angry at him. He has committed a sin. What was that sin? When things were going well for him, when he was successful, he was arrogant and he felt that he deserved the credit for all his successes. He felt that he was a self-made man, and he did not realize how much of what he had achieved in this world was with the help of other people and with the help of God.

This is true of every self-made person. Where would a "self-made man" who now owns a chain of grocery stores be if it were not for the bank that gave him his first loan without which he could not have started his business? And where would this person be without the advertising that promoted his business, and those who sold him merchandise, and those who stocked the shelves, and those who worked at the cash registers in his store from morning to night, and those who greeted every customer with a smile? Without them, would he be the success that he now boasts that he is?

The psalmist now realizes that there is no such thing as a self-made person, because we live in an interdependent world. Forgive me for this example, and please do not misunderstand what I am about to say. I do not mean to suggest, God forbid, that this COVID-19 pandemic was the intent of God. That is not true. In fact, to say that is to blaspheme. But what this virus has done is make us aware, perhaps for the first time, of how interdependent we are.

What you breathe out – I breathe in. And what I breathe out – you breathe in. That is how interdependent we are. And so the psalmist confesses in verse 7: I was wrong and I was arrogant when I said *bal emot l'olam*; when I said in my time of serenity that "I shall not stumble ever."

If we read the psalm this way, it means that the psalmist is confessing his sin of thinking that he deserved the credit for all that he had achieved. Or we can read this statement not as a confession but as a recognition that God's anger is mysterious. We simply do not know what causes it, and so all we can do is hunker down and wait for it to end. All we know is that God's anger does not last as long as God's love does.

Verse 8 is a fact of life. When God wants to, God can make us feel as strong and as safe as a mountain, but when God turns away from us, we're terrified.

In verse 9 we read, "To You, Adonai, I called, and to my Master, I pleaded for grace — *etchanan*." What does *etchanan* mean? It comes from the word *chen*, which means "undeserved, unearned kindness." So the psalmist is saying, "I asked for Your help not because I have earned it but because I hope that You will give it to me out of Your grace."

If you ask the average Jew, they will tell you that grace is a Christian concept. As Paul the apostle says, Jews depend on works; Christians depend on grace. Jews believe that they earn God's love by doing the *mitzvot*; Christians believe that God loves us because of God's grace.

But, that is too simple a distinction. As Dr. Shai Held has taught, throughout the Bible, the Talmud, and everywhere else in the Jewish tradition, there are many requests for kindness that we Jews do not claim that we deserve but that we hope God will show us anyway. We call God *El Rachum Vichunun*, "the God who is compassionate and merciful." God is not a scorekeeper who puts a check beside our names when we do good and a mark against our names when we do bad. God is kind and merciful.

Verse 10 is difficult. It sounds like the psalmist is saying, "Save us for Your name's sake; for if we go under, who will there be on earth left to praise You? You need us as much as we need You." But now look at verse 11: *Shema Adonoy vichaneni* is the same phrase that we found in verse 9. Here it means: "Be gracious to us and help us." In verse 10 the psalmist said, "Help us for Your sake," but here he shakes his head and says to himself, "This is not the proper way to talk to God. You cannot bribe God and so I take back what I said and I ask You to save me, not for Your sake but for mine."

And now the conclusion: God has answered the prayer of the psalmist. The psalmist has recovered from his illness and so in the final two verses says, "You turned my grief into dancing; You untied my sackcloth and wrapped me in joy. I will sing to You with my whole being." The psalm that began with the fact that the dead are silent ends with a declaration: "now that I have recovered, I will not be silent. I will ever praise You."

We all pray fervently when we are ill. The psalmist reminds us to pray gratefully when we recover.

DIGGING DEEPER

What's In a Title?
Rabbi Jack Riemer

Let me begin by asking you to look at the title of this psalm and see if you notice two strange things in it.

The first question is: How can this psalm be called a psalm of David in honor of the dedication of the Temple? David never lived to see the dedication of the Temple. It was dedicated by Solomon, many years after David died.

The second question is: How come this psalm is recited on Chanukah when there is no mention of Chanukah in it?

The answer to the first question is fairly easy. The phrase *mizmor lidavid* does not always mean a song by David. Sometimes it means a song in honor of David. Sometimes it means a song in the musical tradition of David. Sometimes it means a song in honor of the present king who is a descendant of David. And sometimes it means a song in memory of King David.

The fact that a song begins with the words *mizmor lidavid* does not in itself prove that it was written by David, and it does not even prove that it was written in the time of David.

The second part of the title is harder to explain. How can you explain why there is not a single reference to the Temple anywhere in this psalm? And how do you explain that it is recited on Chanukah when there is no reference to Chanukah anywhere in this psalm?

Let me offer you my suggestion for whatever it may be worth: the title somehow got attached to this psalm by mistake. Once it got there, no one had the courage or the chutzpah to take it out. And since it had the word *chanukah* in it, people decided it was a good psalm to say on Chanukah.

But as mentioned in my introduction to this psalm, this psalm was likely written by a person who was very sick, nearly died, and then recovered, and he wrote this psalm in order to give thanks to God for his recovery.

The Power of Prayer
Rabbi Jack Riemer

There is a story that we read every year from the prophets on the first day of Rosh Hashanah. It is the story of a woman named Hannah who was bitter because she had no child. Her whole life felt empty and without purpose. She could not eat and she could not drink because she was so unhappy and so envious of her rival, Peninah, her husband's other wife, who kept turning out children one after another, while she remained childless. Then one day she went into the sanctuary after the services were over and poured out her heart to God.

I imagine she went to services on Rosh Hashanah every year. She always bought a new outfit for this occasion, and her husband always made sure that they had good seats. On the way out, she always made a point of shaking hands with the *kohanim* and telling them how much she enjoyed the services.

But this year she did differently. This year she went into the sanctuary when the services were over and no one else was there. She prayed to God in silence, swaying back and forth. Eli, the High Priest, happened to come by and thought she must be drunk. He rebuked her and told her that she ought to put away her drinking, especially in the House of God. Hannah answered him with simple dignity. She said, "I am not a drunkard. I am simply pouring out my heart before the Lord."

When he heard that, Eli apologized and wished her well and went on his way. There is a certain irony to this scene. Eli, the professional expert on prayer, cannot tell the difference between a drunken woman and a woman who is pouring out her heart before the Lord. But God can!

And then we read this line: *upaneha lo hayoo la od*, "Her face was no longer the same." She did not yet have a child. She was not even pregnant. But the Bible says that when she went out of the sanctuary, "her face was no longer the same."

She looked different because she felt different. She looked different because she had prayed to God many times before, but her words were different this time. In the past she had prayed, "Dear God, please give me a child." This time she prayed, "Dear God, please give me a child so that I can raise him up for your service." *And that* made all the difference. Now, for the first time in her life, she was thinking not only of what she did not have but of what she could give. Now she was thinking of how she could raise a child, if she had one, for service to God.

Hannah had a child that year, but even if she hadn't, I think that her life would have been transformed. I think that she might have become a teacher, a social worker, or something like that, because prayer had changed her whole perspective on life.

It changed her from being frustrated and angry over what she did not have to thinking of what she could do, and that transformed her. I think the reason the Sages chose this story for us to read at prime time on the first day of Rosh Hashanah was to teach us the same lesson, which is that prayer can change us, whether or not our prayers are answered.

That is what I think it means in Psalm 30 when the psalmist says, "I called out to You" — and the very experience of doing so made me see my life differently.

The Taste of Joy
Rabbi Spitz

Psalm 30 celebrates the gift of life by a poet who has approached the abyss. Perspective and celebration emerge. We are uncertain if the grave danger was actual enemies, physical illness, or mental despair. Rabbi Riemer mentioned this psalm in his introduction, with verse 6 as a life-line to resiliency: "In the evening a person lies down with weeping and in the morning sings with joy."

We have each tasted the joy of renewed health, if even when only recovering from a flu. In the extreme, as our psalmist conveys, a person may have reason to fear that the end is near. In recent years, I counseled a mother of small children who was told after repeated brain imaging that she had a brain tumor that had to be removed and that the surgery would reduce her mental capacity. She approached the surgery date with prayers by a synagogue community, meditation affirmations, and much foreboding. On the morning of the surgery, she underwent a final brain scan. Surprisingly, the abnormality no longer appeared. The world-renowned neurosurgeon said that during his career he had seen this only once before. Apparently, he concluded, a swollen artery had appeared as a growth and had receded. No surgery was needed. You can only imagine the relief of the patient and her family and community. In the words of our psalmist, "You turned my grief into dancing for me; You untied my sackcloth and wrapped me with joy" (v. 12).

What Happens After We Die?
Rabbi Elie Spitz

At an earlier phase of my rabbinate, I researched near-death experiences (NDEs), accounts of people whose hearts had stopped or who were in a coma, near death, and were then revived. Reporting on the in-between phase, many described a cluster of the following phenomena: being drawn out of their bodies; watching themselves and their caregivers as if looking down; feeling drawn to a light; seeing their life's events pass before them as if viewing a movie; being given a choice by an ethereal figure to return to their body or move toward the light; choosing to return and suddenly becoming aware of pain.

The first time a person recounted such a near-death experience to me, the synagogue visitor did so at a *kiddush*, the gathering over refreshments after a service. A relative of a congregational leader, he described a motorcycle accident. With his body on the side of the road, he watched the medics work on him as if his consciousness hovered over his body. He described a state of sublime calm. An ethereal figure appeared and offered him a choice: move into the light or return to your body. He chose to return and was immediately zapped back into his body, wracked with pain. I asked him how this experience had changed him. He replied that he no longer feared death and was much more spiritual, "but I do not attend synagogue any more often."

To better understand such phenomena, I read many books, including one by Dr. Melvin Morse. The physician-author describes being called to the emergency room to attend to an unconscious girl who had drowned in a friend's pool. Once revived, she told the doctor of a lit figure who had given her the choice to return to her body. She also described in physical detail the medical team who had worked on her and the precise locations and activities of her family members during that time. After the family arrived, the doctor interviewed them and, sure enough, their whereabouts matched her account, as did her description of the clothing and activity in the emergency room. Morse had not heard previously of near-death experiences and was intrigued. He sought out medical records of pediatric patients in the Seattle Children's Hospital who reported such NDEs, finding twelve such individuals. He interviewed them and did so again twenty years after their hospitalizations. He found that despite the intervening years, each vividly remembered their near-death experience. Remarkably, each had completed high school, tested more positively than peers on a survey of psychological health, and each believed that she or he had come back to earth for a purpose, ranging from being kinder to siblings to training as a scientific researcher. Hence, the title of his book, *Transformed by the Light.*

Psalm 30 focuses on the danger of death with a variety of Hebrew words for the grave or the afterlife. Each is identified with "going down" — to *She'ol, Bor, Shachat.* For this psalmist, once dead, there is an inability to consciously act: "What benefit is there in my blood [death]; in my descent to *Shachat?* Shall the dust praise You? Shall it declare Your truth?" (v. 10). Claims of an end to an active relationship with God upon death are found in other psalms, too:

- 6:6 — "In death there is no mention of You."
- 88:11-13 — "For the dead will You work wonders? Will departed spirits rise to praise You? Will it be told in the grave of Your kindness? Or Your faithfulness in *Avadon?* Will it be known in the darkness of Your wonders? And Your justice in the land of oblivion?"
- 115:17 — "The dead do not praise God, nor do those who go down into the silence [of the grave].

Such lines might lead a reader to conclude that in the Bible, dead is dead. And yet there are other verses that suggest consciousness after death:

- Job 26:5 — "The shades tremble beneath the waters and their denizens."
- Isaiah 14:9-10 — "*She'ol* was astir to greet Your coming — rousing for You the shades of all earth's chieftains, raising from the thrones all the kings of nations. All

speak up and say to you, 'So you have been stricken as
we were; you have become like us!'"

+ Jeremiah 31:15 — "A cry is heard in Ramah — wailing,
bitter weeping — [deceased] Rachel weeping for her
children. She refuses to be comforted."

+ I Samuel 28:3-25 — The account of King Saul com-
municating with the deceased prophet Saul with the
aid of a medium, the Witch of Endor.

As you can see, there is no one biblical position on the afterlife. We
may choose whether to read such biblical lines figuratively or literally. The
realm beyond death is given many names, five alone in Psalm 88. And
yet the psalmists consistently speak of no conscious activity after death.
But the context for the psalmists is an urgent pleading to God for help
to overcome a danger. As a belief in consciousness after life repeatedly
exists among the prophets of the Bible, we may assume that the psalmists
knew those beliefs. What the psalmists believed about the afterlife is open
to speculation as the context for their words is to emphasize regarding
death, "surely not yet."

My first book, *Does the Soul Survive? A Jewish Journey to Belief in Afterlife, Past Lives, and Living with Purpose*, examines belief in the afterlife
by weighing contemporary evidence of near-death experiences, telepathy,
and mediums, while listening to the teaching of Jewish thinkers on these
topics as if fellow jurors. In my own examination as an independent ju-
ror, I grew to identify with the traditional Jewish teaching: "This world
is like a passageway before the World to Come; prepare yourself in the
passageway so as to enter the main room" (*Pirkei Avot* 4:21, quoting Rabbi
Ya'akov). Belief in the world to come exists, but it is downplayed before
the immediate challenges and opportunities of this life.

As a contrast, I recall attending the funeral of Big Mama Thornton,
which took place in the Watts neighborhood of Los Angeles in 1984.
Big Mama was a blues singer and songwriter I admired. Her recordings

of "Hound Dog" and "Ball and Chain" were later transformed into huge hits by Elvis Presley and Janis Joplin. As I entered the chapel, a recording of Big Mama singing "What a Difference a Day Makes" played from the balcony. The officiant was her former bandleader. As he eulogized, he grew in enthusiasm, "There is no reason to cry. Big Mama is now in a boat traveling from these shores to the other side. Soon she will be jamming the most amazing music ever heard with Louis and Lady Day." When a woman in the congregation began to wail, she was ushered out of the room. The preacher had made the next world a destination of rejoicing that surpassed the goodness of this life.

For the poet of Psalm 30, the focus is on living now. He does not want to die and sees those earlier threats as enemies. He celebrates his recovery in physical terms: "You turned my grief into dancing (*machol*) for me." Most likely, the danger that the psalmist describes is that of a serious illness. The words might also apply to a serious setback in life, such as a divorce, loss of a job, or defamation. Overcoming such trauma enables growth. In Hebrew, the word for crisis has the same root (שבר) as that of a birthing stool, stones used by ancient women for support while giving birth.[105] Moving from despair to hope may enable the emergence of a new perspective or phase of life.

Hope Despite Despair
Rabbi Spitz

Extreme despair reoccurs in the Bible. Rachel yearning for a child says to her husband, Jacob, "Give me children, otherwise let me die" (Genesis 30:1). Moses, exhausted from Israelite rebellions, says to God, "I alone cannot carry this entire nation, for it is too heavy for me. And if is how you deal with me, kill me now!" (Numbers 11:14). Jonah the prophet, after reluctantly fulfilling his duty of prophesy to the people of Nineveh, proclaims, "Please, Lord, take my life for I would rather die than live"

(Jonah 4:3). And after Elijah fled the murderous Queen Jezebel to the desert: "He came to a broom brush and sat down under it, and prayed that he might die, 'Now, O Lord, take my life, for I am no better than my ancestors'" (I Kings 19:4).

Some of the greatest Jewish leaders experienced deep depression. Maimonides, a philosopher, physician, and great codifier of Jewish law, wrote that he could not get out of bed for one year after his brother David drowned in the Indian Ocean.[106] A prominent biography of Rabbi Nahman of Bratslav is entitled *The Tormented Master*.[107] And as for modern political leaders, Abraham Lincoln on more than one occasion in his twenties had friends stand guard to prevent him from taking his life. Winston Churchill referred to his "black dog," a lifelong companion of encounters with inner darkness.[108] In each of these cases, the inner struggles would later enhance their respective capacity to deal with the turbulence of life.

My second book, *Healing from Despair: Choosing Wholeness in a Broken World*, written with Erica Taylor, dealt with such inner darkness. My goal was to normalize the experiences of despair, to address the extreme tragedy of suicide with compassion, and to provide hope for those dealing with mental illness. As in Psalm 88's darkness, Psalm 30 addresses a low point in a person or a community's experience and is invaluable in honoring that reality and thereby provides catharsis and hope.

Addressing a God of Deliverance
Rabbi Spitz

The psalmist of Psalm 30 repeatedly credits God with the strength to overcome fatal danger. Yet it was not all smooth sailing. We read further on, "*Adonai*, with Your desire You made me stand strong as a mountain; When You hid Your face, I was terrified" (v. 8). "God's face" is a metaphor for experiencing God's warm, caring presence. There are times when we may feel distant from God.

Martin Buber, the twentieth-century Bible scholar and theologian, spoke of the eclipse of God. God, Buber taught, is always present, but there are moments in our lives when we block out God. We do so by overintellectualizing: we make God into an object, an It. And there is but a step from dogma to magic, which is making God into a tool to manipulate to meet our needs. God, for Buber, is experienced in relationship as Thou, the Other whose very presence is the end goal. Experiencing God's presence evokes an affirmation of life's goodness and even our own self-worth.

Abiding before God's presence we are strengthened, hopeful, and purposeful. As stated in the closing words of the Psalm, "My glory shall hymn to You and not be silent. *Adonai*, my God, forever I will praise You" (v. 13). Repeatedly in Psalms we read that God wants our praise. Gratitude stops short of praise. A thank you acknowledges what God has done for us. Praise is a step higher in that it takes out the "I." To praise God is to exclaim "Wow" over the goodness of God as manifest in a creation of goodness. When we feel love flowing through us from the source of creation, when we are uplifted by the beauty of life, we are then motivated to express that praise to God in deeds of kindness and beauty making, too. And with such praise, we too are lifted up.

Deeply Personal Is Universal
Rabbi Spitz

Psalm 30 is deeply personal. A first-person, singular word (I, my, me,) appears twenty-four times in twelve verses. The psalmist addresses God directly and emotionally. Martin Buber's description of relationship with God is an ideal worthy of pursuit. But in life as lived, we have needs that are also part of intimate relationship. As with a spouse, it is ideal to just value each other as an end in itself. But when we feel awful and ask our lover to bring us a glass of water, our subsequent gratitude is also an expression of love. I honor those who normally describe God in absolute terms and yet before surgery ask friends to say a prayer for healing. We naturally turn to God for a loving presence and also for deliverance — not as a manipulation of God but as an expression of our deepest longings and the awareness that life has an element of both unknown danger and the mystery of deliverance. Love includes seeking caregiving and profound gratitude.

The middle phrase of Psalm 30 is "with Your desire You made me stand strong as a mountain" (v. 8a).[109] This is the core of the psalm. The psalmist has come close to death, an experience of fearful descent. It is precisely the relationship with God that has offered uplift "to stand strong as a mountain." The psalmist had turned to God in need: "To You, *Adonai*, I called and to my Master, I pleaded for grace" (v. 9; see also v. 11a). God's response was an act of grace, unearned kindness. God is the Master, the mighty Source of life. It is not a relationship of equals: "I'm God, You're Not."[110] And yet we are invited to turn to God as a lover who caringly responds to our needs with presence and even deliverance.

During the days of the Temple, a choir of Levites welcomed pilgrims bringing first fruits to the Temple with the singing of Psalm 30.[111] This is a psalm that invites us as readers to make the words our own. For that which is most personal is most universal. Here the psalmist describes an extreme of danger. This psalm invites each of us to turn to God when we are feeling broken, threatened, or in despair. And even when we are feeling "strong as a mountain" — as the pilgrim celebrating first fruits — these words offer an awareness that in turning to God with gratitude and praise we express an enduring love that will give context and add joy to this earthly existence.

Psalm 35:1-3

Its Role at a Crucial Moment in American History

Rabbi Jack Riemer

א לְדָוִד. | 1 For David.
רִיבָה יְהוָה אֶת יְרִיבַי; | Strive, Adonai, against them that
לְחַם אֶת לֹחֲמָי. | strive with me; fight against them that fight against me.

ב הַחֲזֵק מָגֵן וְצִנָּה, | 2 Take hold of shield and armor,
וְקוּמָה בְּעֶזְרָתִי. | and rise up to my help.

ג וְהָרֵק חֲנִית וּסְגֹר לִקְרַאת רֹדְפָי; | 3 And unsheathe the spear and
אֱמֹר לְנַפְשִׁי יְשֻׁעָתֵךְ אָנִי. | battle-axe against my pursuers; say to my spirit, "Your Deliverance am I."

Perhaps I should explain before we begin that our study of this psalm is going to be a little bit different than the way we have studied the psalms until now.

It will be different in two ways. The first is that we will focus on just three lines and not say anything about the rest of this psalm. The reason for this is that this psalm was probably a prayer that the Israelites recited when they set off to war, and it contains very little that speaks to the modern reader, at least as near as I can tell.

And the second way in which our study of this psalm will be different is that usually we study how the ideas and the values that are expressed in a psalm appear in Jewish history, but this time we will explore the way in which this psalm played a role at a crucial moment in American history.

Psalm 35 is a psalm that I confess that I had never read before until I began this series. It appears nowhere in the Jewish prayerbook. It is recited on no Jewish holiday. And yet I recently found out, much to my surprise, that this psalm played an important role in American history.

It was Rabbi Meir Soloveichik who enlightened me on this way of reading the psalm. Rabbi Soloveichik is the head of the Institute for the Study of Torah and Western Civilization at Yeshiva University, and his field of study is the relationship between Jewish and Western Thought. And so, it is understandable that it was he who discovered this psalm's place in American history.

Rabbi Soloveichik began his essay on this psalm by pointing out that there are two kinds of documents in every society. One is the contract and the other is the covenant.

The purpose of a contract is to protect the rights of each party when they enter into an agreement. A contract spells out my rights and your rights so that if either one of us tries to violate the rights of the other, the aggrieved party can point to the violation of the agreement.

The purpose of a covenant is different. In a covenant, both parties spell out the goals that they want to achieve and the values by which they want to live. A covenant transforms the two parties who enter it from two separate entities, who are each concerned with protecting their own rights, into a *we* made up of people who unite for the sake of a common goal.

In Jewish literature a good example of a covenant would be the moment at Sinai when all Israel joined together in agreeing to God's command to be a holy people and declared together in one voice: "*Na'ase vinishma*" — we will do whatever you want us to do! So great is our love for You that we accept this covenant without even waiting to find out its details.

In Jewish literature an example of a contract would be the Torah reading of Mishpatim, which follows right after this declaration at Sinai by listing in very specific terms the obligations that the people of Israel have bound themselves to live by. Its purpose is to transform the enthusiasm that the people felt at Sinai into a regimen of specific responsibilities. It is easy to be carried away in a moment of enthusiasm and to say that I will do whatever you want me to do. It is a very different thing to hear the terms of the contract and then to ask yourself: Is this what I signed up for?

In American literature, the Declaration of Independence was a covenant. The signers pledged to each other "their sacred honor, their wealth and their lives" in order to form one United States.

The Constitution was a contract. In it, each colony set forth its rights and its obligations under the law. The Constitution protected the colonies from the tyranny of a majority. If fifty-one percent of the Congress wants to impose a law that takes away the rights of the forty-nine percent, the minority has the ability to show that this proposed law is unconstitutional.

It is no surprise that the Constitution does not contain the name of God, for it is a legal document, not a vision. The Declaration, in contrast, starts out with a reference to God in its opening words. It is meant to be a vision of the kind of society that its authors wanted to bring into being, and therefore, a prayer for God's blessing and help was appropriate.

There were two incidents that took place during the creation of these two documents that illustrate the difference between them.

During the debates over the Constitution, when the delegates were deadlocked over some issue, Benjamin Franklin rose and suggested that they take a break from their negotiations in order to pray. He addressed the chair and said: "How has it happened, sir, that we have not thought even once of humbly appealing to the Father of lights to illuminate our understanding? If God governs the affairs of men, and if a sparrow cannot fall to the ground without His notice, is it possible for a state to rise without His aid?"

It was an interesting proposal and Franklin was a respected elder statesman, but his proposal was shot down immediately. The delegates were disciples of Locke and Rousseau and they believed fervently in the separation of Church and State. And so the document that they produced was, and remains to this day, entirely secular in its nature. They wanted and needed no reference to God in the contract that they were working on.

But now consider another event. In 1774, at the Continental Congress that produced the Declaration of Independence, someone proposed that the delegates begin their deliberations with a prayer. John Jay, who was later to become the first Chief Justice of the Supreme Court, objected. He pointed out that there were many different religious divisions among those present and therefore no single prayer would satisfy them all. Then Samuel Adams stood up and said that he would happily hear a prayer from any gentlemen of piety and virtue, provided only that he was a friend to his country. One of those present — would that we knew his name — rose and read from Psalm 35. The portion that he read was:

"Plead my cause, O Lord, against those that strive with me. Fight against those that fight against me. Say unto my soul:'I am Thy salvation.'"

That evening John Adams wrote to his wife and reported to her on what happened when this prayer was offered. He told her that "I have never seen a greater effect on an audience than I saw on this day! I cannot begin to describe to you the outpouring of emotion with which the delegates — myself included — turned to Heaven and asked for divine aid. It felt as if Heaven had prepared this psalm centuries ago just so that it could be read today."

Commenting on this story, the Catholic theologian, Michael Novak, notes that "it was precisely the sharp denominational divisions among the colonial Americans that made the Hebrew Bible the unifying force that it was on that day and that it has been ever since. It was the biblical sense of a providential and covenantal mission that has enabled Americans, past and present, to overcome their differences and to unite their individual agendas into a common destiny."

So here you have it: three lines that come from a psalm that most of us have never read had the power to unite the fractious members of the Continental Congress and enable them to work together towards one shared goal! It reminded them that their work and all human work is "under God," as the Pledge of Allegiance would later say, and it made them feel both humble and inspired to do their work.

Three simple sentences — a plea to God to be with them on their journey and to protect them from their enemies — written in the land of Israel, far away from the land in which they heard it, written originally in the Hebrew language which none of them knew, written more than twenty-two hundred years before their time — these three simple sentences had the power to transform the members of the Continental Congress from a group of quarreling delegates, each concerned only about the rights of his own colony, into the United States. As John Adams wrote to his wife: "I have never seen a greater effect on an audience than I saw on this day."

We Jews think of the psalms as our book, and rightly so, but we should realize that it is the book of all humanity as well, and we should rejoice in what it has done to inspire, to teach, and to bless those who have encountered it in many different times and places. It is good to know the crucial role that it played in the days when the Declaration of Independence came into being, and we hope that it will continue to be an influence on this country in all the years to come.

Psalm 36

"In Your Light Do I See Light"

Rabbi Elie Spitz

Psalm 36 draws on the power of faith in a Higher Power to overcome evildoers and the temptations of wrongful acts. The description of those who act badly with no remorse is sadly a cautionary part of life, as well.

א לַמְנַצֵּחַ לְעֶבֶד יְהוָה לְדָוִד.

1 For the conductor. For the servant of *Adonai*, for David.

ב נְאֻם פֶּשַׁע לָרָשָׁע בְּקֶרֶב לִבִּי:
אֵין פַּחַד אֱלֹהִים לְנֶגֶד עֵינָיו.

2 Speaking of crimes of the wicked within my heart; "There is no fear of God before [their] eyes.

ג כִּי הֶחֱלִיק אֵלָיו בְּעֵינָיו;
לִמְצֹא עֲוֹנוֹ לִשְׂנֹא.

3 For [they] smooth it over in [their] eyes lest they find [their] mischievousness to hate.

ד דִּבְרֵי פִיו אָוֶן וּמִרְמָה;
חָדַל לְהַשְׂכִּיל לְהֵיטִיב.

4 The words of [their] mouth are mischief and deceit; [they] have ceased to apply wisdom to do good.

ה אָוֶן יַחְשֹׁב עַל מִשְׁכָּבוֹ:
יִתְיַצֵּב עַל דֶּרֶךְ לֹא טוֹב;
רָע לֹא יִמְאָס.

5 Mischief [they] devise upon [their] bed; [they] establish themselves on a path that is not good;
evil, they do not disdain."

ו יְהוָה בְּהַשָּׁמַיִם חַסְדֶּךָ;
אֱמוּנָתְךָ עַד שְׁחָקִים.

6 *Adonai*, in the heavens is Your kindness; Your faithfulness extends to the skies.

ז צִדְקָתְךָ כְּהַרְרֵי אֵל,
מִשְׁפָּטֶיךָ תְּהוֹם רַבָּה;
אָדָם וּבְהֵמָה תוֹשִׁיעַ יְהוָה.

7 Your righteousness is like the highest mountains; Your judgments like the greatest depths; human and beast You deliver, *Adonai*.

ח מַה יָּקָר חַסְדְּךָ אֱלֹהִים
וּבְנֵי אָדָם בְּצֵל כְּנָפֶיךָ יֶחֱסָיוּן.

8 How precious is Your kindness, God; people in the shadow of Your wings take refuge.

ט יִרְוְיֻן מִדֶּשֶׁן בֵּיתֶךָ;
וְנַחַל עֲדָנֶיךָ תַשְׁקֵם.

9 They overflow with the rich oils of Your house; and from the stream of Your delights, You give them drink.

י כִּי עִמְּךָ מְקוֹר חַיִּים;
בְּאוֹרְךָ נִרְאֶה אוֹר.

10 For with You is the fountain of life; in Your light do we see light.

יא מְשֹׁךְ חַסְדְּךָ לְיֹדְעֶיךָ
וְצִדְקָתְךָ לְיִשְׁרֵי לֵב.

11 Draw forth Your kindness to those who know You and Your righteousness to the upright in heart.

יב אַל תְּבוֹאֵנִי רֶגֶל גַּאֲוָה,
וְיַד רְשָׁעִים אַל תְּנִדֵנִי.

12 Let not overtake me the foot of arrogance and let the hand of the wicked not cause me to wander away.

יג שָׁם נָפְלוּ פֹּעֲלֵי אָוֶן;
דֹּחוּ וְלֹא יָכְלוּ קוּם.

13 Over there have fallen the workers of mischief; they are thrust down and unable to get up.

READING CLOSELY

The Psalmist makes word choices to amplify the message of pursuing righteousness. The introductory line says that this is a psalm "for the servant of God, for David."[112] Although "servant of God" is used elsewhere in the Bible to describe David, Moses, and Abraham, it is only applied to David in one other psalm (18:1). Psalm 36 provides practical guidance on how to serve God rather than serving one's self.[113]

Verse 2 begins *Ne'um*, "Speaking [of crimes of the wicked within my heart]." This is the only place in the entirety of Psalms that the word *ne'um* is used, which is particularly surprising, for the word appears over 370 times in the Hebrew Bible.[114] It usually conveys an oracle from God. *Ne'um* may suggest here how the evildoer's words are spoken with such assuredness as if stemming from the Most High.

Many translators make the second word of verse 2, *pesha* — "crime" — the speaker: "I know what Transgression says to the wicked" or "Rebellion speaks to the wicked, my heart thinks,[115] giving the sinful words a life of their own. Such personification, unique in Psalms, conveys the psychological mechanism where the voice in our head may feel independent. In the words of comedian Flip Wilson, "The devil made me do it." My choice of translation describes a good person reflecting on those who would otherwise seek to lead him astray. As poetry, both work together: an independent voice in the speaker's head and as the anticipated thoughts of the wicked.

The middle of the psalm (vv. 6-10) contrasts the reliability of God with the self-serving superficiality of the evildoer. God is faithful and righteous as if to the greatest heights, whose judgments are to the greatest depths. God is kind and generous, offering refuge and abundance to all.[116] The Ba'al Shem Tov, the eighteenth-century founder of Hasidism, recited verses 7 and 8 as his final words.[117] A Jewish practice emerged of reciting verses 8 through 11, beginning "How precious is your kindness," at the start of morning prayers when wrapping the head in the *tallit*, the prayer shawl, as if physically accepting God's embrace and a light that is found inwardly.

The psalm in its final lines shifts toward prayer, like the teaching of AA (Alcoholics Anonymous) that we may need help from a Higher Power to act rightly. "Draw forth Your kindness to those who know You and Your righteousness to the upright in heart" (v. 11). The righteous are the group with whom the psalmist identifies. And yet verse 12 reveals the uncertainty over his own constancy: "Let not overtake me the foot of arrogance and let the hand of the wicked not cause me to wander away." The use of bodily metaphors suggests a deeply felt physical-like vulnerability.

The final verse, as is often the case in Psalms, presents a shift: "Over there have fallen the workers of mischief; they are thrust down and unable to get up" (v. 13). Here the psalmist looks at the wrongdoers as if from a distance and sees them as failures. It is left to the reader to imagine if their wrongdoing has been exposed causing their downfall by peers or as God's active punishment. Here as well, the two may be intertwined.

DIGGING DEEPER

Loved by a Higher Power
Rabbi Spitz

Abraham Twerski was a Hasidic rabbi and a psychiatrist who dedicated his career to working with addicts. He was the first to introduce me to Alcoholics Anonymous. He shared that whenever he felt emotionally down, he attended an AA meeting. Although he did not have a substance-use problem, he said that the honest sharing of vulnerabilities and the capacity to trust in a Higher Power uplifted him. Rabbi Twerski comes to mind in reading this psalm as if it were read at an AA meeting. Consider verse 10 as an appropriate affirmation of a trusted Higher Power: "For with You is the fountain of life; in Your light do we see light." The guidance of

AA is to turn over one's power to a Higher Power, to see, if you will, our life's choices through the eyes of the Divine.

I know spiritual practitioners who recite this line over and over as both a statement of faith and as an aspiration for divine encounter. To see God as the fountain of life is to yearn to experience the flow of God through us and in each part of creation, a flow experienced as love. To see with God's light is to discern right from wrong. As in the biblical creation account, light is the first act of creation and is nonphysical. Such light is essential for creation to exist. It is not the light of the sun, which is only placed in the sky on the fourth day. Rather, God's light attunes us to values as lenses for seeing the world and our own uniqueness, a light that guides us toward self-discipline and the greater good.

In the biblical account, for instance, we are told that humans were created "in the image and likeness of God." This is not a statement of fact but rather of faith: a way of seeing the world in the "light of God." Such a statement directs us to see all people as equally valuable and worthy of dignity. I once asked Rabbi Twerski regarding his choice to work with those at the lowest rung of society, how much the teaching of "being created in the image of God" factored into his work. He replied, "Totally."

Overcoming Deception and Expediency
Rabbi Spitz

Psalm 36 begins with a portrait of guilt-free mischief-makers. Rabbi Twerski warned in *Addictive Thinking: Understanding Self-Deception,*[118] one of his more than sixty books, that an addict is a liar. For the compulsion to drink alcohol or take drugs overpowers a person's sense of right and wrong. Dr. Twerski characterized addiction as self-medicating to reduce the anxiety of feeling unworthy of love. Such a mindset blocks out God's light: "There is no fear of God before [their] eyes" (v. 2). Psalm 36 describes such self-deception in verses 2 through 5.

What is most striking about this description of wrongdoing is the Teflon-like conscience: "For [they] smooth it over in [their] eyes lest they find [their] mischievousness to hate" (v. 3). I have known too many who have rationalized bad behavior. I recall an adulterer who explained to me after the divorce, "My trysts were only acts out of order." The person who proposed my cooperation in misappropriating public funds responded to my astonishment, "Sometimes, I need to do what I need to do to get by." The psalm continues, "The words of [their] mouth are mischief and deceit; [they] have ceased to apply wisdom to do good" (v. 4). With those in the extreme of self-serving conduct there is often a pattern: an inability to admit wrongdoing; the flattering of others, including indiscriminate expressions of affection; and an assuredness of being the best. Such self-centered people are often perceived as attractive, even possessing charisma. I am reminded of the warning of Proverbs (31:30): "Charm is deceptive; beauty is fleeting, a woman who reveres God is to be praised."

I, too, am tempted to cut moral corners for the sake of meeting goals. We are wired to act with self-interest to survive in a dangerous world. Unexamined fears may prompt us to only focus on immediate needs and to do so with expedient action. And yet religion at its best prepares us for upright behavior: clarifying right and wrong, providing a moral compass, admitting short-coming, and insisting on integrity. Toward the end of the psalm (v. 12), the writer calls on God for help in avoiding the temptations of the mischief-makers: "Let not overtake me the foot of arrogance and let the hand of the wicked not cause me to wander away." Rabbi Benjamin Segal surmises that the author fears a personal relapse.[119] I am unconvinced that this is necessarily the case. For we do not need a personal history of corruption to know its temptations and to actively seek to overcome such wrongdoing.

What Is Spirituality?
Rabbi Spitz

Rabbi Mordecai Finley of Venice Beach, California, is widely known as the rabbi of songwriter Leonard Cohen and as a master teacher of Jewish mysticism and spiritual psychology. In a recent public conversation with him, Rabbi Finley noted that he recites verses 8 through 11 as a daily practice.[120] He emphasized that such lines are best learned by heart so as to become expressions of the heart, adding that he uses his own chant when reciting these words. His brief commentary prompted me to look more closely at these words as a description of spirituality.

"How precious is Your kindness, God; people in the shadow of Your wings take refuge. They overflow with the rich oils of Your house; and from the stream of Your delights, You give them drink" (vv. 8-9). Spirituality begins with gratitude, evoking the kindness that we experience and the sense of safety and trust in God's presence as something that we can metaphorically taste, offering delight. In Hebrew the word for delight, *eden*, is suggestive of the Garden where God placed Adam and Eve as the foundational experience of harmony. "For with You is the fountain of life; in Your light do we see light" (v. 10). When we go deeply into inner stillness, we experience a spiritual flow of love and wisdom as the presence of the Divine. Such encounter on the level of soul goes beyond words. "Draw forth Your kindness to those who know you" (v. 11) conveys that knowing God is the result of experiences rather than propositional beliefs. The Hebrew word *yodei*, "to know," is also used for intimate relationship.

"And your righteousness to the upright in heart" (v. 11). And now to quote Rabbi Finley: "How does one become a knower of God? Has to be upright of heart. . . . Unfortunately, there are moral people who are not spiritual and spiritual people who are not moral. We need to do the work of combining the two. These words recited after putting on the *tallit* are the core of my experience of the Divine and the soul."

Psalm 44

"You Disgraced Us!"

Rabbi Elie Spitz

How can we believe in God in the face of tragedy? This is a deeply emotional question that resonates with the reciting of this psalm, for this is a psalm of protest, as if raising clinched fists heavenward.

א לַמְנַצֵּחַ לִבְנֵי קֹרַח מַשְׂכִּיל.

1 For the Leader; for the Korachites, a *maskil*.[121]

ב אֱלֹהִים בְּאׇזְנֵינוּ שָׁמַעְנוּ אֲבוֹתֵינוּ סִפְּרוּ לָנוּ: פֹּעַל פָּעַלְתָּ בִימֵיהֶם בִּימֵי קֶדֶם.

2 God, with our ears we have heard, our ancestors have storied us: deed that You did in their days, in the days of yore.

ג אַתָּה יָדְךָ גּוֹיִם הוֹרַשְׁתָּ וַתִּטָּעֵם; תָּרַע לְאֻמִּים וַתְּשַׁלְּחֵם.

3 You, Your hand dispossessed nations and You planted them; You smashed peoples and You sent them away.

ד כִּי לֹא בְחַרְבָּם יָרְשׁוּ אָרֶץ, וּזְרוֹעָם לֹא הוֹשִׁיעָה לָּמוֹ; כִּי יְמִינְךָ וּזְרוֹעֲךָ וְאוֹר פָּנֶיךָ כִּי רְצִיתָם.

4 Surely not by their own sword did they inherit the land, nor did their own arm deliver them; but Your right hand and Your arm and the light of Your face, because You wanted them.

ה אַתָּה הוּא מַלְכִּי אֱלֹהִים; צַוֵּה יְשׁוּעוֹת יַעֲקֹב!

5 You are my Ruler, God; command deliverance of Jacob!

בְּךָ צָרֵינוּ נְנַגֵּחַ; **6** Through You we gore our foes;
בְּשִׁמְךָ נָבוּס קָמֵינוּ. through Your name we trample those
who rise up against us.

כִּי לֹא בְקַשְׁתִּי אֶבְטָח **7** Surely not in my bow did I trust,
וְחַרְבִּי לֹא תוֹשִׁיעֵנִי. nor did my sword deliver me.

כִּי הוֹשַׁעְתָּנוּ מִצָּרֵינוּ **8** Surely You delivered us
וּמְשַׂנְאֵינוּ הֱבִישׁוֹתָ. from our foes
and those who hate us
You put to shame.

בֵּאלֹהִים הִלַּלְנוּ כָל הַיּוֹם **9** In God we have we gloried all day
וְשִׁמְךָ לְעוֹלָם נוֹדֶה. סֶלָה. long and to Your name forever we will
give praise. *Selah*

אַף זָנַחְתָּ וַתַּכְלִימֵנוּ **10** Yet, You neglected us and You
וְלֹא תֵצֵא בְּצִבְאוֹתֵינוּ. disgraced us, and You did not go forth
with our forces.

תְּשִׁיבֵנוּ אָחוֹר מִנִּי צָר **11** You turned us back from the foe
וּמְשַׂנְאֵינוּ שָׁסוּ לָמוֹ. and those who hate us plundered us
at their will.

תִּתְּנֵנוּ כְּצֹאן מַאֲכָל **12** You made us like sheep to be eaten
וּבַגּוֹיִם זֵרִיתָנוּ. and among the nations scattered us.

תִּמְכֹּר עַמְּךָ בְלֹא הוֹן **13** You sold Your people for no wealth
וְלֹא רִבִּיתָ בִּמְחִירֵיהֶם. and did not set a profit on their price.

יד תְּשִׂימֵנוּ חֶרְפָּה לִשְׁכֵנֵינוּ;
לַעַג וָקֶלֶס לִסְבִיבוֹתֵינוּ.

14 You made us scornful to our neighbors;
a derision and mockery to those around us.

טו תְּשִׂימֵנוּ מָשָׁל בַּגּוֹיִם,
מְנוֹד רֹאשׁ בַּלְאֻמִּים.

15 You made us a byword among the nations, a shaking of the head among the peoples.

טז כָּל הַיּוֹם כְּלִמָּתִי נֶגְדִּי
וּבֹשֶׁת פָּנַי כִּסָּתְנִי—

16 All day long my disgrace is before me and the shame of my face has covered me —

יז מִקּוֹל מְחָרֵף וּמְגַדֵּף;
מִפְּנֵי אוֹיֵב וּמִתְנַקֵּם.

17 for the voice of the taunter and the blasphemer; before the face of the enemy and the vengeful.

יח כָּל זֹאת בָּאַתְנוּ
וְלֹא שְׁכַחֲנוּךָ
וְלֹא שִׁקַּרְנוּ בִּבְרִיתֶךָ.

18 All this has come upon us;
and we did not forget You,
nor were we false to Your covenant.

יט לֹא נָסוֹג אָחוֹר לִבֵּנוּ,
וַתֵּט אֲשֻׁרֵינוּ מִנִּי אָרְחֶךָ.

19 Our heart has not turned back, nor have our steps strayed from Your path.

כ כִּי דִכִּיתָנוּ בִּמְקוֹם תַּנִּים
וַתְּכַס עָלֵינוּ בְצַלְמָוֶת.

20 Surely You have thrust us down to a place of sea monsters and covered us over with the shadow of death.

כא   אִם שָׁכַחְנוּ שֵׁם אֱלֹהֵינוּ
וַנִּפְרֹשׂ כַּפֵּינוּ לְאֵל זָר;

21 If we had forgotten the name of our God or had we spread out our hands to an alien god;

כב   הֲלֹא אֱלֹהִים יַחֲקָר זֹאת?
כִּי הוּא יֹדֵעַ תַּעֲלֻמוֹת לֵב.

22 Would not God search this out? For [God] knows the secrets of the heart.

כג   כִּי עָלֶיךָ הֹרַגְנוּ כָל הַיּוֹם;
נֶחְשַׁבְנוּ כְּצֹאן טִבְחָה.

23 Surely, on account of You we are killed all day long; we are thought of as sheep for slaughter.

כד   עוּרָה! לָמָּה תִישַׁן אֲדֹנָי?
הָקִיצָה, אַל תִּזְנַח לָנֶצַח.

24 Wake up! Why do You sleep, Supreme? Rouse up, do not neglect us forever.

כה   לָמָּה פָנֶיךָ תַסְתִּיר-
תִּשְׁכַּח עָנְיֵנוּ וְלַחֲצֵנוּ?

25 Why do You hide Your face — forget our affliction and our oppression?

כו   כִּי שָׁחָה לֶעָפָר נַפְשֵׁנוּ;
דָּבְקָה לָאָרֶץ בִּטְנֵנוּ.

26 Surely bowed down to the dust is our neck; cleaving to the earth is our belly.

כז   קוּמָה עֶזְרָתָה לָּנוּ
וּפְדֵנוּ לְמַעַן חַסְדֶּךָ!

27 Get up as a help to us and redeem us for the sake of Your kindness!

READING CLOSELY

The word *You* appears thirty-two times, as the psalmist addresses God with personal immediacy. And six times a verse begins with *Surely*, emphasizing the strength of the feeling.[122] When I read this psalm, my hand reflexively goes to my heart.

The psalmist addresses, on behalf of the community, the immense gap between faith in God who decisively acts in history and the actual suffering of God's covenantal people. The middle words of the psalm, as if characterizing the rage, are "You made us scornful to our neighbors; a derision and mockery to those around us" (v. 14). Even more than martyrdom, which is also presented, these words seethe with humiliation. Yet the psalm's final word provides a glimmer of divine light despite the darkness.

The psalmist assumes that God has unlimited power. For repeatedly the Bible has described the Creator as personally intervening in history: whether bringing the Israelites out of Egypt with a mighty hand and an outstretched arm or promising to reward and punish loyalty to God by bringing or withholding the rains. The biblical metaphors of God's body enable relationship with an otherwise invisible presence. That physicality is also in the Priestly blessing describing God's shining light and "turning God's face to you to grant you peace" (Numbers 6:25-26).

Psalm 44 can be divided into two sections: God's power as displayed in the past (vv. 1-9) and the protest (vv. 10-27). The Hebrew is distinctive for repeated rhymes and rhythmic sounds. The vocabulary is diverse rather than the more common psalm format of repeated words. It is as if the psalmist seeks to convey that the suffering has a steady beat while filled with the unanticipated.

The account of God's loyalty begins (v. 2) with reference to deeds conveyed by ancestors. In describing the Exodus from Egypt, the Bible will have repeatedly emphasized the need for storytelling to the next generation.[123] The psalmist refers to God's "hand" in conquering the land (v. 3).

Victory was God's doing: "Surely not by their own sword . . . but [by] Your right hand" (v. 4).[124] At the middle of this section is the phrase "and the light of Your face" (v. 4), suggesting that once upon a time the people were truly blessed with intimacy with God. The psalmist responds to that past with loyalty: "You are my Ruler, God" (v. 5), which is amplified in each of the verses that follow, reaching the ninth: "In God we have gloried all day long and to Your name forever we will give praise. *Selah.*" The word *selah* in the Psalms marks a literary conclusion. Some scholars link it to the Hebrew word for drum,[125] as if the section ends with a loud, reverberating "boom."[126]

The opening word of verse 10, *af* (yet), marks a dramatic shift. Defeat is made all the more painful, for God could have saved the people. We are not told if there is a specific event for which the psalmist is protesting or an enduring plight, such as protracted exile. The protest is divided into three parts: the current shaming (vv. 10-17),[127] the people's faithfulness (vv. 18-23), and a demand for divine action (vv. 24-27).

In describing the physical suffering and disgrace, Rabbi Riemer points out that the sheep images in this psalm are the opposite of Psalm 23: "You made us like sheep to be eaten" (v. 12) rather than protected. References to the human body are used for us to tangibly see and feel the sorrowful plight: "You made us a byword among the nations, a shaking of the head among the peoples. . . . The shame of my face has covered me" (vv. 15-16).[128] Yet the people remain faithful: "All this has come upon us; and we did not forget You, nor were we false to Your covenant" (v. 18).

Holy protest also has a place in the Bible and will so conclude our psalm (vv. 24-27). When Abraham learns of God's plan to destroy Sodom and Gomorrah, the patriarch has the audacity to say, "Shall not the Judge of all the earth deal justly?" (Genesis 18:25); and a negotiation with God ensues. When, after the infidelity of the Golden Calf, Moses will say to God, "Now, if You will forgive their sin [well and good]; but if not, erase me from the record which You have written"[129] (Exodus 32:32), and God forgives.[130]

The psalmist proclaims, "Wake up! Why do You sleep, my Supreme? Rouse up, do not neglect us forever. Why do You hide Your face — forget our affliction and oppression?" (vv. 24-25). Yet the early rabbis will say that light only emerges after the darkest moment of night.[131] That darkness is conveyed in the next verse: "Surely bowed down to the dust is our neck [*nefesh*]; cleaving to the earth is our belly" (v. 26). The word *nefesh* has both physical and emotional connotations, for it can mean both neck and spirit, and is often translated as "life." On the belly in the dust is a place of a cursed serpent, as if punished by God for wrongdoing in the Garden of Eden (Genesis 3:14). This is the lowest possible place to be, fully down and dark.

Now, the psalmist rises up and challenges: "Get up, [God], as a help to us and redeem us for the sake of Your kindness" (v. 27). "Wake up . . . get up" are words of holy challenge. Martin Buber, the twentieth-century Bible scholar and theologian, entitled one of his books *The Eclipse of God* (1952), an image from this psalm, arguing that a hiding God is also a God that can be found. And that is the thrust of the closing word: *hesed*, "kindness." For the psalmist, God is hidden but fundamentally kind. The word *hesed* in the Bible is often linked to the covenant, such as "God is faithful, guardian of the covenant and kindness" (Deuteronomy 7:9). Kindness is repeatedly identified as at the core of God's nature[132] and a faithfulness to the covenant with Israel. The last word points to hope, as if the psalmist is saying: despite all that I have said, I still look to You as fundamentally kind, as a light in the darkness.

The Talmud records that a group of Second Temple Levites chanted Psalm 44 on the Temple Mount each day.[133] They were known as the *me'orarin*, the wakers, for the phrase of verse 24 directing God: "Wake up! Why do you sleep?" Yohanan, the High Priest of the fourth century BCE, had them stop for fear that the words might be taken literally by too many listeners.[134] This story leads us to wonder: How literally should we take the psalm as a whole as describing the nature of God? [135] Very likely, the psalmist was grounded in a theology of an actively intervening God, which leads to a paradox: Here is an address to an all-powerful God that rebukes God. For it is precisely God's nature, the psalmist conveys, to welcome human honesty, for that receptivity also defines God. To have a personal relationship with God means to both extoll and rebuke. In the prayerful words of a figure in the writings of Elie Wiesel, "Be with me, when I have need of You. But above all, do not leave me when I deny You."[136]

Digging Deeper

How We Hear
Rabbi Spitz

My mother use to tell the following story. A father hands a letter to his wife and says, "Can you believe what our son has written!" Then he reads with a demanding tone, "Please! Send money!" and thrusts the letter over to his wife.

"I hear it quite differently," she responds, and in a gentle, pleading voice reads, "Please send money."

How we hear what is on a page often describes as much about ourselves, if not more, than the intention of the writer.

In reading Psalm 44, I hear the voice of protest. Others in the more traditional Jewish community read the same words as an admission of guilt for justified punishment. Consider, for instance, the introduction to Psalm 44 of ArtScroll, a publisher of Orthodox rabbis in America:

> The sons of Korach depict the early triumphs
> of our people as they entered the Promised
> Land — invincible and armed with Torah laws.
> They mourn the bitter defeat which our people
> suffered when they abandoned these divine

weapons. Nevertheless, these inspired singers are filled with hope, for even in the exile, the Jewish people have displayed undaunted loyalty to Torah by sacrificing their lives for the sanctification of God's name. Surely this merit will unlock the gates of redemption.[137]

We hear what we read with preconceptions, which can lead to quite divergent takeaways.[138]

How to Respond to Tragedy
Rabbi Spitz

As for the Holocaust and the tension with biblical descriptions of a God who intervenes, I pause to acknowledge the enormity of the topic. I am a child of Holocaust survivors. The evil of those events is quite emotional for me. I am identified with Elie Wiesel, the Holocaust survivor and Nobel Peace Prize recipient. His accent and the events that he describes ring familiar and familial. In *Night* (1960), his riveting account of life in the death camps, he describes a Jewish boy dangling from a noose at Auschwitz. Behind him a man says, "Where is God?" Wiesel thought to himself, "This is where — hanging from the gallows."[139] Wiesel had grown up with the traditional belief in God's protective presence, rewarding and punishing. He would later say that he retained faith but quite differently from his childhood.

I once consulted with Wiesel after a tragic loss in my family. I have a cousin who is like a brother to me. His nine-year-old became ill one night. The nurse of their HMO said over the phone, "It sounds like the flu. If he is still sick in the morning, then bring him in. For now, keep him drinking fluids." The boy continued to drink Cokes and died during the night from undiagnosed diabetes. The funeral on a December day was chilling. Just before this event, I had engaged in a public conversation with Rabbi Harold Kushner, the author of *When Bad Things Happen to Good People* (1981). When Kushner's son, Aaron, was dying from progeria, a genetic disease that leads to rapid aging, Kushner wrote that he had a need to pray but could not to a God who would cause such suffering. His theology shifted to believing in a caring God but not an all-powerful God. This shift has a place in Judaism among the mystics who say that God chose to limit divine power in order to create. Still feeling the pain and disorientation of the boy's sudden death, I met with Wiesel, who listened caringly.

"How do you relate to Rabbi Kushner's understanding of God?" I asked.

"I cannot agree," he responded. "I do not know God's intent or power. God is a question mark."

I next spoke with Rabbi Zalman Schachter-Shalomi and asked how he would respond to the role of God in this particular tragedy. He said that the four worlds of Jewish mysticism were his approach. *Asiyah*, the physical plane, meant that he would first want to hear what happened medically. *Yetzirah*, the emotional plane, meant that he would just hold those who grieved. *Beriah*, the intellectual plane, limited what he could understand; Kushner's theology took him as far as he could go rationally. And yet there was a fourth plane, *atzilut*, the spiritual or intuitive plane, where we encounter a caring Presence for whom the world is ordered. On this plane of seeking God, we gain acceptance by acknowledging mystery and a glimpse of purposefulness.

When I met with Kushner afterward, I told him of my family's tragedy and the theological responses. I asked him what he would say concerning this fourth level of intuition. He responded, as I paraphrase, "When my son was suffering, I could only go as far as I did in describing God. But, now years later, I too would acknowledge that there is a quality of God's presence that transcends my intellectual knowing. Yes, I too intuit a caring God and the mystery of that Presence."

This experience with tragedy has shaped how I have dealt as a rabbi with the suffering of others: taking time to acknowledge the physical, emotional, intellectual, and spiritual. In my own life, as does the psalmist, I too address God directly: to express wonder and gratitude and upset. I do not expect God to intervene in response to my prayer. I do not hold God as the perpetrator of the Holocaust, for to do so would be to pray to a God who is brutal and unjust. Yet I pause with humility to acknowledge God on the emotional and intuitive level as a mystery, who invites me to raise my hands upward as if with clenched fists to protest human suffering — whether mine, my community's, or that of fellow human beings.

What Kind of Shepherd?
Rabbi Riemer

Psalm 44, verse 12, introduces the sheep metaphor: "You made us like sheep to be eaten and among the nations scattered us." This is an expression that was used in Israel when the first survivors of the Holocaust arrived. The Israelis could not understand why they had not fought back, why they had gone like sheep to the slaughter — as if they could have fought back, as if they had weapons, as if they had allies, as if they were not exhausted from lack of food, as if the fences were not electrified, as if they had a choice.

This line about being sheep is the total opposite of Psalm 23. There, shepherd means a protector. There, the psalmist says, "*Adonai* is my shepherd; I shall not lack" (v. 1). Here, it is the total opposite. In verse 12 he says, "You are the shepherd who neglects me. You are the shepherd who turns his back on me. You are the shepherd who does not do what a shepherd is supposed to do. You are the shepherd who has let me down."

There is an echo here of Leviticus 27 in which the shepherd counts his sheep one by one and takes the tenth one and sacrifices it. The tenth lamb is sacrificed for no fault of its own but just because it happens to be the tenth one. And that is how this psalmist feels. He too is being sacrificed, and he too feels that it is for no fault of his own.

And then in verse 13 the psalmist essentially says, "You sold us cheap. It is bad enough that you sold us, but you sold us cheap. You treated us as though we were worthless. You treated us like garbage. You gave us away without even asking a decent price for us. You sold us the way people sell things at a flea market. You sold us the way someone sells a piece of junk that he just wants to get rid of — at any price, just so long as he can get rid of it."

It reminds me of what used to happen at a slave market in this country. If the slave that was being sold was of some value, its owner would hold up his arms in order to show what good muscles he had. Then the slave owner would open the slave's mouth to show what good teeth he had. He would do this in order to get a good price for his slave. But if the slave was old and weak or handicapped, the owner would say, "Slave for sale — any price will be accepted."

The psalmist feels that this is how God sold them. What hurts the psalmist the most is not so much the defeat in battle but the shame and the humiliation that followed after the defeat.

Rabbi Shai Held gives a contemporary parallel.[140] You and I may not agree with his politics, but try to listen to this parallel just the same. Held says that this is how some Palestinians feel today when they have to stand in line for hours and hours at a checkpoint waiting to get into Israel so they can obtain some work. And then, when they finally get to the head of the line after standing in the hot sun for hours, they have to go through a demeaning body search from head to foot in order to make sure that they have no hidden weapons. Then finally, finally, finally, after standing in line in the hot sun for hours and after going through a humiliating body search, they are allowed to cross the green line. And what kind of work are they given to do when they get there? They are put to work tearing down the very houses in which they used to live and putting up new houses in their place, which are meant for the new immigrants who are coming into the land.

Think of that. When they finally get across the green line, they are put to work tearing down the houses that they used to live in and building new houses in their place to be used by new immigrants! Can you imagine any greater humiliation than this? It is this humiliation and this shame that is worse than defeat in battle.

Wake Up, God
Rabbi Riemer

In the book of I Kings (18:21-39), there is a scene where the prophet Elijah calls to the four hundred pagan priests of Baal and challenges them to a contest. Elijah puts a sacrifice on one altar, and he tells them to put their sacrifice on another altar. He puts water on his sacrifice, which will make it harder for it to catch fire; and he tells them to put water on their sacrifice, which will make it harder for their sacrifice to catch fire. And then he challenges them to call on their gods to come down and burn their sacrifices. They call, they yell, they sing, they dance — but nothing happens.

And Elijah teases them. He says to them, "Why don't you yell a little bit louder? Maybe your gods are sleeping. Maybe if you yell louder, you can wake them up."

And so they yell and yell and yell; and they dance and dance and dance; and they scream and scream and scream — but their gods do not answer.

And then Elijah gives one mighty cry to God, and fire comes down from heaven and consumes his sacrifice. And all the people call out, *Adonai hu ha Elohim*, "The Lord is the one true God."

In Psalm 44, verse 24, the psalmist calls on God to wake up. Here, the God of Israel is sleeping. Here, the words from Psalm 121:4 — *shomer Yisrael lo yanum vilo yishan*, "the guardian of Israel does not sleep and does not slumber" — have been reversed. Now God is like one of the pagan gods and the psalmist must try to wake God up and he is unable to do so.

In the book of Kings and Psalm 121, God never sleeps. In Psalm 44, God has to be awakened. There, the prophet teases the priests of Baal to wake up their god. Here the psalmist tries to wake up God and he fails.

This is probably the bottom of the Bible. I can think of no other place in the Bible in which anyone speaks so brutally, brazenly, and bluntly to God. I know of no other place where a psalmist says to God, "Wake up already. Stop sleeping." He continues, "Listen to me God; do something! Wake up and do something, for Your people need you."

The implication is that if God doesn't wake up, then God is no different and no better than the pagan gods, Baal and Ashtoreth. How do you explain how the editors let this psalm into the book of Psalms?

The only answer I can offer you is that it was placed here because whoever edited the book of Psalms valued honesty and truth more than flattery or empty praise. If that is the reason, then this is what makes the book of Psalms such a remarkable book.

I believe that any book and any religion that can make room for love songs like Psalm 23 and songs of trust like Psalm 8 to coexist side by side with songs of rage and anger like Psalm 44 is a book and a religion that deserves to be respected.

One People, Many Views
Rabbi Riemer

Up until this year I had never read Psalm 44, and I am sure that this is true for many of you as well. If it were not for Rabbi Shai Held, who teaches Bible at the Hadar Institute in New York, I might still not have discovered this psalm.

Psalm 44 appears nowhere in the prayerbook and nowhere in the cycle of the Jewish year. I can understand why. And I can understand why nobody ever taught me this psalm: it is beyond question the angriest and the most bitter psalm in the entire Bible. It is a psalm that accuses God, rants against God, and cries out in rage against God.

How on earth did this psalm with its anger, venom, and fierce hostility to God ever get into the Bible? How can you explain why whoever edited the book of Psalms did not censor this chapter out?

I am sure that there must have been some people who came out of the concentration camps after the war who were unable to say Psalm 23, Psalm 8, or Psalm 145 — the *Ashrei*. The words must have stuck in their throats. How could they praise God and declare God all powerful after what they had gone through? They must have felt that if God was all good and if God was all powerful, how could that God have allowed a million and a half children to be murdered? How could that God have allowed six million Jews to be slaughtered?

I can understand those Jews being unable to recite these psalms.

But I imagine that if they were given Psalm 44 to read, they would have agreed with every word that it says, and they might even have said amen.

Psalm 44 is just the first in a long tradition of songs and stories that denounce God and demand justice from God. For example, there is the *din torah* with God by Levi Yitzchak of Berditchev in which the Hasidic master says, "I have come to have a *din torah* — a court case — with you, God. Everywhere you look in the Bible, it says speak to the people of Israel; everywhere you look in the Bible it says, 'Command the people of Israel.' *Vos vilst du fun dayn folk Yisrael?* What do you want from your people, Israel? Why do you impose yourself upon your people? Why don't you command some other nation instead of us for a change — O God of Israel!"

He goes on and on like this for three verses in which he compares the people of Israel with the Russians, the Germans, and the English. He ends with these words: "Let there be an end to the *golus* already. Let there be an end to Jewish suffering already. But until that day comes — *yitgadal viyitkash shmey rabbah.*"

After all these complaints, he ends by praising God.

A poem by the Yiddish poet Katya Maladowsky says, "You have made us the chosen people? Why don't you choose some other people for a while?"

And, of course, there are the writings of Elie Wiesel, which constitute an unending challenge to God. Wiesel declares on almost every page that he will not give up faith in God but that his heart is full of questions to God.

There are many other poets and playwrights in this tradition, including Chaim Grade, who wrote "My Quarrel with Hersh Rasseyner," one of the greatest pieces of literature to come out of the Holocaust.[141] I seek below to maintain some of the drama in their encounter, albeit in a very short summary, for this exchange highlights the nature of Psalm 44's protest in contrast to much of the Bible's trust in God, such as Psalm 23.

Chaim Grade of Vilna started out in a mussar yeshiva when he was young, hence his nickname Chaim Vilner. A mussar yeshiva is a place where you learn to deny the pleasures of this world and instead try your best to concentrate only on correcting your soul and on serving your God. As someone once said, if you leave the mussar movement, you may sin but you will never enjoy it.

Chaim Grade left the yeshiva because he wanted to make it as a writer in the outside world. He went to the West, and Rabbi Hersh Rasseyner, his classmate in yeshiva, stayed and ended up in one of the concentration camps.

After the war Grade happens to bump into his old classmate outside Hotel de Ville in Paris. Above their heads on the wall of the museum that was located next door to the hotel were statues of all the great heroes of the Renaissance and the Enlightenment. When they meet, one says, "Can you still believe in God after what happened?" And the other one says, "Can you still believe in humanity after what happened?"

The two of them sit down on a bench underneath those statues and they begin to talk.

Grade says, "Reb Hersh, you ought to have respect for these statues for these are the philosophers, scientists, and poets who brought wisdom to the world."

And Reb Hersh says, "Really? What kind of wisdom did your heroes bring to the world? They were thinkers, but the minute they had to put their theories into practice, their systems of thought broke down. They were like well-trained dogs who follow their master obediently until they see a bitch, and then they break away and go for her. Don't you know, Reb Chaim, that Germany was the center of philosophy, science, and art; and it was these heroes of yours who were the first to obey the Nazis when they came to power?"

Grade responded, "And what about you, Reb Hersh? I remember how you used to walk the streets with your head down because you were afraid to see the temptations in the world. I remember how the women who worked in the marketplace used to bring you food at the end of the day. And what did you give them in exchange, Reb Hersh? You gave them sermons on how sinful they were and on how much they needed to repent. You sold your share in the World to Come to those women a dozen times, Reb Hersh. Don't be so afraid of the world."

To which Reb Hersh replied, "I am not afraid of the world. I have seen the face of the evil and I know what it is like. But let me tell you something, Reb Chaim. If God had come to me even at the worst time in the concentration camps, if God had said to me even when the Nazi had his boot on my face, if God has said to me, 'Would you like to trade places with this Nazi? If you say yes, I can do it for you.' Do you know what I would have said to God? I would have said, 'No, thank you.' And I would have thanked God for having made me a Jew and not a Nazi."

Reb Hersh told Reb Chaim that after going through all the hell of the Holocaust, he has now opened up a yeshiva in Germany, of all places.

Grade said, "God may not be an orphan, but the Jewish people are. We have lost a third of our people and you still believe in the Torah? How can you still believe?"

The debate goes on for many pages. And neither one is able to persuade the other.

And then in the last lines after this long and fierce debate, Chaim Grade says to his old classmate, "Our paths are different, both in spirit and in practice. The storm that has torn us apart from our roots has scattered us both. It has scattered you to a yeshiva in Germany, it has blown me to a writer's café in France.

"Who knows when or whether we will ever meet again?

"May we both have the merit of meeting again someday, somewhere, and who knows? Perhaps then we will be able to agree on which of us is right.

"And until then, *Vos mir zenen, zenen mir, ober yiden zenen mir,* 'Till then, whatever we may be,' we are both still Jews and may we both continue to be, even though I regard you as a twisted and perverted fanatic and you regard me as a sinful idolator.

"And until then, I beg you, Reb Hersh, do not exclude me from the Jewish people. Instead let us embrace each other and let us wish each other well until we meet again."

And on that note, they hug as the curtain falls.

I have a fantasy that what happens in this story may happen someday between the psalmist who wrote Psalm 23 and the psalmist who wrote Psalm 44. May they too hug and embrace someday, somewhere. May we too read Psalm 44 with all its anger at God with respect and appreciation for the truth that it contains, and may we be able to read Psalm 23 with all the love of God with respect and with appreciation as well. For if we can learn how to do that, we will be one people who can listen to each other, who can learn from each other, who can live with each other.

And if not? We will surely die as a people and be no more.

Psalm 95
"The Prelude to Shabbat"

Rabbi Jack Riemer

Beginnings are taken seriously in Judaism. We begin the evening service with a key phrase from Psalm 78: *Vihu rachum yichaper avon*, "He in His mercy forgives sin." But what sin are we talking about here? If you read the psalm in its context, you will see that the lines above it say, "That they praised God with their lips, they flattered Him with their tongues but inwardly they were not loyal and yet in His mercy God forgives sin." That means that praying without sincerity is not prayer.

We begin the morning prayers with the words *Modeh ani*, "I am grateful to You," which remind us of how much we have to be thankful for and how great is God's faith in us. We begin the afternoon service with the word *ashrei*, "happy," to remind us of what constitutes real happiness.

And then we have Psalm 95, which is the prelude to the Friday night service. What does this psalm mean? Why do we begin our Friday night service with this psalm when it has no mention of Shabbat in it?

א לְכוּ נְרַנְּנָה לַיהוָה; נָרִיעָה לְצוּר יִשְׁעֵנוּ.	**1** Let us go sing joyfully to *Adonai*; let us shofar blast to the Rock of our deliverance.
ב נְקַדְּמָה פָנָיו בְּתוֹדָה; בִּזְמִרוֹת נָרִיעַ לוֹ.	**2** Let us advance before [God's] presence with thanks; with psalms, let us raise voices to [God].
ג כִּי אֵל גָּדוֹל יְהוָה וּמֶלֶךְ גָּדוֹל עַל כָּל אֱלֹהִים.	**3** For a great *El* is *Adonai* and great King over all gods;

אֲשֶׁר בְּיָדוֹ מֶחְקְרֵי אָרֶץ ד
וְתוֹעֲפֹת הָרִים לוֹ.

4 in Whose hand are the depths
of the earth; the heights of the
mountains are [God's];

אֲשֶׁר לוֹ הַיָּם וְהוּא עָשָׂהוּ ה
וְיַבֶּשֶׁת יָדָיו יָצָרוּ.

5 for the sea is [God's] and [God]
made it
and the dry land, [God's] hands
formed.

בֹּאוּ נִשְׁתַּחֲוֶה וְנִכְרָעָה; ו
נִבְרְכָה לִפְנֵי יְהוָה עֹשֵׂנוּ.

6 Let us bow down and let us fall to
our knees; let us bend the knee before
Adonai our Maker;

כִּי הוּא אֱלֹהֵינוּ ז
וַאֲנַחְנוּ עַם מַרְעִיתוֹ וְצֹאן יָדוֹ;
הַיּוֹם אִם בְּקֹלוֹ תִשְׁמָעוּ.

7 for [God] is our God, and we are
the people of [God's] pasture, and the
flock of [God's] hand;
today, if only to [God's] voice would
you listen:

אַל תַּקְשׁוּ לְבַבְכֶם כִּמְרִיבָה, ח
כְּיוֹם מַסָּה בַּמִּדְבָּר.

8 "Do not harden your heart as at
Meribah, as on the day of Massah in
the wilderness;

אֲשֶׁר נִסּוּנִי אֲבוֹתֵיכֶם: ט
בְּחָנוּנִי גַּם רָאוּ פָעֳלִי.

9 when your ancestors tested Me,
tried Me, though they had seen My
deed.

אַרְבָּעִים שָׁנָה אָקוּט בְּדוֹר וָאֹמַר, י
עַם תֹּעֵי לֵבָב הֵם וְהֵם לֹא יָדְעוּ דְרָכָי.

10 Forty years I loathed a generation
and I said,
'A people of straying hearts are they
and they did not know My ways';

יא אֲשֶׁר נִשְׁבַּעְתִּי בְאַפִּי,   **11** So I swore in My anger,
אִם יְבֹאוּן אֶל מְנוּחָתִי.   "They shall never come to My resting place!'"

READING CLOSELY

The Scandinavian school of biblical scholarship stressed the need to look for the *sitz in leben* (setting in life) of every page in the Bible. They taught us to ask: What is the occasion in the life of the community for which this story, law, or psalm was composed? What is the situation in life that it reflects? The questions are in order but easier to ask than to answer.

This is true of all poetry, which is what the psalms are. As my teacher Dr. Shalom Spiegel once said, "The original meaning of a poem died on the speaker's lips. When the listeners try to retell what they heard, the result is already commentary." And so we should never claim to be sure that we know an author's precise meaning of any psalm or poem.

I remember an experience I once had that taught me this lesson. I was asked to give a talk at the 92nd Street Y on the meaning of some of the stories by Elie Wiesel. Just as I was about to begin my talk, much to my surprise in walked Elie Wiesel.

If I could have found a way to get out of the room I would have, for how could I explain his stories in his presence? But he insisted, and so I had no choice but to continue my talk. And lo and behold — when I got through explaining what the first story meant, he took out a pen and a piece of paper and made some notes.

I walked him home after the talk, and I asked him why he took notes on what I said his story meant. He said, "From the moment you finish writing a story and send it to the publisher, it no longer belongs to you. And so, if someone else finds a meaning in a story that you wrote that you never thought of — that is his privilege, and he may very well be right."

And so let me tread lightly with Psalm 95. If I say things that the psalmist never meant to say, let me tell you that these words of mine may be worth considering, even if they were not what the psalmist had in mind.

The predominant theory among modern Bible scholars is that Psalm 95 is an entrance psalm that was recited when the pilgrims came to the Temple sanctuary. These scholars point out that entrance to a temple in antiquity was an awesome event that was marked by a special ceremony. They say, for example, that at the Babylonian Temple of Marduk, worshippers had to pass through twelve gates and that they had to recite a special declaration of faith at each gate. They say that similar entrance ceremonies were held at the Oracle of Delphi in Greece and at the sacred shrines of Egypt. At many of these shrines, scholars say, an examination was held in order to make sure that no one who had a physical handicap or who was ritually impure could enter. And they say that similar entrance ceremonies were held at the Holy Temple in Jerusalem.

That may be true; but if it is, you must take notice of the difference between the entrance ceremonies of their neighbors and the entrance ceremony that the Israelites carried out. The entrance ceremony that took place at the sanctuary in Jerusalem stressed wholeness of heart and cleanliness of character as prerequisites for entry — not health of body or purity from disease. They taught the people who came from all corners of the country on the pilgrim festivals the true meaning of their coming. They set a mood by instructing the pilgrim that the prerequisite for being in the Temple was not physical purity but purity of intention. And so does Psalm 95, in which the psalmist calls on heaven and earth to join him in acknowledging the Creator.

But there is another question that we must deal with: What does this psalm mean to us now, when there is no longer a Sanctuary in Jerusalem?

Ever since the sixteenth century, this psalm and the four psalms that follow are the opening prayers of the Sabbath Eve service. Why did the

Kabbalists of Safed choose these psalms with which to open the Sabbath Eve service? Why did they choose these psalms even though there is not a single mention of the Sabbath in any of them?

My guess is that they chose these psalms for three reasons. The first is because they loved them, and love is reason enough in choosing a psalm with which to begin a service. These are stirring hymns, and they make a majestic entree into the service.

The second possible reason why they chose these psalms may have been because they sing out the glory of God as the creator of heaven and earth, and they call upon heaven and earth, the sand and the sea, to join with us in praising God. This is surely an appropriate theme with which to begin the Sabbath, whose central theme is the celebration of God's creation.

The third reason may have been because it was a constant aim of the Kabbalists of Safed to make a connection between the laws and the ideas associated with the Temple and the laws and ideas associated with the Sabbath. It was as if they wanted to suggest that the people of Israel have two sanctuaries: a Temple in space that is temporarily destroyed, and a Temple in time that still stands in all its glory. There is a Temple in space where God once dwelled, and there is a Temple in time where God may still be found. There is a Temple in Zion, and there is a Temple — the Sabbath — that is with us wherever we may go.

In Psalm 95, they were able to make this connection because of the last word of the psalm, the word that became for them its key word. The psalmist did *not* say "So I swore in My anger that they will not enter the land of Israel," which is what you would expect. Instead, he said, (v. 11), "So I swore in My anger, 'They shall never come to My resting place (*menuchati*)!'"

Menuchah is a word with many levels of meaning in the Bible. It is the biblical term for peace, harmony, calm, serenity, and the good life. "You have not yet come into *menuchah*," says Deuteronomy 12:9, which means both the land of Israel and true peace. "There the wicked will cease from troubling, and there the weary will find *menuchah,"* says Job of the grave (3:17). "He makes me to lie down *al mey minuchot* — "alongside tranquil waters" says Psalm 23:2, when the psalmist wants to picture tranquility.

Menuchah is clearly more than just physical rest in these passages. It has a sense of serenity. It has a sense of the harmony that comes from knowing the shelter of God's presence. It has a sense of trust. It is this — and not just the land of Israel — that our psalm says that the generation of the wilderness did not receive. They increased wrath and therefore they did not know *menuchah.*

Menuchah is the word that caught the attention of the Kabbalists and enabled them to see in this psalm a lesson about the Sabbath. From this word they derived a law of the spiritual life that they who increase anger and they who increase strife do not receive the gift of *menuchah.* People who rely on their own power and strength may achieve many things in this world. They may acquire pleasure and power. They may acquire wealth, honor, and strength. But they will not have *menuchah.* A person cannot have *menuchah* until and unless their soul is at peace. The Sabbath is meant to be more than a day off from work. It is meant to be a day of contentment and trust — a day of receiving the gift of *menuchah.*

If this is so, then the psalm's place at the beginning of the Sabbath service becomes clear. The Sabbath is the goal of the six days of the week. One cannot be cruel and callous six days a week and then sanctify the Sabbath. One cannot be obsessed with greed six days a week and enjoy tranquility on the seventh. The Sabbath is the product of the way we live during the week and the goal of the creation. The Greeks and Romans were baffled by the Sabbath for they could understand a people who rested one day a week so that they could work better on the other six days, but they could not understand a people who worked six days a week in order to achieve tranquility on the Sabbath. That debate has gone on in many countries and in many cultures ever since.

Therefore in the Jewish tradition, ever since the sixteenth century we are bidden not only to clean the house and our bodies, dress in our best garments, and set the table as if royalty were coming to dinner, but also to say Psalm 95. It is a prayer of self-judgment. By reciting it we ask ourselves: Where are we? What have we done with the week that has gone by? Are we really ready to turn off brooding over the past and worrying about the future so that we can really rest?

The Shabbat is a partnership between God and us. Those who try God's patience as our ancestors did at Meribah by not trusting that if they rested, they would nevertheless have what they needed to eat on the morrow, and those who angered God as our ancestors did at Massah by wanting to go back to Egypt, will never know the blessing of *menuchah*.

Why does the psalmist make mention of these rebellions that took place at Massah and Meribah long, long before his time? There are two possible reasons. One is because these were especially unjustified acts of rebellion. The people had been liberated from Egypt. They had passed through the Reed Sea and emerged safe. They had seen the army of their taskmasters drowned. They were being given manna every day. And yet they rebelled? And yet they complained that they didn't like the food? And yet they said sarcastically (Exodus 14:11), "Was there a shortage of graves in Egypt that you had to bring us out here to die in the desert?" (That is my favorite example of Jewish humor, by the way.)

The nineteenth-century theologian Rabbi Samson Raphael Hirsch offers a different explanation. He says that the forty years they spent in the wilderness was the first exile the Jewish people experienced, and our lives ever since the fall of the Second Temple are the second exile. Therefore it is important that we learn not to commit the sins of the first exile. It is important that we do not do what they did at Massah and Meribah.

For the Kabbalists, Psalm 95 was a fitting note on which to begin the Sabbath service, for it provides us with a plumb line by which to measure our readiness for the Sabbath. It asks us: Are you ready to enter the day that is God's Temple? For that is what the Sabbath really is.

This question is as valid in our time as it was when the sanctuary in Jerusalem still stood.

DIGGING DEEPER

The Messiah's Arrival Depends on Us
Rabbi Riemer

Ilana Kurshan, a remarkable teacher of the Talmud and its relevance to our lives, retells the story in the Talmud about how Rabbi Yehoshua ben Levi once met the prophet Elijah in the marketplace.[142] He went over to him and asked him the question that many Jews of his time would have asked: "Can you tell me when the Messiah will come?"

Elijah answered, "Why don't you ask him yourself?"

"I would if I could," said Rabbi Yehoshua, "but where can I find him?"

Elijah directed him to go to the gates of Rome, where the Messiah sat among the sick and the wretched, who were changing the bandages on their wounds.

Rabbi Yehoshua ben Levi said, "How will I know which one he is?"

Elijah said, "All the other beggars take off all their bandages first and then put new ones on again. The Messiah takes his bandages off one at a time, so that if he should get the call, he will not have to delay for even a minute."

So, Rabbi Yehoshua went off to Rome and found the beggars who were sitting under the bridge unwrapping and then rewrapping their bandages. He saw which one was the Messiah and approached him to ask, "When are you going to come already?"

The Messiah answered, "Today."

Rabbi Yehoshua went back to Elijah and said, "The Messiah promised me that he would come today, but he has not kept his promise."

Elijah explained, "The Messiah was in fact quoting from a verse of Psalm 95 where it says, 'Today, if only to [God's] voice would you listen.'" In other words, he was telling you that the Messiah will come the very same day that the people commit to doing God's work in the world. This work means sitting among the sick and the wretched at the gates of the city and all those at the margins of society, helping them find hope and healing.

The notion of the Messiah, then, is a metaphor for the redeemed world to which we aspire. The world will not be redeemed when the Messiah comes; rather, the Messiah will come when we redeem the world. And then Ilana Kurshan quotes the Israeli philosopher Yeshayahu Leibowitz, who says that a false messiah is any messiah who has already come.

That story in the Talmud should remind us every time we say Psalm 95 that when and if the Messiah comes depends on us as much as on God. And that is surely a lesson worth considering when we begin the Sabbath.

The Spirit of Shabbat
Rabbi Riemer

I learned a story from Dr. Abraham Joshua Heschel that throws light on the spiritual nature of Eastern European Jewish life.

Rabbi Solomon of Radomsk once arrived in a certain town where he was told there lived an old woman who had known the famous Rabbi Elimelech of Lizhensk. She was too old to go out, and so he went to see her, and he asked her to tell him what she knew about the great master.

She answered, "I do not know what went on in his room or in his study hall because I only worked as one of the maids in the kitchen of his house. But one thing I can tell you. During the week, we maids would often quarrel with each other. But on Friday, when the Sabbath was about to arrive, the spirit in the kitchen was like the spirit on the eve of the Day of Atonement. Everyone would be overcome with an urge to ask forgiveness of each other. We were all seized with a feeling of affection and inner peace."

May the spirit of *menuchah* prevail in our homes on Erev Shabbat!

A Seesaw Journey
Rabbi Spitz

Psalm 95 contains opposites: joy and foreboding; calls to action and reflection; universal praise and a specific threat; and a transcendent God who speaks directly to us. Building on Rabbi Riemer's beautiful description of this psalm as leading to *menuhati*, "My rest," let us also examine this psalm as a spiritual seesaw that initiates a preparation for repose.

As liturgy, Psalm 95 opens a passageway from the work week to the holy day of repose. In chanting the six psalms of Friday night, we are prompted to review the previous six days one-by-one in order to let go of tensions and unfinished business while savoring our newly-formed, sweet memories. These psalms lead us to *Lecha Dodi*, the sixteenth-century mystical ode to the Sabbath personified as a bride and queen.

The first five of the six psalms of Kabbalat Shabbat are 95-99. Chanting psalms sequentially conveys the steady flow of a week. These five "Royal Psalms" address God as the sovereign creator of the world, which is a key motif of the Sabbath day along with joy. It is the custom of a mourner to refrain from entering the synagogue until after *Lecha Dodi*, for the six psalms are celebratory, evoking emotions at odds with mourning.

Psalm 95 has seven exhortations of "let us" in the opening six verses. The number seven is purposeful, conveying a complete array of actions: sing; trumpet praise; advance; raise voices; bow down; fall to our knees; and bend the knee. The sequence suggests an approach to the Temple and worship. In chanting these "Royal Psalms" in our Friday night liturgy, we share in a seesaw journey — marked by internal tensions and shifting themes — that moves us inwardly and forward toward repose.

Two Distinct Parts
Rabbi Spitz

Psalm 95 is composed of two sections seemingly at odds with each other, conveying that relationships and rest demand preparation. Writing in the plural, the psalmist sings of a communal pilgrimage with purposeful word choices, images, and structure.

Verses 1 through 7 are the first unit. They describe God as Creator of all, and yet point to worship by a particular people. The opening two verses and the closing two verses of this section focus on praise. The middle three verses (vv. 3-5) describe God's unique, expansive might. Verse 3 proclaims, "For a great *El* is *Adonai* and great King over all gods (*elohim*)." This line echoes Moses's words to the Israelites before they entered the Promised Land, "Hear, O Israel, the Lord (*Adonai*) our God (*El-oheinu*) the Lord (*Adonai*) is One" (Deuteronomy 6:4). *El* is a job description. It is the name used for gods worshipped throughout the ancient Near East. In this verse, the plural, *elohim*, is distinctly not a description of the Israelite God, who is "the King." Rather, *elohim* describes those with power, whether a human judge or a natural force; each is inferior to their Creator.[143] In these opening seven verses God is three times called *Adonai* (YHVH), the name identified with God upon liberating the Israelites from Egyptian bondage. Verse 3 emphasizes that God is uniquely supreme over all. Verse 4 is vertical — God's hand encompasses the depths of the earth and heights of the mountains; and verse 5 is horizontal — whose hands formed the seas and the land. Yet the use of YHVH emphasizes God is a caring presence with a distinctive relationship with the Israelites.

That distinctive relationship comes to the foreground in the second half of the psalm. Verses 8 through 11 shift from a tone of joy to painful memory and a grave warning. God recounts Israelite rebellions at Meribah and Massah. Let us review the Biblical history. This location is first described soon after the Exodus, when the memory of miracles was still fresh but thirst was immediate. "'Give us water to drink,' they said, and Moses replied to them, 'Why do you quarrel with me? Why do you try the Lord?'" (Exodus 17:2). The people continued to grumble: "Why did you bring us up from Egypt, to kill us and our children and livestock with thirst?" God directed Moses to strike a rock with the same staff he had used to part the waters of the Reed Sea. Water flowed from the rock. And yet "the place was named Massah and Meribah, because the Israelites quarreled and because they tried the Lord, saying, 'Is the Lord present among us or not?'" (Exodus 17:7).

The second time the location is named is toward the end of the Israelite's desert journey. Miriam has just died. Bereft of water, the people once again speak sarcastically of their exodus. God tells Moses to draw water from a rock, but this time God says to Moses, "You and your brother Aaron take the rod and assemble the community, and before their very eyes order the rock to yield its water (Numbers 20:8). Moses gathers the people, calls them rebels, and says, "Shall we get water for you from this rock?" And he strikes the rock twice (vv. 10-11). Water flows and so does punishment to Moses and Aaron for failing to "affirm My sanctity in the sight of the Israelite people" (v. 12). The Bible notes that this place is known as the "Waters of Meribah." We do not know if this is the same physical location or more likely named similarly as a place of rebellion over water.

The concluding two lines of Psalm 95 (vv. 10-11) actually conflate history: "Forty years I loathed a generation and I said, 'A people of straying hearts are they and they did not know My ways'; so I swore in My anger, 'They shall never come to My resting place.'" The incident that barred the Israelites from entering their land was their refusal to enter the Promised Land. Moses had sent twelve spies. Ten of them reported that the Promised Land's inhabitants were insurmountable: "We were like grasshoppers to ourselves and so we must have looked to them. The whole community broke into loud cries. . . . 'Let us head back for Egypt'"

(Numbers 13:33-14:4). God responded, "How long will this people spurn Me, and how long will they have no faith in Me despite all the signs that I have performed in their midst?" (14:11). God is enraged, telling Moses of the desire to destroy the former slaves and to start over with Moses. The leader talks God down from such an extreme act, but the verdict against their incessant muttering against God is that they are to die in the desert and only their children will enter the Promised Land.[144]

How do we understand the shift from "Let us sing [to God]" to God's painful memory of forty years of "loathing a generation." First, I take the words of God as the psalmist's imagining rather than God's actual words; an act of cosmic empathy. For the psalmist, the magnificence of creation is matched by God's shepherding the Israelites to freedom despite their human failings. Seen in the context of pilgrimage, Rabbi Edward Feld comments that the leader calls on the fellow travelers to anticipate the joy of communing with the source of heaven and earth and yet warns them not to complain amidst the challenges of the actual journey: "the generation that wandered in the wilderness had closed the their hearts and covered their eyes — seeing only the difficulties, but not the majesty, of the enterprise — and so did not enter God's 'resting place.'"[145] As we move toward Shabbat each week, we are likewise to feel as if on a pilgrimage with anticipation of the celebration of the glory of God's creation. And yet, to come to that place of peace and joy we will need to let go of our griping.

"For [God] Is Our God . . . Today"
Rabbi Spitz

A word count often reveals the bulls-eye, the central message. The middle words of Psalm 95 in Hebrew begin: "For [God] is our God" (v. 7). This is a statement of loyalty to divine relationship. This looks back toward the verses that extolled God's uniqueness as Creator and forward to the God who led the Israelites in the desert. The verse continues, "And we are the people of [God's] pasture, and the flock of [God's] hand; today, if only to [God's] voice would listen." The reference to God's hand repeats the image as used for God as Creator. The Vilna Gaon of eighteenth-century Lithuania emphasized that God as shepherd conveys God's affection. And yet the relationship comes with expectations — "if only."

The emphasis on "today" has another significance. Rabbi Nahman of Bratslav (Ukraine, 1772-1810) said that living up to God's expectations might feel like too big a task. Here we are told by the psalm, as Rabbi Nahman interprets it, to sustain the relationship by taking it one day at a time. Bill Wilson (1895-1971) and Alcoholics Anonymous would mirror this insight by teaching that to overcome compulsions, live one day at a time. The last word of verse 7, "listen," focuses us on paying attention now: to what we might take for granted; to what is before us; and to the pitfalls of self-pity, fear, and complaining — like the Israelites did in the desert — for that leads to a hardened heart. In sum, Psalm 95 calls on us to choose to pay attention now, for doing so will enable celebration.

The Wisdom of Paradox
Rabbi Spitz

Amid a Jewish wedding celebration is a warning. At first impression this seeming break in mood is actually part of a larger whole. The shattering of a glass to conclude the ceremony conveys that in the midst of our greatest joy, we should recollect our greatest communal sadness, the destruction of the Temple in Jerusalem. For the two brought together are a reminder that the love of a bride and groom are precious as fragile and that they are duty bound to use the strength of their love to heal a broken world.

Paradox is a seeming contradiction that actually describes a greater whole. We seesaw in our thoughts and feelings. And yet it is essential to know the fulcrum, the center point that defines our core values. For the psalmist, that central point is also a paradox: loyalty of belonging to a distinctive people along with honoring the Source of Creation as transcending any one people. Faith requires holding together deep truths that are seemingly opposite.

As Rabbi David Wolpe explained the nature of paradox: "Which is true? 'Nothing ventured nothing gained' or 'Fools rush in where angels fear to tread'? 'He who hesitates is lost' or 'Look before you leap'? 'Out of sight out of mind' or 'Absence makes the heart grow fonder?'" Holding together opposites, the nineteenth-century Rabbi Menachem Mendel of Vorki described a true Jew as "uright kneeling, silent screaming, motionless dance." [146]

Psalm 95 takes us on a journey. We are guided to praise the wonder of God's creation. We move toward Shabbat as if awaiting the entry of the bride, which the rabbis see as the essence of anticipatory joy. And simultaneously, we are reminded that the wedding celebration — the day of Shabbat — exists in a broken world. And yet (the phrase that marks the moving of the seesaw), the psalmist bids us to lean into the joy, "Come let us sing!"

Psalm 137

"By the Rivers of Babylon"

Rabbi Elie Spitz

Abounding in musical adaptations of key verses,[147] Psalm 137 ironically notes an inability to sing. Opening with the woeful mourning of Judean exiles in Babylonia, the psalm ends with a surprisingly violent call for vengeance.

א עַל נַהֲרוֹת בָּבֶל שָׁם יָשַׁבְנוּ,
גַּם בָּכִינוּ בְּזָכְרֵנוּ אֶת צִיּוֹן.

1 By rivers of Babylon, there we sat and surely wept when we remembered Zion.

ב עַל עֲרָבִים בְּתוֹכָהּ
תָּלִינוּ כִּנֹּרוֹתֵינוּ.

2 Upon the willows in its midst, we hung our lyres.

ג כִּי שָׁם שְׁאֵלוּנוּ שׁוֹבֵינוּ
דִּבְרֵי שִׁיר וְתוֹלָלֵינוּ— שִׂמְחָה—
שִׁירוּ לָנוּ מִשִּׁיר צִיּוֹן.

3 For there our captors demanded of us words of song and our tormentors — joyfully — "Sing for us of the songs of Zion."

ד אֵיךְ נָשִׁיר אֶת שִׁיר יְהֹוָה
עַל אַדְמַת נֵכָר?

4 How can we sing a song of *Adonai* on alien soil?

ה אִם אֶשְׁכָּחֵךְ יְרוּשָׁלָ͏ִם
תִּשְׁכַּח יְמִינִי.

5 If I should forget you, Jerusalem, let me forget my right [hand].

ו תִּדְבַּק לְשׁוֹנִי לְחִכִּי אִם לֹא אֶזְכְּרֵכִי; **6** Let cling my tongue to my palate

אִם לֹא אַעֲלֶה if I do not remember you; if I do not

אֶת יְרוּשָׁלַ͏ִם עַל רֹאשׁ שִׂמְחָתִי. raise Jerusalem at the head of my joy.

ז זְכֹר יְהוָה לִבְנֵי אֱדוֹם **7** Remember, *Adonai*, for the children

אֵת יוֹם יְרוּשָׁלָ͏ִם, הָאֹמְרִים of Edom the Day of Jerusalem, who

עָרוּ! עָרוּ! עַד הַיְסוֹד בָּהּ! said, "Destroy! Destroy! Even until

the foundation of it!"

ח בַּת בָּבֶל הַשְּׁדוּדָה: **8** Daughter of Babylon, the

אַשְׁרֵי שֶׁיְשַׁלֶּם לָךְ אֶת despoiled, happy who will repay your

גְּמוּלֵךְ שֶׁגָּמַלְתְּ לָנוּ. acts that you have acted upon us.

ט אַשְׁרֵי שֶׁיֹּאחֵז וְנִפֵּץ **9** Happy who will grab and

אֶת עֹלָלַיִךְ אֶל הַסָּלַע! hurl your babes against the rock!

READING CLOSELY

This lyrical poem is widely sung, except for its last three lines, which are largely ignored and even actively omitted.[148] Why end with such a brutal yearning: "Happy who will grab and hurl your babes against the rock!" As for structure, Psalm 137 is divided into thirds: The sorrowful plight of the exiles (vv. 1-3); a response to their tormentors (vv. 4-6); and the cathartic song of exile (vv. 7-9).[149] In each section, the psalmist chooses words for sound as well as weave.[150]

The Sorrowful Plight of the Exiles (vv. 1-3).

"By rivers of Babylon" (v. 1) describes the exile after the Babylonian destruction of the First Temple in 586 BCE, an exile that would end in its seventh decade.[151] "Rivers" is in the plural. The Euphrates had many tributaries and rivulets. The image of water is a contrast with Israel, a dry land that is largely dependent on rain for its crops. We do not know the actual date of the composition or the composer's identity.[152] Some scholars, such as Robert Alter, hold that the intense emotions convey an immediacy as if at the outset of exile. Others place the timing after the return, suggested by the past tense of the phrase "there we sat."[153] When we read that the exiles wept, we can imaginatively fill in many sources of pain: the uprooting from all that was familiar; the separation of families and neighbors; the cruel violence witnessed and even received; the destruction of the Holy Temple; and the loss of independence as a people.

In verse 2, *kinor*, the last word, is translated by some, as in the King James Version, as "harp." A lyre is specifically a small harp that corresponds in size to the image of hanging from the willows. "The willows," translated by some as "poplar," grow alongside water. The motive for hiding the lyres is either for safekeeping or to renounce their use due to their identification with King David's singing and the service of the Temple.

In verse 3, the captors humiliate the exiles by demanding to hear the songs from the old country. For the captors, the songs' appeal may be just an enjoyable melody. But for the captives, Zion songs are sacred, evoking memories of the joy of the Temple service and the pain of spiritual dislocation. The word *tolalainu* occurs only here in the Bible and is usually translated by context as "tormentors."[154] The word's sound approximates *sholalainu*, which means "plunderers," or *li'hala*, "causes weeping." Choosing a unique word poetically conveys the unprecedented nature of the torment. "Joyfully," here set apart by dashes, may refer either to the mood of the captors or the type of song requested. As a post-Holocaust reader, I painfully bring to mind images of Nazi soldiers mocking Jews by having them dance on a Torah scroll. Humiliation by violating that which is most sacred comes through this portrayal of the demand for songs of Zion.

Response to the Tormentors (vv. 4-6)

The middle three verses present the thoughts of the captives in response to the tormentors' musical demands: "How can we sing a song of *Adonai* on alien soil?" (v. 4). We do not know if the rhetorical question, stated in the plural, is a pledge of civil disobedience or just a lament of the difficulty of meeting the captors' demands. This is the first use of God's name in this psalm. It is the intimate divine name identified with service in the Temple.[155] National identity and the Promised Land are intertwined. How to live in relationship with God when the sacred place of worship is destroyed and the people are ripped from their land is a challenge that will resonate during the two thousand years of exile following the Roman destruction of the Second Temple.

Verses 5 and 6 are an oath. Jerusalem is addressed directly as if a lover, a living relationship. These are the middle words of the psalm. Although at a physical distance, the psalmist swears that Jerusalem will never be forgotten and memory will retain the bond. The psalmist speaks for the first time in the first person, conveying a raw, personal longing. The word in Hebrew for "my right" refers throughout Psalms to the right hand:[156] identified with strength and as a second nature part of a person — namely, to forget Jerusalem would be like forgetting my very person. The right hand would have also been needed for playing the lyre.[157] These verses present a conditional self-curse: "If I forget you, Jerusalem . . . let cling my tongue to my palate."[158] The vow of silence is juxtaposed with the demand for song. And more, the identification with Jerusalem as "the head of my joy" pokes at the captors' demand for joyful song.

Cathartic Song of Exile (vv. 7-9)

Rabbi Edward Feinstein, spiritual leader of Valley Beth Shalom in Encino, California, sees these last verses as if sung in response to the captors' request, but with the words of a foreign language.[159] The captors hear only the melody. The Israelites speak to God and mock their enemies, gaining emotional release.

How should we understand these brutal words of vengeance? Verse 7 begins with Israel's neighbors to its southwest, Edom. In the Bible, Edom is identified with Esau, Jacob's brother and therefore part of the extended family.[160] And yet the prophets — Jeremiah, Ezekiel, and Obadiah[161] — when describing the Temple's destruction, decry Edom for complicity with the Babylonians. Those who conquered in the ancient world tended to preserve the temples of the vanquished, absorbing their gods into their polytheistic pantheon. When Edom on the Day of Jerusalem's destruction chanted to destroy or raze the Temple,[162] as the psalmist emphasizes, "the foundation of it." For the Temple was the foundation of Jewish belonging and closeness to God. To destroy the Temple was as if to demolish the very identity and will of the Jewish people.

The Edomites goading the Babylonians to destroy the Temple was an utter betrayal by a neighbor.[163] In pausing with this painful image, I bring to mind my mother's account of being marched in 1944 through her hometown, Munkacs, Czechoslovakia. Her neighbors lined the streets to the train station, jeering and cheering. She said that seeing those she trusted turning against her endures as among the most painful memories of the Holocaust, which would include Auschwitz.

In both verses 8 and 9, the word "happy" is used. It is that same word, *ashrei*, that begins Psalm 1. Happy is more than a passing feeling. As used in the Bible, it is an enduring sense of wholeness of heart and mind. But here in verses 8 and 9, surprisingly, the word is used in the context of revenge of the Babylonians: "Happy who will repay your acts that you have acted upon us. Happy who will grab and hurl your babes against the rock!"[164] The final word, "rock," contrasts with the opening image of Babylonian rivers. A rock suggests the land of Israel. Clearly these are words of a traumatized people. Living after the Holocaust, we naturally bring to mind more recent images of horror against the Jews and the naturally evoked feelings for revenge.[165]

What is remarkable is that these lines are largely absent in the public, non-Orthodox Jewish chanting of the Psalms.[166] Psalm 137 is recited along with the reading of the book of Lamentations on the Ninth of Av, the annual commemoration of the destruction of the First and Second Temples. And yet in my synagogue, those last lines are omitted from the standard text prepared for this distinctively sad Memorial Day. Although Jews have repeatedly suffered across history, Jewish teachings rarely take a posture of victimization or violence; revenge is left to God.[167] And yet in Psalm 137, rage is expressed, which has a legitimate place amid the suffering described.

For when we ignore our wounds and our emotional reactions, we run the danger of distorted feelings emerging inappropriately. Rather than pointedly expressing anger against the perpetrators of evil, those suffering from violence may reflexively direct their pain against those closest to them. This psalm ends pointedly with an image of violence. And yet the psalmist does not say, "Let's do it! Let's kill those bastards!" This is not a call to arms but an act of searing honesty and catharsis that enables reclaiming a view of life as a gift.[168]

DIGGING DEEPER

Words of the Huppah
Rabbi Spitz

A groom smashes a glass to mark the end of a Jewish wedding, as was mentioned earlier regarding Psalm 95 and paradox. That custom emerges in the shadow of the Second Temple's destruction. The Mishnah, edited in Israel at the start of the third century, records: "Mar bar Ravina made a marriage feast for his son. He observed that the rabbis present were ecstatic. So, he seized an expensive goblet worth 400 *zuzim* and broke it before them. Thus, he made them sober."[169] The shattered glass reminded those present of the charge of Psalm 137:6 of placing "Jerusalem at the head of my joy."[170] For the rabbis, a wedding is the happiest day in a person's life. Precisely then we are to remember the destruction of the Temple and the longing for its rebuilding.

In that light, there is also the widely practiced custom of grooms reciting verses 6 and 7 of Psalm 137 under the huppah just before breaking the glass, clarifying the intention. There is also a custom for the groom to place ashes in his hair for the ceremony as a reminder of the Temple's destruction.[171] In recent years in Israel, grooms have even obtained ashes from the archaeological digs of the Temple Mount, inspired by a Yemenite custom and enabling even greater symbolic immediacy.[172] Jerusalem and the destroyed Temple have endured as symbols of loss, giving context to the joy now experienced by Jews in that sacred place.

Saved by a Song
Rabbi Spitz

The song of the captive brings to mind a family tale. Before and during World War II, my grandparents owned a tavern in Munkacs, Czechoslovakia. The occupying Hungarians, allied with the Germans, made it a crime to aid a person fleeing from outside their jurisdiction. In 1943, the Hungarians arrested my grandfather, Marcus Mordechai Smilovic. He languished in a jail near Budapest. His wife, Hannah, came to visit just before the Jewish holiday of Purim, marking the salvation from the Persian decree to destroy the Jews. She brought a bowl of beet borscht for her husband.

Purim was a particularly significant holiday for my grandfather. He served as the head of the Society for Bridal Dowries in his city in which there were many Hasidic Jews like himself. Each Purim he would travel with a few musicians upon a wagon pulled by horses festively decorated with bells and colorful cloth. They would stop at the homes of leading potential contributors. Arriving after their lunch, Mordechai would ascend the table and sing and dance to the music, raising funds for poor brides.

In the jail, so the family lore goes, my grandfather brought out his bowl of borscht with a spoon. He got up on a table and encouraged the people to celebrate Purim, offering them each a spoonful of the treat. He stood on a table and sang *Szol a Kakas Mar*, a Hasidic song at least a hundred years old that mixed Hungarian, Yiddish, and Hebrew: [173]

> Crows the rooster now; sun is rising now. In green forests and open fields walks a little bird. But what kind of bird is it? But what kind of bird is it? Its feet are yellow, blue are the wings, waiting for me there. Bird, wait a little bit! You must always wait — if God gave me only to you, yours I would be then. But when will that happen? But when will that happen? When the Temple stands again and Zion is rebuilt again. Then will it happen! Why does it not happen? Why does it not happen? Because of our sins were we exiled from our homeland. That's why it doesn't happen.

The fellow Jewish inmates danced and sang along. The guards could make out select Hungarian words but not the nature of the song and its longing. They looked on with amazement at the joyful celebration.

The next day, my grandfather was brought for the first time to the administrative office. "I heard of the party that you made yesterday. Sing to me your song," the warden demanded. And so Mordechai sang.

"What are the charges against you?" the warden inquired.

"I have been here for close to nine months and have not had a hearing. So I am unsure as to why I am imprisoned."

"Where are you from?"

"Munkacs."

"Okay, I release you. Go home."

And so a song freed my grandfather — a song that conveyed yearning for Jewish dignity, marked by the rebuilding of the Temple in Jerusalem. In honor of this story and her love of her father, my mother's older sister in Israel would each year at Purim put on a gold dress and sing this song in multiple senior care facilities and encourage dancing.

The Hasidic song is linked to Psalm 137 with its focus on the Temple's rebuilding as a precious yearning with the promise of reclaimed strength and dignity just up ahead. As conveyed in this Hasidic song, classic Jewish theology put the blame on the Jews for their Temple's destruction. The book of Lamentations presents Jerusalem with human emotions, longing for her dispersed children and describing the uprooting as justified divine punishment. The rabbis of the Talmudic period would state that the First Temple was destroyed due to violating the cardinal sins of idolatry, bloodshed, and sexual misdeeds; and the Second Temple due to baseless hatred among Jews.[174] Seeing the destruction and exile as self-inflicted allowed for a sense of control in reclaiming what was lost. If the people renewed their loyalty to God as expressed in the covenant, they could return to former glory. This sense of control moved Jews away from a mindset of victimhood and served to empower. Zionism, the political movement of Jews returning to the Promised Land, emerged as an expression of that two-thousand-year-old longing. Rather than waiting for God to take action by bringing the Messiah and the promised return, Jews acted.

Empathize, Not Judge
Rabbi Riemer

Psalm 137 is one of the most difficult in the whole book of psalms. The first part is universally loved. It is sung at Jewish camps every year on Tisha B'Av, which is the anniversary of the destruction of the Temple. A great many composers, including Beethoven and Bach, have set it to music. It was even set to a reggae melody by a composer in Detroit.

The last part is, to put it mildly, not loved at all. There are some people, both Jews and Christians, who abhor this part of the psalm. It is considered by some to be the most offensive passage in the entire Bible.

At the Second Vatican Council, the Catholic Church decreed that it should no longer be recited in the Catholic liturgy. The Anglican Church recently made the same decision. And Jews never sing the last part. One line from the first part of the psalm is recited at some weddings, but I have never heard anyone recite the last part.

The psalm begins with the words *Al niharot bavel*, "By the rivers of Babylon." When you hear these words, what memories come to your mind? Do you remember when you last heard these words sung? *Al niharot bavel* expresses the loneliness and the despair that the Jewish people experienced when they were taken away into exile after the destruction of the Temple. Psalm 137 is one of the very few psalms that is possible to date. It was written either in 586 BCE, when the Temple was destroyed and the people were carried off to Babylon or sometime soon afterward, which makes it one of the earliest of the psalms.

"By the rivers of Babylon, there we sat and surely wept": Why does it say "rivers"? Because Babylon was a land that was rich in rivers and lakes. The most famous of them were the Tigris and the Euphrates, but there were many more. And so when they arrived, the Israelites must have felt the contrast between this land and the land that they came from. Israel is a dry country. It has only the Jordan, the Dead Sea, and the Kinneret. I think that one of the implications of this line is that even though this land had water and Israel did not, nevertheless the Jewish people missed their home. They were not envious or impressed by the abundance or the beauty of these rivers. They wished they could be back in the land of Zion.

Up until now, this psalm is a poignant lament over the loss of a homeland. It is a touching account of what it feels like to be a refugee. In an age like ours, when so many millions of people have become refugees from Ukraine, when so many people have drowned in frail boats from Africa to Europe, and when so many people have been stopped and sent back while trying to get from Venezuela or Mexico or other lands of poverty and oppression to the United States, this is a very powerful poem that speaks to the hearts of all displaced people, wherever they might be.

But now comes the difficult part of this psalm: verses 7 to 9, the part that offends many people. Verse 7 says, "Remember, *Adonai*, for the children of Edom the Day of Jerusalem, who said 'Destroy! Destroy! Even until the foundation of it!'" Why this anger at Edom? They did not conquer Israel; Babylon did. All they did was stand on the sidelines and cheer for Babylon.

The Edomites in Jewish tradition are the descendants of Esau, and that is what makes what they did so painful. It is bad enough when strangers are cruel to you, but when your own kin — your own family — is cruel to you? When those who are your kinsmen, who ought to do whatever they can to help you, stand on the sidelines and cheer when you are conquered, *that is really painful.*

There is a passage in the book of Deuteronomy in which God says to Moses, "You are about to enter the land of Israel. But in order to do so, you will have to cross over the land of Edom. Do not fight them. Do not pillage them. Do not steal from them. For they are your kin." And then the text goes on to say, "If you need food and water, you may purchase it from them, but you must not invade their property or pillage their land or take food from them without paying — for they are your kin." The Bible is reminding the Israelites that kin do not mistreat kin.

Now look at our psalm and see what our kin have done to us. See how they stood on the sidelines and cheered as the enemy destroyed our Temple and our land and our people. It was an act of betrayal. Kin do not do what they did.

Now the psalmist turns from Edom to Babylon and says, "May what you did to us be done to you. Blessed be whoever smashes your children's heads against the rock . . . as you did to our children." It does not say that they are going to do it. It only says that they wish that it be done to the tormentors. It is the fantasy of the helpless and the persecuted in all times. It is the wish of those who cannot fight but who can dream: "May someone do to you what you have done to us."

Now let us consider three comments on the curse in the last lines of this psalm.

The first comment comes from Mark Brettler, a biblical scholar who teaches at Duke University. He hates this passage. He says if it were up to him, he would take it out of this psalm. In fact, he says that he would sooner take the entire book of Psalms out of the Bible than allow this passage to remain. He says that it is the most vicious statement in all of Jewish literature, and we should be ashamed that it is in the Bible. That is pretty extreme, but that is what he says.

The second comment comes from one of the early Church Fathers, John Chrysostom. He says this line is a typical example of the vengefulness and vindictiveness and hatred that was characteristic of the Jewish people until Jesus came to give them the qualities of mercy and compassion. Coming from the leader of a people that carried out inquisitions, crusades, and pogroms in the name of the God of love, this is a terrible distortion, is it not?

And now comes my favorite commentary. Back in the nineteenth century there were many small towns, especially in the South and the West, that did not have ministers. And so there sprang up a number of lay ministers who would preach on Sundays. The only problem was that most of these lay ministers did not know very much. Some of them did not know more than the congregants did. And so the regional headquarters of these churches would send out packages that contained a month's supply of sermons that these lay preachers could read from every Sunday. One of the preachers whom they commissioned to write these sermons was Samuel Spurgeon. He would provide material for every passage that was read in church during the year. When it came to the last line of Psalm 137, he wrote, "Anyone who has stood by helplessly and watched his wife raped before his eyes, and anyone who has stood by helplessly and seen his children murdered before his eyes, and anyone who has seen the sanctuary that he considers to be most holy reduced to ashes before his eyes has a right to criticize this passage. The rest of us should keep a respectful silence." In other words, if you have not gone through what the Jews went through, you have no right to judge them for having uttered these words.

I think this is a wonderful comment on the last verse of Psalm 137. If you have not gone through what they went through, how dare you judge them? I think of some of the Holocaust survivors whom I know who are bitter, who do not trust non-Jews, and who speak of Germans with contempt even though those who committed these atrocities are no longer alive and even though some of their children and grandchildren have done noble things for Jews. What can we say when we see the bitterness with which some of these people speak? We who did not go through what they did have no right to sit in judgment on them.

So here is the bloodiest passage in all the book of Psalms. I hope that you agree with Reverend Spurgeon that it is a prayer that we should not dismiss lightly but that we should understand in the light of what the Jews who wrote it experienced. It as the lament of a battered and bereaved people that should be empathized with and not judged.

A Two-Part Truth
Rabbi Riemer

"May what you did to us be done to you. Blessed be whoever smashes your children's heads against the rock . . . as you did to our children" is one of the few cries for retribution that we have in Jewish liturgy. Considering how much persecution the Jews have endured, you would think that there would be much more, but there is only this one, the prayer in the Amidah against those who betray us, and the prayer that we say when we open the door for Elijah at the beginning of the second half of the seder: *Shfoch chamatcha al hagoyim asher lo yidacho*, "Pour out Your wrath upon those nations that do not recognize You and on those kings who do not accept Your authority."

Notice that the statement of the Passover Haggadah is not a condemnation of all nations. It is only a condemnation of those who do not accept God's authority. Why? *Ki ochal et Yaakov, vi-et naveyhu hishmadeu*, "For they are consuming the house of Jacob and are destroying his home."

Why did they say these words on seder night? Because they were literally true! The seder was often interrupted by mobs who broke in and pillaged and plundered under the influence of sermons that they heard on Easter about how Jews use the blood of Christian children in the making of their matzahs. After they left, the Jews would look around at their ruined seder table and say these words. Can you blame them?

In 1943, the Reconstructionist Movement published a new Haggadah in which they deleted these words. They did so because they felt that they were outdated, since we now live in a land where all people live together in freedom. Dr. Abraham Joshua Heschel responded to this deletion with these words: "Are there any other words that were more appropriate for Jews to say as they were being stuffed into the railroad cars and taken to be killed in the crematoria than these?"

The new Conservative Haggadah keeps this text but adds another passage to it that says *Shfoch ahavatcha al hagoyim…,* "Pour out your love upon those who do know Your name and who do recognize your authority, for they have saved some of our people and rescued the good name of humanity." This prayer is meant to be a tribute to those non-Jews who risked their lives in order to save Jews during the Holocaust. It is recited not instead of, but in addition to, the traditional *shfoch chamatcha,* for both are true. I believe that to recite either text without the other is to distort history.

This two-part truth is reflected at Yad Vashem in Jerusalem. The memorial to those who were slaughtered has a garden at the entrance in honor of those righteous gentiles who saved Jews.

Psalm 145

"Opening Your Hand and Satisfying Every Living Being"

Rabbi Elie Spitz

Why is Psalm 145, which is traditionally said twice during the morning service and as the opening prayer of the afternoon service, the most repeated of all the psalms in Jewish liturgy? And what are the spiritual messages of this most universal of all the psalms?

תְּהִלָּה לְדָוִד׃ **א** **1** A praise of David.
אֲרוֹמִמְךָ אֱלוֹהַי הַמֶּלֶךְ I exalt You, my God the Sovereign,
וַאֲבָרְכָה שִׁמְךָ לְעוֹלָם וָעֶד׃ and I bless Your name
forever and ever.

בְּכָל יוֹם אֲבָרְכֶךָּ **ב** **2** With all days I bless You and
וַאֲהַלְלָה שִׁמְךָ לְעוֹלָם וָעֶד׃ I praise Your name forever and ever.

גָּדוֹל יְהוָה וּמְהֻלָּל מְאֹד **ג** **3** Great is *Adonai* and much praised
וְלִגְדֻלָּתוֹ אֵין חֵקֶר׃ and [God's] greatness
is not fathomable.

דּוֹר לְדוֹר יְשַׁבַּח מַעֲשֶׂיךָ **ד** **4** Generation to generation extolls
וּגְבוּרֹתֶיךָ יַגִּידוּ׃ Your doings
and of Your mighty acts, they tell.

הֲדַר כְּבוֹד הוֹדֶךָ **ה** **5** Of the splendor of Your glorious
וְדִבְרֵי נִפְלְאֹתֶיךָ אָשִׂיחָה׃ majesty and accounts of Your
wonders, I converse.

ו וְעֱזוּז נוֹרְאֹתֶיךָ יֹאמֵרוּ
וגדלותיך (וּגְדֻלָּתְךָ) אֲסַפְּרֶנָּה.

6 And of the strength of your wonders, they speak, and of Your greatness, I recount.

ז זֵכֶר רַב טוּבְךָ יַבִּיעוּ
וְצִדְקָתְךָ יְרַנֵּנוּ:

7 Remembrance of Your abundant goodness they pour out and of Your righteousness, they sing joyfully:

ח חַנּוּן וְרַחוּם יְהוָה;
אֶרֶךְ אַפַּיִם וּגְדָל חָסֶד.

8 Gracious and merciful is *Adonai;* slow to anger and of great kindness.

ט טוֹב יְהוָה לַכֹּל
וְרַחֲמָיו עַל כָּל מַעֲשָׂיו.

9 Good is *Adonai* to all and [God's] mercies are over all [God's] creatures."

י יוֹדוּךָ יְהוָה כָּל מַעֲשֶׂיךָ
וַחֲסִידֶיךָ יְבָרְכוּכָה.

10 All Your creatures shall acclaim, *Adonai,* and Your faithful bless You.

יא כְּבוֹד מַלְכוּתְךָ יֹאמֵרוּ
וּגְבוּרָתְךָ יְדַבֵּרוּ.

11 Of the glory of Your sovereignty, they speak and of Your might they declare.

יב לְהוֹדִיעַ לִבְנֵי הָאָדָם גְּבוּרֹתָיו
וּכְבוֹד הֲדַר מַלְכוּתוֹ.

12 To make known to humanity [God's] mighty acts and the glorious majesty of [God's] sovereignty.

יג מַלְכוּתְךָ מַלְכוּת כָּל עֹלָמִים
וּמֶמְשַׁלְתְּךָ בְּכָל דּוֹר וָדֹר.

13 Your sovereignty is a sovereignty for all times and Your reign is for all generations.

יד סוֹמֵךְ יְהוָה לְכָל הַנֹּפְלִים
וְזוֹקֵף לְכָל הַכְּפוּפִים.

14 *Adonai* supports all who are fallen and uplifts all who are bent.

טו עֵינֵי כֹל אֵלֶיךָ יְשַׂבֵּרוּ
וְאַתָּה נוֹתֵן לָהֶם אֶת אָכְלָם בְּעִתּוֹ.

15 The eyes of all look expectantly to You and You give them their food on time.

טז פּוֹתֵחַ אֶת יָדֶךָ
וּמַשְׂבִּיעַ לְכָל חַי רָצוֹן.

16 Opening Your hand and satisfying every living being with favor.

יז צַדִּיק יְהוָה בְּכָל דְּרָכָיו
וְחָסִיד בְּכָל מַעֲשָׂיו.

17 Righteous is *Adonai* in all [God's] ways and kind in all [God's] doings.

יח קָרוֹב יְהוָה לְכָל קֹרְאָיו,
לְכֹל אֲשֶׁר יִקְרָאֻהוּ בֶאֱמֶת.

18 Near is *Adonai* to all those who call upon [God], to all who call upon [God] in truth.

יט רְצוֹן יְרֵאָיו יַעֲשֶׂה
וְאֶת שַׁוְעָתָם יִשְׁמַע וְיוֹשִׁיעֵם.

19 Favor for those who revere [God], [God] does, and their outcry [God] hears and delivers them.

כ שׁוֹמֵר יְהוָה אֶת כָּל אֹהֲבָיו
וְאֵת כָּל הָרְשָׁעִים יַשְׁמִיד.

20 *Adonai* protects all those who love [God], but all the wicked [God] destroys.

כא תְּהִלַּת יְהוָה יְדַבֶּר פִּי
וִיבָרֵךְ כָּל בָּשָׂר
שֵׁם קָדְשׁוֹ לְעוֹלָם וָעֶד.

21 Praise of *Adonai* my mouth shall declare and may all flesh bless [God's] holy name forever and ever.

READING CLOSELY

Psalm 145 opens with the distinctive inscription, "A psalm for David." The word *tehillah*, "psalm," is the name that the sages will give to the entire book, *Tehillim*. Remarkably, Psalm 145 is only focused on praise. There are no requests. There is no mention of Zion, the Temple, or the service of the Priests. This psalm suits any time or occasion and serves as a summation of what came before and the transition to what comes after: exultant psalms of praise.[175]

Why is Psalm 145 repeated three times a day? Because as an acrostic, praise is expressed with the entire alphabet: a way of saying that praise for God is from A to Z, encompassing the fullness of human expression. And such praise for God is not just for the beauty of creation but also for God's abiding, merciful caregiving. Echoing such praise evokes an awareness of what might otherwise go unnoticed as indeed glorious.

This psalm of praise is composed of couplets and imperfect verbs, conveying ongoing action.[176] The psalm is structured for clarity of themes as follows:[177]

1. Prelude: verses 1-2, beginning, "I exalt You, my God the Sovereign," describes the overall goal of the psalm, beginning with the words of an individual addressing God directly.[178]

2. God is great: verses 3-6, "Great is *Adonai* and much praised." These four verses shift to the "they" proclaiming God's wonders and doing so across generations.[179] The specific phrase, *dor l'dor*, "generation to generation," that will become part of the liturgy and a popular expression, appears only here in scripture.

3. God is merciful: verses 7-9 continue with the third person plural. And "they sing joyfully" is a paraphrase of a fuller quote from Torah: "*Adonai, Adonai,* a God compassionate and gracious, slow to anger, abounding in kindness and truth" (Exodus 34:6). God spoke the original words after forgiving the Israelites for their infidelity of worshipping the

Golden Calf.[180] The final verse, acknowledging that "Good is Adonai to all," will be quoted by Rabbinic commentaries as a directive for human kindness for all creatures.[181]

4. Interlude: verse 10 speaks directly to God: "All Your creatures shall acclaim, *Adonai*, and Your faithful bless You." "The faithful"[182] are the bridge between personal praise and the hope of universal acknowledgment. The Code of Jewish Law will later hold that this verse requires intentionality of focus, and if not, needs to be repeated.[183]

5. God is sovereign: verses 11-13 direct telling all living mortals of God's glorious sovereignty (v. 12) and those in the future, too: "Your sovereignty is a sovereignty for all times[184] and Your reign is for all generations" (v. 13). The initial letter of each verse in reverse spells out *MeLeKh*, meaning "sovereign." The psalm now shifts from looking up to praise God to God looking down on creation with acts of kindness.

6. God is beneficent: verses 14-20 provide examples of God in action, including supporting the fallen, raising up the bent, giving food in its proper time, and giving favor to the faithful. The word "all," which will appear seventeen times in this psalm, is especially repetitive in this section as God's universal kindness is emphasized.[185] There is a custom for a person to open a hand when chanting verse 16: "Opening Your hand and satisfying every living being with favor."[186]

7. Finale: Verse 21 comes full circle, returning to the same opening word for praise (*tehillah*), but now expanding with a universal call: "May all flesh bless [God's] holy name forever and ever." God's intimate name (YHWH) is repeated ten times in this psalm, signifying a wholeness of connection.

Amid the last several verses, the poet acknowledges an "outcry" to God and the faith that "all the wicked [God] destroys." Despite the primary focus on the goodness of life, the poet has — as does each of us — enemies and vulnerabilities of temptations. God's forgiveness appears in this psalm in a subtle but pointed way. The psalmist (vv. 8-9) paraphrases a biblical quote (Exodus 34:6-7) and omits the Torah text's use of "truth." Why? For truth implies strict justice. When we stand before God's greatness and might, we express the belief that God mercifully accepts us despite our shortcomings.

Why is this psalm the staple of Jewish prayer? The presented motifs are the essence of prayer: amazement before a God who displays before us the might of magnificent works and kindness, although we are fragile and incomplete. Psalm 145 gives us confidence that God hears us appreciatively despite our shortcomings, as God mercifully forgave our ancestors after the Golden Calf. We praise God, starting with our own words, and tell of God's glory to the next generation. We sing with our Jewish community and, finally, we call on the whole of creation to sing God's praises. For to praise God is to celebrate God's relationship with us as individuals, with the Jewish people, and with each element of creation. In the words of the Talmudic sages, reciting this psalm three times a day will place us before God in the Messianic era, which the Sages teach is also any moment when we are fully and selflessly present.[187]

Yet, above all, Psalm 145 is repeated three times a day because of its central message: God's greatness is God's goodness. Specific statements are offered as to how God mercifully helps the weak, upholds those who are faithful, and justly punishes the evildoer. The test of the efficacy of prayer is whether it motivates positive action. When we praise, we are reminded that we are beloved by God and that prompts us to share that love. The image of God is that of our collective Parent. The key source of joy for a parent is seeing God's children take care of each other, living purposeful lives and valuing the parent's legacy. Chanting this psalm implicitly prompts us to perform the kindnesses and acts of justice that God models.

DIGGING DEEPER

The Reward of the World to Come
Rabbi Spitz

Among the very first set of debates in the Talmud, we find the rabbis already asking about the prominence of Psalm 145 in the daily liturgy of the Levites in the Temple. Their immediate focus concerns how linking the blessing for redemption and the start of the Amidah prayer warrants being worthy of the World to Come. In that context, the Talmud shares the following quote:

> Rabbi Elazar said in the name Rabbi Avina, "Anyone who recites 'A praise by David' [Psalm 145] three times every day can trust that he [or she] is a child of the World to Come."[188]

The discussion then debates why this psalm is singled out for such a great reward. One sage says that it is due to its acrostic format, organized by the letters of the Hebrew alphabet. Another counters that if that is the case, then Psalm 119, with eight verses for each Hebrew letter, is an even more remarkable acrostic. Another says that it is due to verse 16, which acknowledges God's beneficence: "Opening Your hand and satisfying every living being with favor." A rabbi rebuts that this generosity is also stated in Psalm 136:25: "[God] gives nourishment to all flesh, for [God's] kindness endures forever." The discussion ends with stating that Psalm 145 is uniquely an acrostic that emphasizes God's beneficence. The rabbinic claim of the reward of "the World to Come" will go a long way in explaining why the rabbis made Psalm 145 a thrice-daily repeated recitation.

A Prescription for Spiritual Health
Rabbi Spitz

When Psalm 145 was placed in the liturgy in the early Medieval period, two verses were added upfront that three times repeat *ashrei*, "happy," and gives the psalm its liturgical name.[189] A final verse was also added from Psalm 115:8 — "We shall praise *Adonai* now and always. Halleluyah!"

The tale is told of the Hatam Sofer, who headed the Pressburg Yeshivah in nineteenth-century Slovakia.[190] A Jew visiting the revered teacher said, "I am too busy to study or to regularly perform Jewish rituals, but I do recite the *Ashrei* three times a day and thereby feel assured of my entry to the World to Come." Just then a student entered coughing. The rabbi paused to ask if he could give the young man something for his cough.

"I have a bad cold and sadly it is recurring. You see, I am a boarder in a damp, cold basement."

"If so, then all the pills in the world will not solve your problem, for you are in a place that breeds sickness anew each day. Consider finding another place to reside."

And then turning to the errant Jew, the Hatam Sofer said, "The Ashrei is a prescription for enhanced spiritual health. But if you are in an environment that breeds spiritual neglect, no matter how many times you recite the Ashrei, it won't assure you elevation of soul."

This story links with the opening word, *ashrei*, in Psalm 1, whose message is that the company that we keep and the values that shape our worldview will determine our sustained contentment. When the rabbis in the Talmud say that reciting Psalm 145 three times a day brings a great reward, it is not a magical automatic pass to the World to Come. Rather, this psalm is an aid to purposeful, appreciative living and action, whose rewards are many and enduring.

A Child's Prayer
Rabbi Spitz

The acrostic form of Psalm 145 conveys that the psalmist marshals all possible language to praise God and is an aid to memory. The use of the Hebrew alphabet and a specific line from this psalm are contained in a popular folk tale, which I retell as follows:

Once upon a time, there was a poor, unschooled shepherd boy who lived in the countryside far from any synagogue. He was illiterate, but he had memorized the Hebrew alphabet (the *aleph-bet*) in the form of a song. He would often sing those letters to the sheep, who seemed to enjoy his sweet voice.

One Shabbat, the boy and his parents were in a town visiting family and attended the synagogue for morning service. There were so many well-dressed people gathered in one place. The boy felt excited and intimidated. He listened to the cantor chant the beautiful prayers to God. People came up to the Torah and recited blessings, and the ancient words washed over him. He listened attentively to the rabbi's teaching about the Torah reading. As the prayers resumed, the young boy felt so moved that he recited the *aleph-bet* over and over, his voice growing louder each time. Some people smiled due to the beauty of the boy's voice and others as if his failure to use the actual words revealed the boy's ignorance. The boy was oblivious to those reactions and instead spoke directly to God.

"Ruler of the Universe, I know I am only a child. I want so much to sing the beautiful prayers to you, but I don't know them. Please, dear God, take these letters of the alphabet and rearrange them to form the words of my heart that I would want to say to you."

The rabbi overheard the boy's words and tears formed in his eyes. He thought to himself, "For the heartfelt words of this boy, God's heart is opened and our prayers will surely come before God as well. For as King

David said, 'Near is *Adonai* to all those who call upon [God], for all who call upon [God] in truth'" (Psalm 145:18).[191]

Stepping away from the story, it is worth noting that each verse of Psalm 145 is a couplet joined by a *vav*, the Hebrew letter signifying "and," with two exceptions: verse 8 omits the word "truth" from the quote from Exodus 34:6 and verse 18, where calling on God "in truth" draws God close. These exceptions draw our attention to the nature of truth. We avoid God's judgment of truth for fear that we could not withstand such honesty, and yet when we speak to God, our utter sincerity is what draws God near. We are reminded that we differ from God, who welcomes our truth.

The Missing Nun
Rabbi Spitz

Remarkably, one letter is missing in Psalm 145's acrostic: the *nun* (נ). Why?

Let's enter into the thicket of scholarship to see the diversity of answers and why persuasively, the omission of the fourteenth letter is artistically purposeful.

Already the Talmud pointed out this discrepancy and explained the absence of the *nun* as a letter identified with Israel's failure, citing the verse from Amos (5:2): "She has fallen [*naflah*] and will no longer rise, the maiden of Israel."[192] Another sage points out that the word "fallen" appears in the very next verse (v. 14), "God supports the fallen ones," and explains that King David wrote with prophetic power of a fall ahead with the assurance that God would help.

Professor Robert Alter, a contemporary scholar who has translated the entirety of the Bible, surmises that the absence is inadvertent: "Evidence strongly suggests that this line was in the original psalm and somehow was dropped in the tradition of scribal transmission that became the Masoretic text."[193] He quotes the *nun* verse in a Dead Sea Scroll from Qumran (on or before the first century CE): "Trustworthy [*ne'eman*] is God in His ways and faithful in all His deeds." Alter notes that the ancient translations and one medieval Hebrew manuscript also have a verse for *nun*.[194]

Rabbi Benjamin Segal and Professor Reuven Kimelman persuade me that the omission is purposeful. They note that the Qumran quote deviates from the rest of the psalm in its choice of God's name, the verbal form, and does so with a stock liturgical, non-Biblical phrase.[195]

But intentionally leaving out a letter in an acrostic is not uncommon in ancient poetry. There is even a word for this poetic technique, namely a lipogram. Of the nine acrostic psalms, four omit a letter.[196] In Psalm 145, the omission offers poetic gains: first, drawing the reader's attention to a shift in theme to the longest section, verses 13-20, which focuses on how God acts with beneficence; and second, enabling the middle (v. 11) to serve as the thematic bull's-eye. And finally, the intentional omission conveys a vital teaching: all praise of God is ultimately incomplete.

The Three Elements of a Blessing
Rabbi Spitz

The word "bless" is used three times in Psalm 145, demarcating the poem and providing the ingredients for the standard blessing formula.[197] "Bless" is used in the following verses: 1 — "I bless Your name"; 10 — "Your faithful bless You"; and 21, the final verse — "May all flesh bless [God's] holy name forever and ever." The rabbinic formula for a blessing likewise begins with the "I" addressing God directly, shifts to the "we" with describing God, and culminates with expansiveness: Blessed are You/ Adonai, Our God/ Sovereign of the universe..." The final Hebrew word, *olam*, can mean both "universe" and "eternity." The blank at the end of the blessing formula invites filling in the immediate prompt, such as "who brings forth bread from the earth." Psalm 145 in structure and content goes to the core of relationship with God, who is simultaneously transcendent and immanent and who gives care three-dimensionally: to "me" individually, the "we" of community, and the entirety of creation.[198]

What Do These Words Really Mean?
Rabbi Riemer

I want to study Psalm 145 with you as I learned it from my teacher, Dr. Arthur Green, who probably learned it, as I did, from the one who was the teacher of us both, Dr. Abraham Joshua Heschel.

But before I do this, I want to make one observation about the way most of us recite Psalm 145 in our synagogues today and the way the Sages say that we should say this prayer.

My observation is that if a traffic cop ever came into one of our synagogues today and saw how most of us say this prayer, he would give out traffic tickets for speeding.

It is understandable that we rattle off this prayer at full speed. We have said it many times before, and it is arranged in alphabetic order and so we know each line by heart. And yet, there is a statement in the writings of the Sages that says that this prayer, above all others, should be recited slowly and carefully.

The Sages say that whoever recites the Ashrei with intention — *muvtach lo she hu ben olam haba*. Most of us misunderstand this passage. We think that it means that if you say the Ashrei sincerely you will be admitted into the world to come. But that is not what it says. It says that whoever says the Ashrei *is* in the world to come. For these few minutes, while we say these words, we are in the world to come. And so it is wrong to rattle off these words quickly as so many of us do.

And now, let me turn to the text of the Ashrei. I will share the insights of Dr. Arthur Green and tell you the story of how both of us learned the meaning of the Ashrei from the same teacher.

We Are the Cantors of the Universe
Rabbi Riemer

I had the honor of working as Dr. Abraham Joshua Heschel's secretary during my years at the seminary. One day when he gave me some pages to type for him, and I came across a line that I simply did not understand. He had written "Man is the cantor of the universe," and I just did not know what that meant. Man is the cantor of the universe — really? Does that line make sense to you? It didn't to me.

I went back up to Dr. Heschel's study and I knocked on the door. When he let me in, I said to him, "I am not going to type this sentence until you tell me what it means, because if I don't understand it, your readers won't either."

I don't know where I got the chutzpah to say that, but that is what I said to him.

And I still remember what he said to me in response. He smiled and he said to me gently, "Tell me, my friend, have you never recited Ashrei? May I suggest that you go back downstairs and daven minchah [the afternoon prayers], and this time pay attention when you say the Ashrei. And then if you still don't understand what this line means, come back and tell me, and maybe I will take it out."

And so I went back to my room and I davened *minchah* and this time I looked at the Ashrei, which was essentially Psalm 145, in a whole new way than I had ever looked at it before: Ashrei is the song that we sing together with and on behalf of all.

The Talmud says something about the Ashrei that it does not say about the Shema, the Amidah, or any other prayer in the prayer book. The Talmud says *Kol mi sheomer ashrey shalosh pa-amim bayom bikavanah, muvtach lo shehu ben olam haba*, "Whoever says Ashrei three times a day and who does so with sincerity is in the World to Come."

I always thought that what that comment meant was that if you said the Ashrei with sincerity three times a day, you would be rewarded by being admitted to the World to Come after you leave this world. But that is *not* what it says!

It does not say that if you say the Ashrei sincerely three times a day you will be admitted to the World to Come in the future, as a reward for doing so. It says that whoever recites the Ashrei sincerely *is* living in the World to Come during the time that he or she is reciting it!

This is the real definition of the Ashrei. It is a prayer that takes us out of the mundane world in which we usually live and lifts us up into a higher spiritual reality, at least during the time that we say it.

And that is why we should take the Ashrei seriously, and this is why we should say it as slowly and as carefully as we can.

A Cosmic Address
Rabbi Riemer

What is so special about the Ashrei? Why is this the only prayer that the sages say enables us to experience the World to Come while we say it?

As I learned from Dr. Arthur Green, a former student of Rabbi Heschel and founding dean of Boston's Hebrew College, the Ashrei is one of the very few prayers in the siddur in which we address God *not* as individuals, *not* as members of the congregation, *not* as members of the Jewish people, and *not* even as members of the human race. Instead, we address God on behalf of the entire cosmic system — all the planets, all the stars, all the galaxies that exist in the cosmos.

The Ashrei is one of the very few prayers in the entire siddur in which there is not a single Jewish reference. There is not a single mention of the Torah or mitzvot — not one. There is not a single mention of the going out from Egypt in the entire prayer — not one. There is not a single mention of Jerusalem in this whole prayer — not one. The Ashrei is not a prayer about the Jews, and it is not even a prayer about human beings. It is a prayer that celebrates the glory of God that is manifest throughout all creation.

Let me prove it to you by asking you this question: What is the word that appears the most often in the Ashrei? What word appears more times than any other word? The word is *kol*. There are twenty-one verses in the Ashrei — one for each letter of the Hebrew alphabet with the exception of the letter *nun*. But notice this: the word *kol*, which means "all," appears seventeen times in these twenty-one verses. Let me provide some examples:

In verse 10 it says *Yoducha adonay kol ma-asecha*, "All your creatures shall acclaim, Adonai, and your faithful bless You." This means not just us and not just the human race but all God's creatures will acknowledge God.

In verse 13 it says *Malchutcha malchut kol olamim*, "Your sovereignty is a sovereignty for all times." Look at that term *kol olamim*. Here is a psalm that is at least two thousand years old, if not more, and yet it says that God rules not only over this world in which we live but over *kol olamim* — over all the worlds.

In verse 16 it says *Poteach et yadecha, umasbia lichol chay ratson*, "Opening Your hand and satisfying every living being with favor." This is the central passage in the Ashrei. This is the one at which some people have the custom of kissing their tefillin or opening their hands. And notice that this is saying that God is opening God's hand "to every living being."

[By the way, if I may digress for a moment, do you know that there is a wonderful kosher restaurant for poor people in Brooklyn? I read a story about it in the New York *Jewish Week* recently. It is a place where people can come in with their families and pay or not pay, whichever they choose to do. This place is concerned not only with giving food to poor people but also with preserving their dignity. That is the reason why they give out token money.

This restaurant has a wonderful name, Masbia, which comes from this line in Ashrei. *Masbia* comes from the same root as *sovea*, and what it means is not only to feed someone but to feed them generously or sufficiently. You or your children can tell the waiter that you want seconds, and they will bring a second serving to you without question. And the Ashrei says the same thing about God.]

So you see that the Ashrei is a prayer in which everyone — not only Jews, not only human beings, not only this planet, not only this galaxy, but the entire universe — joins together in a song of celebration of the glory of God. A person is the cantor of the universe in that we praise God with words, whereas the rest of creation praises God by its very being.

Sing Out the Glory of God
Rabbi Riemer

For some reason, two lines — both of which begin with the word *ashrei* — have been taken from other psalms and added as preludes to the Ashrei.

The first prelude begins with the words *Ashrei yoshvey beytecha*, which means "Happy [or blessed or fortunate] are those who dwell in Your house." Where is God's house? I used to think that *beytecha* referred to the synagogue, to the Temple in Jerusalem, or to the *mishkan* in which the Israelites worshipped in the wilderness. But now I realize that *beytecha* does not mean that at all.

Ashrei yoshvey beytecha means "Blessed are the people who live in this dazzling, amazing, complex, fascinating and wondrous universe that God has made, and who are fortunate enough to be aware that they do."

The second line of the prelude says *Ashrei ha am shekacha lo*, which means "Happy [or blessed or fortunate] is the people who knows this truth." That is, happy is the people who is aware of the glory and the beauty of this planet, this galaxy, this entire universe within which we live.

Do you recognize that phrase *shekacha lo*? It comes from my very favorite blessing in the whole prayerbook, the blessing that you are supposed to say when you see something that is very beautiful. If you see the Grand

Canyon, Niagara Falls, a work of art that is very special, you are supposed to say *Baruch atta Hashem Elokeynu Melech ha olam shekacha lo b'olomo*, "Blessed are You, O Lord our God, ruler of the universe who has made something as gorgeous as this is in His world."

> [May I suggest that if you want to have a successful marriage, you should say this *bracha* to your spouse at least once a day. The first thing you should do before you get out of bed, before you get dressed, and before you say *Modeh Ani*, the prayer upon awakening, should be this *bracha*. You should turn to your spouse and say *Baruch... shekacha lo b'olamo*, "Thank you, God, for making something as beautiful as you are in this world." Trust me — if you say this blessing to your spouse once a day every day, it will improve your marriage greatly.]

But what does it mean here in the Ashrei? Here I think that it means: Glory be to God who has made this amazing universe, this incredible galaxy, these many planets, and many satellites — those that we can see with a telescope and those that are beyond our ability to see, even with a telescope — who has made those planets that are within this solar system in which we live, and those that are millions and millions of light years away from this planet on which we live. Glory be to God for having created a cosmic system in which the stars and the planets go on their appointed rounds and not one of them ever collides with another one.

For that is amazing. That is not to be taken for granted . . . and therefore at least once a day, we are supposed to say *Ashrei ha am shekacha lo*, which means: Glory be to God, who has made this solar system of ours; in which there is just enough sunlight so that we can live — because if there were a little bit less sunlight coming to our planet from the sun, we would freeze; and if there were a little bit more sunlight coming from the sun, this planet of ours would burn up. And glory be to God, who has made Saturn, Mars, and Venus in such a way that they rotate in the heavens on their appointed paths and never collide with each other, because if they did, there would be no world.

Glory be to God — *shekacha lo b'olomo* — that such it is to God in God's world.

The Creator Determines Value
Rabbi Riemer

And now I want to share with you one more comment about the Ashrei that I learned from my colleague and teacher Rabbi Benjamin Blech. He began by telling his congregation in a sermon the following story: "Has everyone here heard what happened at Sotheby's this year? Someone — we don't know who it was but someone — bought a twenty-one-inch painting called *Salvator Mundi* at an auction that was held at Sotheby's. It is a painting that is believed to have been done by Leonardo Da Vinci. And here is the news: this anonymous buyer paid the sum of 450 million dollars for this painting."

Who bought this painting? And more important, why? Did whoever it was buy it as an investment? That is possible. But it is hard to believe that this person will find someone who will buy this painting from them for much more than they paid for it. I am not a big expert on these matters, but it seems to me that buying something for 450 million dollars in the hopes of someday being able to sell it to someone else for more is not a very good investment strategy.

So, if it is not a good investment, why did this person buy the painting? Did they buy it just so they could have the pleasure of exhibiting it in their living room and thereby making all of their friends and neighbors jealous? Maybe. But there is one catch with this plan. In order to do that, they would have to be sure that it really is a da Vinci. And the experts and the art critics are not really sure that it is.

Some art historians believe that it was done by da Vinci, and some believe that it was done not by da Vinci but by one of his students, perhaps under his supervision. Some art historians believe this painting was done in the style of da Vinci but half a century after his death. And some art historians believe this painting is a complete forgery; they claim it uses a certain kind of ink and a certain kind of paper that were not invented until a century after da Vinci's death.

Sotheby's wanted to make sure that they were not sued for selling a forgery, and so they protected themselves by writing in the booklet that they gave to every bidder at the auction these words: "We are not in a position to affirm or deny this painting's authenticity." They were not saying whether it is an authentic da Vinci or whether it is a fake.

What's the difference if it is a forgery? Whether or not it is beautiful is irrelevant. It's *who created it* that determines its value.

Why did Rabbi Blech tell this story to his congregation?

Rabbi Blech said, "I tell you this story because the same thing that is true in the art world is true about the world around us. According to the psalmist, the heavens declare the glory of God, but this is only true for those who believe that the heavens are the work of God.

"According to Isaiah, 'Holy, Holy, Holy is the Lord of Hosts. The whole earth is full of His glory.' But this is only true for those who discern the work of God within them.

"According to the prayerbook, *Ma rabu ma-asecha, Adonai; Maley chol ha-aretz kinyanecha,* 'How marvelous is Your creation, O God. The whole earth is full of ways of acquiring you.' But this is only true for those who see the handiwork of God within the world. How we feel about the world depends on who we believe created it."

Rabbi Blech says that just about every educated person today believes in the theory of evolution. And rightly so. Evolution is true. All scientists agree on this. But there are two different ways of understanding what evolution means. You can believe in the theory of evolution from a religious or secular perspective. You can believe that evolution is the gradual unfolding of God's plan for the universe, or you can believe that evolution has no goal and that it has no purpose. You can believe that evolution is the work of God, or you can believe that evolution is random.

You can believe that planets and stars have simply come into being for no reason and that they have no ultimate goal. Or you can believe that the unfolding of the universe over the billions of years it has taken — which climaxed with the moment when the first creature climbed out of the water onto solid earth and then stood up on two legs and then began to utter sounds and then learned how to talk — was the work of God. When I say the moment when the first creature stepped out of the water, I am speaking metaphorically, for each of these events must have taken many centuries. But this is what I mean when I say that each of these moments was a turning point in the history of evolution.

And which of these two concepts of evolution you choose to affirm will determine what you feel is the worth of the world.

If you believe that evolution is the working out of the divine plan of the Creator, then the world is wondrous and sublime, and the heavens declare the glory of God. If you believe that the world is just a cosmic accident and that there is no divine purpose to the universe, then you look upon nature as without meaning and without wonder. And that will determine how you look at your own life. To put it bluntly, as I see it, if the world was made by God, then life is worth living.

And that is the whole point of the Ashrei. The Ashrei declares that the universe is not a cosmic accident; it is the work of God. It declares that it is God who sustains and nurtures not only us, not only the human race, but the stars and planets in our universe.

The Ashrei declares that the Earth is not our mother, as the pagans believed. The Ashrei declares that the Earth is our sister and that it is our task to join with our sister and sing out the praise of God for having made us both. That is why the Ashrei ends with these words: *Tihilat Adonay yidaber pi, vayivarech kol baser et shem kodsho,* "My mouth will declare the praise of the Lord, and let all flesh" — all that lives, all of creation — join with me and sing in harmony with me, and "praise the name of the Lord together" with me forever.

The Ashrei comes to teach us that even after you know all the details of evolution — even after you know how oxygen and hydrogen come together to form water, even after you know how the laws of gravity work, even after you know all the other rules by which nature operates — nature should still be a wonder. And that is why we should thank God every day, together with nature and on behalf of nature and in partnership with nature.

We should thank God for the many, many, many wonders that occur every single day, as it says in the siddur: We thank you for all the miracles that occur *erev uvoker vitsaharayim,* "evening, and morning, and afternoon."

By the way, notice that it does not say that wonders occur *every* evening, morning, and afternoon. It says that the very existence of evening, morning, and afternoon are wonders in themselves and that they should not be taken for granted.

Let us recite the Ashrei as if we are the cantors of the universe, and as if we human beings have been chosen to sing out the glory of God on behalf of the stars, trees, lakes, planets, and all the rest of the natural world. As it is written toward the end of Psalm 145, *Tehillat Adonai yidaber pi* — "May my mouth declare the glory of God; *vayivarech kol basar et shem kodsho* — "and may all flesh"— not just the people in my place of worship, and not just the Jewish people, and not just the human race, but all flesh — join us in singing out the praise of the Lord.

Now I understand what my teacher, Dr. Heschel, and Dr. Green were teaching when they said that "man is the cantor of the universe."

Psalm 148

"Halleluyah!"

Jack Riemer

א הַלְלוּיָהּ!	**1** Halleluyah!
הַלְלוּ אֶת יְהוָה מִן הַשָּׁמַיִם:	Praise *Adonai* from the heavens;
הַלְלוּהוּ בַּמְּרוֹמִים.	praise [God] in the heights:
ב הַלְלוּהוּ כָל מַלְאָכָיו;	**2** Praise, all [God's] angels;
הַלְלוּהוּ כָּל צְבָאָו.	praise [God], all [God's] hosts.
ג הַלְלוּהוּ שֶׁמֶשׁ וְיָרֵחַ;	**3** Praise [God], sun and moon;
הַלְלוּהוּ כָּל כּוֹכְבֵי אוֹר.	praise [God], all stars of light.
ד הַלְלוּהוּ שְׁמֵי הַשָּׁמָיִם	**4** Praise [God], heaven of heavens
וְהַמַּיִם אֲשֶׁר מֵעַל הַשָּׁמָיִם.	and the waters above the heavens.
ה יְהַלְלוּ אֶת שֵׁם יְהוָה,	**5** Let them praise the name of
כִּי הוּא צִוָּה וְנִבְרָאוּ.	*Adonai*, for [God] commanded and they were created,
ו וַיַּעֲמִידֵם לָעַד לְעוֹלָם;	**6** and [God] stood them up forever, for all time; a decree [God] gave and
חָק נָתַן וְלֹא יַעֲבוֹר.	it will never pass away.
ז הַלְלוּ אֶת יְהוָה מִן הָאָרֶץ:	**7** Praise *Adonai* from the earth:
תַּנִּינִים וְכָל תְּהֹמוֹת.	Sea-monsters and all depths;

ח אֵשׁ וּבָרָד שֶׁלֶג וְקִיטוֹר; **8** fire and hail, snow and vapor,
רוּחַ סְעָרָה עֹשָׂה דְבָרוֹ. storm wind fulfilling [God's] word;

ט הֶהָרִים וְכָל גְּבָעוֹת; **9** the mountains and all hills, fruit
עֵץ פְּרִי וְכָל אֲרָזִים. trees and all cedars;

י הַחַיָּה וְכָל בְּהֵמָה; **10** wild beasts and all cattle,
רֶמֶשׂ וְצִפּוֹר כָּנָף. crawling creatures and winged birds;

יא מַלְכֵי אֶרֶץ וְכָל לְאֻמִּים, **11** sovereigns of earth
שָׂרִים וְכָל שֹׁפְטֵי אָרֶץ. and all peoples,
officials and all judges of the earth;

יב בַּחוּרִים וְגַם בְּתוּלוֹת; **12** young men and also maidens,
זְקֵנִים עִם נְעָרִים. elders with youths.

יג יְהַלְלוּ אֶת שֵׁם יְהוָה **13** Let them praise the name of
כִּי נִשְׂגָּב שְׁמוֹ לְבַדּוֹ: *Adonai*, for [God's] name alone is
הוֹדוֹ עַל אֶרֶץ וְשָׁמָיִם. sublime; [God's] splendor is over the
earth and heaven.

יד וַיָּרֶם קֶרֶן לְעַמּוֹ— **14** And may [God] raise up a horn
תְּהִלָּה לְכָל חֲסִידָיו for [God's] people —
לִבְנֵי יִשְׂרָאֵל, עַם קְרֹבוֹ. praise of all [God's] faithful,
הַלְלוּיָהּ! for the children of Israel,
a people near to [God].
Halleluyah!

READING CLOSELY

If the book of Psalms begins on a didactic note, it ends with exultation. The last five psalms are exuberant declarations that call upon all humanity and all creation to sing out the glories of God. We can hear the clang of the cymbals and the sound of the trumpets, and we can hear the sounds of every other musical instrument that was known in the time of the Second Temple in these psalms, in which the choir in the Temple was joined by the orchestra in belting out this triumphant chant.

The key word in each of these five psalms is *halleluyah*. Halleluyah is one of the words that the psalms have contributed to the English language, and yet its power is no longer felt as much in the Jewish worship service as it once was. Let me tell you about the experience from which I learned this truth.

I once belonged to a storefront synagogue that was located next door to a Black church. *Yontif* [a Jewish holiday] came out one year on a Sunday, and so the contrast between how we prayed and how they prayed became very clear to all of us. We sat politely and prayed demurely. We seldom lifted up our voices and we never stood up and called out the words of the prayerbook with exultation. And meanwhile, the sounds of the service that was being held next door came resounding through the wall that separated us from them. We could hear the halleluyahs that came from out of the voices of those that were present at their service, and we could feel the exhilaration and the enthusiasm that was evident in their shouts.

And I could not help but wonder about two questions. The first one was which service was more beloved to the Lord above who made us all? And the second one was which of these two services would the authors of the last five psalms in the psalter feel more at home in?

I have still not overcome my inhibitions about singing out the glory of God at the top of my voice, like the people in the church next door did that day. But, thanks to Dr. Shai Held of the Hadar Institute in New York who taught me how to understand these psalms, I now have a greater appreciation of what they meant in the context of the time in which they were written and a greater appreciation of what they should mean to us here and now.

And so, what I am going to try to do in this chapter, by means of Dr. Shai Held's insights, is to set these psalms against the beliefs of the pagan world around the people of Israel in antiquity and to understand them as a response by the psalmist to two revolutionary ideas that the first chapter of Genesis brought into the world.

Radical Ideas
Rabbi Riemer

The first chapter of Genesis, according to Dr. Held, teaches two new and radical ideas —one about humanity and one about nature.

The first is what he calls "the democratization of humanity." And the second he calls "the desanctification of nature."

He says that in the pagan worldview the king — and only the king — was considered to be made in the image of God. That was what gave him the authority to rule over his people. He was supposed to be kind to his people, but it was the claim that he — and he alone — was made in the image of God that gave him the power to rule.

Chapter One of Genesis demolishes this claim and declares instead that all human beings — not just the king — are made in the image of God. If this is so, then the king's authority is only relative. It comes from the consent of the people and from the permission of God. As Reinhold Neibuhr, the Protestant thinker, once put it: "The equality of all human beings is what makes democracy possible. The sinfulness of all human beings is what makes democracy necessary."

The second revolution that Genesis Chapter One brought about was in the realm of nature. The pagans believed that nature was divine. To put the difference between biblical faith and pagan faith succinctly: pagans believed that nature was to be worshipped; the Bible says that nature should worship. The Bible considers nature precious. The human being is told to guard over nature and to protect it. Nature is to be respected for it is the work of God…But nature is not God.

With these two principles in mind, we can understand Psalm 148. In this psalm the speaker makes a rousing call to all of nature to join together with us in praising God. This psalm goes even beyond Psalm 150 which calls upon all those that have breath to praise the Lord. This psalm calls upon even those that do not have breath, such as the stars or the sea, the trees of the forests, and the flowers in the gardens to praise the Lord.

The only difference between nature and humanity is that nature praises God by its being; humanity praises God by means of words. And perhaps there is a subtle hint here that we humans should learn from the example of nature and praise God, not only and not even primarily, by means of our words, but by our being and by our actions, as nature does.

The psalm follows the order of creation that is found in Genesis. It begins by calling on the heavens and the heavens above the heavens to sing out the praise of the Lord. It calls on *malachav* — which probably means God's agents — and it calls upon God's hosts — which probably means God's armies, and tells them all to join together with us in praising the Lord. It tells the sun and the moon and the stars to join together in a cosmic song of glory to God. It calls on the heavens that are above the heavens and on the waters that are above the heavens to praise the Lord.

And now, for the first time, in verse five, the psalmist gives the reason why these bodies should praise the Lord. It is *ki hu tsiva vinivra-oo* — For God commanded and they were created. He brought them into being and so they should be forever grateful to Him.

And then the psalmist announces another rule of nature: *Hok natan vilo ya-avor*. God has set boundaries for everything in nature, boundaries that nature cannot defy.

The sun and the moon and the stars may be divine beings according to the pagans, but these lines make very clear that, for the psalmist, they are creatures and not creators, and they are under the authority of God, who sets limits on how far they can go and what they can do.

And then the psalmist moves, just as the first line of Genesis Chapter One does, from the heavens to the seas and then to the earth. He calls on the sea monsters and all those who dwell in the depths of the sea to sing out to God. And here again, we have a clear contrast with the view of the pagan world. The *tannin* in pagan mythology was a ferocious sea monster. The pagans tell legends about how the gods fought the sea monster and ripped off its skin, with which they made the world.

Dr. Held pauses here to raise an age-old question: If the sea monster is the embodiment of evil, and if God has defeated it, why is there still so much evil in the world? To put it in modern terms, why are there still cancer cells that ravage our bodies? And why is there now a virus that has us all in fear?

He cites Dr. Jon Levenson of Harvard who has a book that offers one answer to this question. He says that the Sages transferred the victory over the sea monster from the past to the future. The sea monster was not defeated during the creation of the world, but it will be defeated at the End of Days. How do we know this? The proof he brings is: what is the meal that the righteous will eat on that great day? It is the Leviathan — which is another name for the sea monster, and which represents the forces of evil.

The psalm goes on to say that fire and thunder, snow and fog all obey God's word. The mountains and the hills, the fruit trees and the most precious trees, the wild animals and the tame ones, the creeping things and the birds — all of them are God's creatures and the psalmist calls on them all to join in singing out to God.

Sing Praises
Rabbi Riemer

And now the psalmist turns to the human beings and calls on all of them to join with him in singing out to God.

He says: The kings of the earth and all its governors and judges, the young men and the young women — let them all join together in the praise of the Lord for He alone is exalted, and His splendor is over the heaven and the earth.

Notice that the kings appear far down on this list. They come after the crawling things and after the birds, after the fish and after the animals, in order to make clear that they are only humans and not gods.

And then the psalm ends with a statement that seems out of place. It says that "God will raise the horn of His people and bring praise to His faithful ones, the ones who are close to him — Halleluyah!"

What is Israel doing here at the end of this psalm when all the rest of the psalm has spoken about the entire cosmos?

Some scholars say that this line must have been added afterwards. That could be, but we have no evidence that that is what happened. And it does not answer the question of why it was added, if that is what happened. Dr. Held uses this line as a springboard to discuss the tension that he says always goes on between universalism and particularism in every society. Universalism is a noble goal. It seeks to unite all humanity in the service of God. But universalism carries with it one great risk. We have seen many times in history how a universalist religion, such as Christianity or Islam, has tried to unite the world in joint belief in its faith by forcing conversion on non-believers, and by killing them if they will not convert.

Particularism, he says, is also a noble goal. It seeks to persuade believers to focus on the goal of improving themselves instead of imposing their faith on others by force. But particularism also has one danger. It can lead to isolationism in which a group focuses only on its own welfare and ignores the needs of other groups around them.

Rabbi Held then makes an observation that is worth thinking about. He says that one of the by-products of hailing God as our Creator is that it protects us from self-centeredness. It keeps us from thinking that we are the be-all and the end-all of our lives.

He makes a comparison that startles us when we first hear it. He says that by coincidence the philosopher Descartes and the author of the Modeh Ani prayer lived around the same time. And he suggests that the two of them were polar opposites in how they looked at life. Descartes taught that the *I* is central, and that everyone can only see the rest of the world from where they are. But the author of the prayer which we say upon arising each day did not say: *Ani Modeh*. He did not put the I first in the prayer. If he had, it would not have been an authentic Jewish prayer. He chose *modeh* as the first word and *ani* as the second because gratitude precedes and protects us from self-centeredness. And this is one of the lessons that Psalm 148 conveys.

Modern Meaning
Rabbi Riemer

Let me finish with just three brief comments on what this psalm should mean to us who live today. This psalm says that the praise that is offered to God by the sun and the moon and the stars, the fish of the sea and the birds in the sky may be just as precious to God as our praises are, even though they praise God with their being, and we praise God with words. Could it be that the psalm is hinting that the real praise of God is not through the words that we say during worship — which are sometimes sincerely meant, and which are sometimes recited by rote — but that the real praise of God is when we worship God with our very being, as the cosmos does? Could it be that the psalmist is suggesting that we praise God best when our gratitude at being alive overflows the sanctuary and flows out into the street? Could it be that we express our praise of God best by doing what we were made to do: by doing deeds of lovingkindness for those around us who are poor and weak and helpless?

If that is what this psalm is teaching us, then we can surely join with all creation in saying Halleluyah! And in being grateful, not only to God, but to this anonymous poet who has given us the gift of teaching us what it means to give thanks to God by our very being.

The second suggestion that this psalm makes to the modern reader is about our relationship to the world around us. This psalm, just as Genesis Chapter One does, envisions the human being not just as the ruler of the world but as its caretaker and its guardian. Dr. Held expresses this truth with a striking metaphor. He says that our lives on this earth are like a grand symphony in which each person and each generation has a role to play. Sometimes we get a solo and sometimes we have just a bit part. But it is only if every single player does his part that the symphony comes out right. If the violinist were to try to drown out the cellist or if the harpist were to try to drown out the pianist, the work would be ruined.

And so it is with our world. One of the key words in the creation story is the word *limineyhem*. The Torah takes time to point out that the animals and the fish and the plants were not made all alike, but that they were made according to their kinds. That phrase suggests that biodiversity is an essential part of the divine plan. If there were only one kind of plant or one kind of bird, the beauty of the planet on which we live would be diminished. And so, guarding the universe means caring about and preserving every species, and not letting any form disappear. In an age like ours, in which so many different mammals and plants and birds have disappeared, some because of climate change and some because of the greed of human beings who hunt down animals for sport and who set no limits to their killing, the reminder that is found in Genesis and in this psalm needs to be taken to heart.

If Psalm 148 teaches us these three lessons: the equality of all human beings, the responsibility of human beings to care for and protect all the species of all the creatures on the earth, and the call to all the creatures in the universe to sing out the glory of God for having made them — how grateful we should be!

And how sincerely we should sing out: Halleluyah!

Now that I have learned these three lessons on the meaning of Psalm 148, I have new empathy for the people in that Black church that was in the storefront next door to our synagogue. Perhaps they shouted out the words of Psalm 148 so enthusiastically because they understood these three spiritual truths that we need to absorb.

DIGGING DEEPER

"Coming Full Circle"
Rabbi Spitz

As daily prayer, Psalm 145 starts with the word, *ashrei* — "Happy is the person who dwells in Your House...."[199] The opening two verses are attached from other psalms, both which begin with the word *ashrei*, as if for emphasis. This opening word points to the very start of the Psalm journey, *Ashrei*... "Happy is the person who has not walked in the counsel of the wicked...."

At the end of the Ashrei prayer is another borrowed psalm line: "We shall praise now and always. Halleluyah".[200] Halleluyah means "praise Yah." *Yah* is one of the names of God. There is a dot in the final Hebrew letter signifying the need for prolonged breath in pronouncing this exhale-like word.[201] Psalm 145 is the bridge to the final cluster of psalms that each begin and end with the word Halleluyah. Psalms 145-150, which are read together in traditional morning prayer, are exuberant calls for all humanity and all creation to sing out the glory of God. We can hear the clang of the cymbals and the blasts of the trumpets and the Temple choir belting out these celebratory chants.

Conclusion

The final verse of the book of Psalms (150:6) addresses who should praise: "Let all *ha'neshamah* praise *Yah*, Halleluyah!" The word *neshamah* may translate as breath, life, or soul. With the lingering words, we are aware that the divine gift of life is contained in each breath. Rabbi Menachem di Fano (Italy, 15th-16th centuries) focused on the added "the" of *ha'neshamah* — "the soul" — as conveying praise "with a person's entire being."[202] The goal of Psalms is to engage our whole self — body, emotions, mind, and spirit — in responding to the awareness of God's sustaining presence.

The book of Psalms addresses war and wonder, pain and protest, and also contains much gratitude. Upon reaching the end of the book, we are sensitized to look back on what has moved us — forward with universal longings, and deeply within reality to perceive a loving divine Presence and Mystery. The book of Psalms thereby comes full circle in its quest for happiness by repeatedly and joyfully exclaiming divine praise with the final ringing word — Halleluyah!

Endnotes

Introduction: Falling in Love with Psalms

[1] James Bennett II, "WXQR Editorial — 10 Days of 'The Psalms Experience' at Lincoln Center's White Light Festival," WQXR, October 25, 2017, https://www.wqxr.org/story/psalms-experience-lincoln-center/.

[2] To watch my Zoom recordings of psalms, go to: https://www.cbi18.org/events/psalm-a-day-sessions/

[3] The Buber quote is also paraphrased in Harold Kushner's *When Bad Things Happen to Good People* (New York: Schocken, 1981), chap. 9, "Out of the Whirlwind."

[4] The Hebrew poet laureate Hayim Bialik is widely quoted as saying that "all translations are like trying to kiss a bride through a veil," but I could not find an original source for this apt image.

[5] Another example of the impact on meaning by adding a comma: *Happy New Year's Eve* or *Happy New Year's, Eve* — as if addressing a person named "Eve."

[6] Hebrew's perfect tense is past and present; imperfect is present and future and sometimes jussive/a command (for example, "let's").

[7] A Rastafari song written and recorded in 1970 by Brent Dowe and Trevor McNaughton of the Jamaican reggae group The Melodians and made famous as part of the soundtrack for the 1972 film *The Harder They Fall*, which is how I grew to know and love the song.

[8] Services memorializing the destruction of the First and Second Temples, marked by chanting the biblical Book of Lamentations and including the reading of Psalm 137.

[9] Rabbi Jack Riemer, in a recent Zoom teaching of Psalm 145, spoke of serving as secretary for Rabbi Abraham Joshua Heschel. Heschel used the phrase "cantor of the universe" in his writing. Riemer asked about it and Heschel told him to reread Psalm 145 as a universal celebration. Rabbi Riemer used the phrase "Sister Earth" rather than "Mother Earth" in order to convey that the earth, like humanity, was a creation of God.

[10] Rabbi Riemer has recently published selections from those sermons in two books: *Finding God in Unexpected Places: Wisdom for Everyone from the Jewish Tradition* (2018) and *The Day I Met Father Isaac at the Supermarket: Lessons in How to Live from the Jewish Tradition* (2018).

[11] Together we approach the texts to understand the meaning of the words in context, traditionally called *p'shat*. Such an understanding is largely drawn from close reading, the use of a biblical concordance (which lists each place that a particular word appears in the Bible) and modern, historic scholarship. *Drash* is the "interpretive meaning," which relies heavily on traditional commentaries over an expanse of two thousand years and the entirety of the globe.

[12] Secular songs, like literature, creatively describe life as lived and heartfelt needs. I once had a conversation with Rabbi Harold Kushner who told me that he started off in college

as a psychology major but found that the studies largely focused on the quantifiable, such as perception studies. He switched to literature, allowing him to more fully explore the inner life and the human condition.

Psalm 1
"Happy Is the Person"

[13] Paul Plotkin, *The Lord is My Shepherd, Why Do I Still Want?* (Sunbelt Eakin Press, 2003), x.]

[14] Israel Zangwell, *Children of the Ghetto* (London, 1892), 142-143.

[15] The pronouns in this psalm are "he," which I have made "they" so as to avoid gender limitation.

[16] A sampling of translations finds a preponderance among modern Jewish translators for "happy" (Jewish Publication Society, Robert Alter, Richard Levy, Benjamin Segal, Martin Cohen, Oxford Jewish Study Bible), but there are other choices: "blessed" (King James, Stephen Mitchell, Edward Feld); "fortunate" (Metsudah), "of the joys" (Martin Rozenberg, Bernard Zlotowitz); "in bliss" (Zalman Schachter-Shalomi); "praises" (ArtScroll); "praiseworthy" (Schottenstein Talmud, ArtScroll).

[17] In *The Art of Happiness: A Handbook for Living* (New York: Riverhead, 1998), the Dalai Lama writes, "I believe that the very purpose of life is to seek happiness." And when asked if he was happy, he responded, "Yes, I believe that happiness can be achieved by training the mind" (13-14).

[18] An example taught by Jewish mystics: *ayin* with an *ayin* means "eye," suggestive of the visible; with an *aleph*, it means "nothing" — no thing, that which is unseen yet present. Also consider the word *ani*: with an *ayin*, it means impoverished (externals); with an *aleph*, it means "I," suggesting an inner identity.

[19] Maimonides, *Mishneh Torah, Hilchot Tumat Tzora'at* 16:10.

[20] For examples of *hegeh* linked to speech, see Isaiah 38:14 and 31:4, as a sound made by pigeons and lions; in Joshua 1:8, where it is the swallowed Torah that enables Joshua to "*hageh*"; in Psalm 115:7, where it is linked with the throat; and in Psalm 71:24, where it is linked with the tongue.

[21] Benjamin D. Sommer links the choice by the redactor of placing Psalm 1 at the outset, followed by Psalm 2, as presenting an ongoing debate between what is of greater importance: study (Psalm 1 with its emphasis on keeping company with Torah, which he links to Moses and *mitnagdim*) or prayer (Psalm 2) (linked to David and *hasidim*). He cites Talmudic debate on what takes precedence regarding the sale of a House of Study or a House of Prayer as another example of this tension of needing to choose between mind and heart (*BT Megillah* 25b-26a; also see *Shabbat* 11a). He says that the redactor balanced his choice of placing study first by concluding with Psalm 150 that conveys that the ultimate praise of God is universal and goes beyond words. "Psalm 1 and the Canonical Shaping of Jewish Scripture," *Jewish Bible Theology: Perspectives and Case Studies,*" ed. Isaac Kalimi (Winona Lake, IN, Eisenbrauns, 2012), 199-221.

Sommer also presented on this topic via Zoom for The Jewish Theological Seminary on January 31, 2022.

[22] Harold Kushner, *Who Needs God?* (New York: Summit Books, 1989).

[23] Quoted by her son, Rabbi Joseph Telushkin in "Ways To Reduce Envy," *A Code of Jewish Ethics* (New York: Bell Tower, 2009), Volume 1, 307.

[24] Abraham Twerski, *Happiness and the Human Spirit: The Spirituality of Becoming the Best You Can Be* (Woodstock, VT: Jewish Lights Publishing, 2009).

[25] I had the privilege to work for Robert Cialdini as an assistant during my freshman year of college (1971-1972) at Arizona State University.

[26] See Steven Pinker, "in memoriam" of Judith Rich Harris (1938-2019)," *American Psychologist* 75, no. 7 (2020): 1024-25, https://stevenpinker.com/files/pinker/files/pinker_2020_judith_harris_obituary.pdf; and Malcolm's Gladwell, "Do Parents Matter?" *New Yorker*, August 17, 1998, https://www.newyorker.com/magazine/1998/08/17/do-parents-matter.

[27] Sadly, a common feature among violent, city-gang members is the lack of a father. Having a pair of parents contributes to personal stability, provides a model of how to deal peacefully with disagreement, and offers the motivation to take on worthy challenges.

Psalm 8
"The Work of Your Fingers"

[28] David Curzon, "Psalm One," from *What Remains: Selected Poems*. Used by permission of Ben Yehuda Press.

[29] Erich Fromm, *The Art of Loving: An Enquiry Into the Nature of Love* (New York: Harper, 1956).

[30] Some Jewish commentators view God as speaking to the angels or to the rest of creation; many Christian commentators use the plural "us" as evidence of the trinity.

[31] Based on a story in II Samuel (6:11) in which the caretaker of the Holy Ark is called Obed-edom the Gittite.

[32] Abraham Joshua Heschel, *Who Is Man?* (Stanford, CA: Stanford University Press, 1965), 39.

[33] Rav Saadya Gaon notices that the use of God's finger is identified with three very different kinds of creation: the stars and planets (Psalm 8), the tablets of the covenant (Exodus 31:8), and the plague of lice (Exodus 8:15).

[34] This is an insight of Jonathan Alter in his commentary on Psalms.

[35] The Jewish mystics spoke of four worlds: the physical (*assiyah*), the emotional (*yetzirah*), the intellectual (*briah*), and the spiritual (*atzilut*). Humans and animals squarely share the first two realms. Yet qualitatively, the human capacities for understanding and creativity in the intellectual realm set us apart. It is in the fourth realm where we intuitively marvel at the orderly nature of our world and are potentially at one with the source of creation.

[36] Brian Toon, "I Have Studied Nuclear War for 35 Years, and You Should be Worried,"

TEDxMile High, February 1, 2018, https://www.ted.com/talks/brian_toon_i_ve_studied_nuclear_war_for_35_years_you_should_be_worried?language=en.

[37] Also see a similar warning in Exodus 23:8.

[38] Paraphrase of *Mishnah, Sanhedrin* 4:5.

[39] Abraham Joshua Heschel, *Man Is Not Alone* (Philadelphia: Jewish Publication Society, 1951), 211.

[40] Abraham Joshua Heschel, *God in Search of Man* (New York: Farrar, Straus & Cudahy, 1955), 46.

Psalm 19
"The Heavens Declare the Glory of God"

[41] "i carry your heart with me(i carry it in". Copyright 1952, (c) 1980, 1991 by the Trustees for the E. E. Cummings Trust, from *COMPLETE POEMS: 1904-1962* by E. E. Cummings, edited by George J. Firmage. Used by permission of Liveright Publishing Corporation.

[42] William Wordsworth, "Immortality Ode," 58-68.

[43] The language is reminiscent of Psalm 8:4: "For I behold Your heavens, the work of Your fingers, the moon and the stars that You set in place." Psalm 8 seems to look to the night sky, while 19's focus is daytime. Also see Psalm 148:1-6 in which the sun, moon, and heaven praise; and Job 38:7, describing "morning stars chanted in unison; all divine beings shouted for joy." The verbs *declare* and *tell* in verse 2 are in the Hebrew participle form, conveying continuous action.

[44] Maimonides (1135-1204, Spain/Egypt) quotes in *Guide* 2:4; and the idea that every star has a soul is stated in *Mishneh Torah, Yesodei* 3:9: "Every star has a soul and is endowed with knowledge and intelligence…and as they apprehend God, so they are conscious of themselves and of the angels above them." The Vilna Gaon of nineteenth-century Lithuania would write that the motions of the sun created airwaves that made sound heard all over the globe (*Avnei Eliyahu*, 242).

[45] The last word of verse 6, *orach* — "on course" — is a pun, but it also sounds like "your light."

[46] This last word of verse 7, *michamato*, "its heat," is also used for the sun; see Job 30:28 and Isaiah 24:23, 30:26.

[47] Each of these verses has the verb *yatzah*, "going out," a repetition that conveys movement.

[48] See Nahum Sarna, in his *On the Book of Psalms: Exploring the Prayers of Ancient Israel* (New York: Schocken Books, 1993), 69-96.

[49] Sarna will say that the psalm was composed following the reforms by King Josiah (622/621 BCE) as a polemic against the cult of sun worshippers.

[50] Radak (Rabbi David Kimche, Narbonne, France, 1160-1235) will comment, "Just as Heavenly lights sustain the earth, Torah sustains the soul. But, as a person may suffer from overexposure to the sun, the more Torah the greater the benefit."

⁵¹ A position presented by Rabbi Shai Held in a public teaching of Psalm 30: https://www.youtube.com/watch?v=d6Oq-WPIr-Q

⁵² The Vilna Gaon advised this psalm for Shavuot, the holiday celebrating the gift of Torah.

⁵³ The reward may be physical, spiritual, or both.

⁵⁴ With gratitude to Shai Held for pointing out this wordplay.

⁵⁵ The second word of verse 14, *zeidim*, is a double entendre, referring either to the arrogant or to willful sin, conveying a vulnerability to temptation. Note that this verse is quoted in the Rastafarian song "Rivers of Babylon."

⁵⁶ Verse 13 suggests that the human limitation compared to God is that we may even be unaware of our wrongs and faults.

⁵⁷ An ambiguity regarding "meditations of my heart," as either words of the heart spoken out loud or words spoken internally.

⁵⁸ Johann Sebastian Bach in the cantata *Die Himmel erzahlen die Ehre Gottes*, BXV 76 (1723); note other notable settings to German texts of Psalm 19: Joseph Haydn in *Die Himmel erzahlen* ("The Heavens are Telling"); and Ludwig van Beethoven in his 1803 song for voice and piano, *Die Himmel runmen des Ewigen Ehre*.

⁵⁹ Consider https://www.youtube.com/watch?v=jCvhni9fyn0 to hear the exuberance of Psalm 19:8 as a hypnotic religious song.

⁶⁰ This insight of Professor Jacob Milgrom was shared in my synagogue in a public talk many years ago. The worship of the sun also has a place in the Bible and even in a description of the Second Temple. Moses will warn against worship of the astral bodies and the sun (Deuteronomy 4:19-20); and taking King Manasseh to task for setting up altars for astral deities (2 Kings 21:3-5; 23:4-5, 11-12); and Ezekiel (8:16), describes those "with their backs toward the Sanctuary of the Lord and their faces toward the east and they worshipped the sun toward the east." *Mishnah* (*Sukkot* 5:4) describes worshippers during the Sukkot celebration of water offerings (*Bet HaShoa'va*) who turned from the east to the west, proclaimed the quote from Ezekiel and added, "And we, our eyes are turned to the Lord." Also see 2 Kings 22-23; 2 Chronicles 24; Jeremiah 7:18.

⁶¹ Cited in Wikipedia for Psalm 19: David Guzik, "Psalm 19 — The Heavens, The Word, and the Glory of God," *Enduring Word*, June 22, 2020 (2019).

⁶² See Shai Held, "Finding God in Nature and Torah: Exploring Psalm 19," January 30, 2022, https://www.youtube.com/watch?v=ATLEH2SeXcg.

⁶³ A teaching of Rabbi Menahem Mendel of Rymanov (Poland, 1745-1815), cited in *Etz Hayim*, p. 441, in the commentary edited by Rabbi Harold Kushner and also noted by theologian Franz Rosenzweig (Germany, 1886-1929).

⁶⁴ Jacob Milgrom has pointed out that the most repeated line in the Torah is "And God spoke to Moses saying," which remarkably lacks explanation among the classical commentators. He said that to understand the verse, it helps to know a story of the Talmud (*Menachot* 29b): Moses saw God writing the Torah with beautiful calligraphy, "What do the crowns on the letters signify?" Moses asked. "One day a teacher,

Rabbi Akiva, will reveal many laws through them." "Let me see this great teacher," Moses said, and Moses's request was met with him being transported in time to the Roman period in Israel. Moses took a seat in the back row of Akiva's academy. Moses was unable to understand the teaching and felt his energy waning. A student asked, "From where do you derive this teaching?" The sage replied, "Such is the law given to Moses at Mount Sinai." With that, Moses's mind was put at ease. Likewise, Milgrom continued, "The inspired teachers of Israel in composing the Torah would attribute to God the teachings that rang true for them and their community as fulfilling God's will and were described as 'God said to Moses, saying.'" "The Nature of Revelation and Mosaic Origins," *Etz Hayim: Torah and Commentary* (New York: Rabbinical Assembly, 1985), 1405-7.

[65] Michael Fishbane, *Text and Texture: Close Readings of Selected Biblical Texts* (New York: Schocken, 1979), 89.

[66] Alan Lew, *This Is Real and You Are Completely Unprepared: The Days of Awe as a Journey of Transformation* (New York: Little Brown, 2003), 126-27.

[67] Elie Spitz "Letters to and from God," *Conservative Judaism* 45, no. 1 (Fall 1992).

[68] The quotes of C. S. Lewis, Samuel Pepys, Maria Johnson, and Charles Caput are presented without citation in the essay of Rabbi Meir Soloveichik's "Love and the Law," *Commentary* (June 2017), https://www.commentary.org/articles/meir-soloveichik/love-and-the-law/.

Psalm 23
"Stages of Life"

[69] "The Lord is my shepherd, I shall not want" is among the best-known lines of Hebrew scripture. This familiar translation is taken from the seventeenth-century King James Bible. The opening image popularly defines this psalm. In some Jewish communities, such as the Persian community, it is recited before each meal. Psalm 23 is universally recited by Jews and Christians at funerals.

[70] Rabbi Harold Kushner wrote an entire book as a commentary on this psalm, *The Lord Is My Shepherd: Healing Wisdom of the Twenty-Third Psalm* (New York: Alfred A. Knopf, 2003). He points out that the opening image evokes the calm of blues and greens rather than the more energetic reds, oranges, and yellows.

[71] Robert Alter translates the phrase "pathways of justice" and comments, "With this phrase, the speaker glides from the sheep metaphor to speaking of himself in human terms." *The Book of Psalms* (New York: Norton, 2007), 78.

[72] Translated in the King James Version: "That which is altogether just shalt thou follow . . ."

[73] Kushner, *The Lord Is My Shepherd*, 78-79.

[74] I am grateful to Rabbi Richard Steinberg for this insight regarding the healing of grief and "through."

[75] Rabbi Kushner points this out in another of his books, *Conquering Fear: Living Boldly*

in an Uncertain World (New York: Anchor, 2009). The phrase, "do not fear/*yirah*" occurs at least seventy-nine times in Hebrew scripture, plus the many times "do not be afraid/ *tifchad*" is commanded.

[76] Rabbi Richard Levy imagines this as a banquet with former foes after having achieved peace. Rabbi Zalman Schachter-Shalomi, as Rabbi Riemer recounted, spoke of creating an imaginary annual gathering of all his enemies to express gratitude for all that he had learned from their criticisms and his struggles with them.

[77] I owe this insight to Bible scholar Dr. Ahuva Ho, my congregant.

[78] See Commentary of Metzudat David (Rabbi David Altchuler, Yavoriv, Ukraine-Prague, 1687-1769).

[79] Maimonides (*MT, Hilchot Teshuvah* 8:4) says that biblical references like "the house of God" refer metaphorically to the World to Come; also Alshich (sixteenth century, Turkey/Israel).

[80] This story is attributed to Levi Yitzhak of Berditchev (Ukraine, 1740-1809).

[81] This idea also appears in *Midrash Shocher Tov*, commenting on this verse and predating Rashi.

Psalm 27
"Adonai Is My Light"

[82] Recited from the start of the month of Elul until Hoshanah Rabbah, the seventh day of Sukkot. This Ashkenazic custom began in the Middle Ages among most Eastern European Jews, but not all. It was not the practice of the Vilna Gaon, nor the other diverse Jewish groups: *Eidot Hamizrah*/Sephardic, Italian, Yemenite, and Romani.

[83] See, for instance, Psalm 51.

[84] Rabbi Benjamin Segal suggests several possible prompts for the psalm: a king's coronation; a person falsely accused; struggling with a difficulty and looking back for confidence; struggling with faith in a protecting God in the midst of a reality of evil.

[85] See for example, ישע – deliverance (vv. 1, 9); צרי – enemy (vv. 2, 12); לבי/לבך – heart (vv.3, 8, 14); קום – arise (vv. 3, 12); בקש – seek (vv. 4, 8); חיי/חיים – life (vv.4, 13); and God's pleasantness or goodness of vv. 4, 13. In total there are fourteen words that are repeated twice; three words repeated thrice; and two words repeated five times. God's name as YHVH is repeated thirteen times, repeated twice in the opening and closing verses and the only word to be used in both.

[86] The trust may refer backward regarding lack of fear or forward to longings described in verse 4 (Rashi and Radak).

[87] In the context of service in the Temple, see 2 Kings 16:15. The phrase *bikur holim*, for instance, means "to take care of the sick," which in antiquity was more than just visiting but included tending to the needs of the person: feeding, grinding medicine, bathing, swathing sores. . . It is as if the psalmist yearns for a responsibility that will keep him in the Temple, pointing perhaps to a Levite composer or to the message that God must be served to be known intimately.

[88] Hasidic sages will often define the foes as the *yetzer harah,* the evil inclination, which is identified with self-serving, impulsive behaviors.

[89] Note that the King James Version keeps the pronouns a bit obscure: "When thou saidst, Seek ye my face; my heart said unto thee, Thy face, Lord, will I seek."

[90] As understood by Rashi and Radak; Meiri sees David initiating his heart's response.

[91] The Vilna Gaon understands the three mentions of God's face in verses 8 and 9 as referring to the three pilgrimage holidays.

[92] The sixteenth-century Italian rabbi Sforno understands the context as, "My parents sent me away to be on my own after adolescence."

[93] "Integrity" is the ArtScroll translation of *mishor,* here translated as "upright." At the end of the verse, שוררי, translated as "watchful foes," is similar in sound and is a word that appears six times in Psalms and nowhere else in the Bible.

[94] The problem of self-chastisement is quite contemporary in the setting of cognitive behavioral therapy, where a person learns to attend to inner false accusations and respond with a prepared rational rebuttal.

[95] "Had I not" – Metsudah, JPS, ArtScroll; "Were I not" – Benjamin Segal.

[96] The present world (Metsudat Zion); the World to Come (Maimonides); or the land of Israel (Malbim).

[97] In biblical Hebrew, the nuance of the word *keveh* is to wait expectantly. As to this repetition of hope, Rabbi Yitzhak Zev HaLevi Soloveitchik (1886-1959), known as the Brisker Rav, explained that by placing trust in God, the reward is strength for an even higher level of trust in God. Rabbi Benjamin Segal asks if the repetition of hope serves as an assurance or conveys doubt.

[98] Deuteronomy 31:6-7; also see Joshua 1:6, 7, 9, 18; 10:25; 2 Samuel 10:12; Daniel 10:19; 1 Chronicles 28:20; Isaiah 35:4; Psalm 31:25.

[99] *Vayikra Rabbah* 21:3.

[100] Psychotherapist and Holocaust survivor Viktor Frankl shared a similar observation in *Man's Search for Meaning* (1946). Prisoners in Nazi concentration camps usually died around Christmas time, surmising that they had anticipated being out by Christmas and when that did not happen, they died of hopelessness.

[101] Benjamin Sommer, "A Faith that Includes Doubt — Psalm 27," https://www.thetorah.com/article/a-faith-that-includes-doubt-psalm-27

[102] Richard Levy, *Songs Ascending: The Book of Psalms,* 2 vols. (New York: CCAR Press, 2017).

Psalm 30
"I Have Recovered: Thank You So Much, O God!"

[103] Debra J. Robbins, *Opening Your Heart with Psalm 27* (New York: CCAR Press, 2019).

[104] Shai Held quote and insights found in his lecture on Psalm 30, found at "Reading Psalms (Tehillim) with Shai Held (Psalm 30)," YouTube video, 59:45, March 30, 2020, https://www.youtube.com/watch?v=d6Oq-WPIr-Q.

[105] See Rashi's comment to Exodus 1:16 describing the midwives Shifra and Puah, who "looked upon the stones," identified as the *mashber* referred to in Isaiah 37:3.

[106] The statement is contained in a letter of Maimonides, cited by Abraham Joshua Heschel, *Maimonides: A Biography* (New York: Farrar, Straus and Giroux, 1982; originally, 1935).

[107] Arthur Green, *The Tormented Master: A Life of Rabbi Nahman of Bratslav* (New York: Schocken, 1987).

[108] The accounts of Abraham Lincoln and Winston Churchill are the focus of Joshua Wolf Shenk, *Lincoln's Melancholy: How Depression Challenged a President* (New York: Mariner, 2005).

[109] The middle is determined by the Hebrew word count, excluding the opening verse that is viewed as an introduction to the content that follows.

[110] Title of the book by Lawrence Kushner, *I'm God, You're Not* (Woodstock, VT: Jewish Lights Publishing, 2010), with the phrase a reference to the first of the Ten Commandments.

[111] *Mishnah Bikkurim* 3:4.

Psalm 36
"In Your Light Do I See Light"

[112] Malbim (Meir Leibush ben Yehiel Michel Wisser, Ukraine, 1809-1879) holds that the description of David as servant is to convey that the psalm's goal is to provide guidance for the person who wants to be a servant of the Lord.

[113] The guidance of avoiding the company of sinners and identifying with the righteous is similar to Psalm 1.

[114] The precise number is 373.

[115] Richard Levy. Likewise, Robert Alter: "Crimes utterance to the wicked within his heart" (p. 12), which Alter characterizes as "an anomalous rhetorical device." Robert Alter, *The Book of Psalms: A Translation with Commentary* (New York: Norton, 2007).

[116] Verse 7 speaks of God's deliverance of "human and beast." Citing this verse, the Talmud (*Chullin* 5b) has Rav Yehudah, quoting Rav, explain that some people can make themselves as simple in understanding as a dumb beast; *Genesis Rabbah* 33:1 states, God saves humans for the sake of the merit of animals.

[117] Abraham Joshua Heschel, *God in Search of Man* (New York: Farrar, Straus and Giroux, 1976), 394.

[118] Abraham Twerski, *Addictive Thinking: Understanding Self-Deception* (New York: HarperCollins, 1990).

[119] Benjamin Segal, *A New Psalm: The Psalms as Literature* (Jerusalem: Gefen and Schechter), 166.

[120] For the public conversation with Rabbi Mordecai Finley, see "Moral Philosophy, Spiritual Psychology, and a Crisis of Consciousness (Mordechai Finley and Elie Spitz)," June 9, 2022, YouTube video, 1:01:25, https://www.youtube.com/watch?v=1egysLDRAps.

The focus on Psalm 36 begins just after the thirty-minute mark.

Psalm 44
"You Disgraced Us!"

[121] This is the third of the Korach psalms. The exact meaning of the term *maskil* is unknown. Some hold that the word is related to "informed" or "learned" and as a title informs the reader that what follows is an important lesson.

[122] In biblical Hebrew, *ki* signifies emphasis, therefore translated here as "surely" or by others as "rather." In modern Hebrew, the same word usually means "because," which is also used in some contemporary translations.

[123] [Signs and wonders are multiplied] "for the sake that you will tell into the ears of your children" (Exodus 10:2); "And you shall tell your children" (13:8, 14).

[124] This phrase is similar to Joshua 24:12.

[125] *Sal* is a basket, which can also be used as a drum.

[126] Reoccurring four times in this section are variations of *oshea* (deliverance) as the key motif.

[127] This section is distinctive for nonrepeating words, as if to emphasize the scope of suffering.

[128] Verses 14-17 are particularly rhyming and rhythmic in the Hebrew, a quality that does not translate. Robert Alter comments that the rhythm suggests the march of suffering of exile.

[129] Translation, including the brackets, from Jewish Publication Society, as contained in *Etz Hayim*, 536.

[130] A dramatization of this idea is at the heart of Elie Wiesel's play *The Trial of God*, in which the sole Jewish survivors of a pogrom in the village of Shomgorod in 1649 ask Jewish visitors to serve as a court to put God on trial.

[131] *Shemot Rabbah* 1:9.

[132] Also see Exodus 34:6 and God's self-description of kindness and truth.

[133] *Sotah* 48a.

[134] The Talmud (*Sotah* 48a) will explain that the psalm refers to a time of suffering when the idolaters are in a state of peace and prosperity, and it metaphorically equates God's disregard with sleep and states that a more literal understanding of the nature of God is Psalm 121:4 — "Behold, the Guardian of Israel does not sleep nor slumber."

[135] Some sages, such as Maimonides (1135-1204), attempted to even read descriptions of God's active intervention metaphorically. For instance, the Torah recounts that "God hardened Pharaoh's heart" (Exodus 9:12), implying the taking away of human free will. Maimonides pointed out that the phrase occurs twenty times in Exodus: the first ten times with Pharaoh hardening his own heart and the next ten with God so acting. Maimonides explains that Pharaoh initially had free will, but by repeatedly changing his mind and not freeing the Israelites, his behavior became the reflex of a deeply in-

grained habit. Maimonides explains that in the language of Torah, we identify natural consequences with the ultimate source of Creation. Maimonides, *Shemoneh Perakim* (Introduction to Ethics of the Sages); also see *Mishneh Torah, Hilchot Teshuvah* 5-6; and David Silverberg "The Hardening of Pharaoh's Heart," Maimonides Heritage Center, https://mhcny.org/parasha/1013.pdf. Also note that in the Midrash, too, Resh Lakish will say that Pharaoh brought on the condition of a hardened heart by his repeated stubbornness (*Exodus Rabbah* 13:3).

[136] Elie Wiesel's *The Town Beyond the Wall* (1995) describes Michael, who once overheard the following prayer to God.

[137] *Tehillim*, trans. Avrohom Feuer (New York: Mesorah Publications, 1985), 543.

[138] Confirmation bias is the term used for the natural inclination to only see what we expect to see and to disregard the rest. This comes into play powerfully in how people read the news.

[139] Elie Wiesel, *Night*, trans. Marion Wiesel, (New York: Hill and Wang, 1960, 1985), 65.

[140] The references to Shai Held's teaching come from his class on Psalm 44, recorded on April 20, 2022: https://vimeo.com/409890826

[141] Chaim Grade's Yiddish short story is translated with an introduction by Ruth Wisse, *My Quarrel* (New York: Toby Press, 2022). Previously, the work was made into a film, with screenplay by Joseph Telushkin and David Brandes, as "The Quarrel" (1991), directed by Eli Cohen; and performed as an off-Broadway play in 2008.

Psalm 95
"The Prelude to Shabbat"

[142] BT *Sanhedrin* 98a.

[143] The use of *elohim* here is translated divergently, as seen in the following sampling: gods (King James Version; Robert Alter; Benjamin Segal); "heavenly powers" (ArtScroll); divine beings (Jewish Publication Society).

[144] The psalm's final word, *menuchati*, "My resting place," is also used in the Bible for the land of Israel (see Deuteronomy 12:9).

[145] Rabbi Edward Feld's commentary is found in *Siddur Lev Shalem* (New York: The Rabbinical Assembly, 2016), 11.

[146] Rabbi David Wolpe, "Paradox," Off the Pulpit, August 26, 2022, https://www.sinai-temple.org/learn/off-the-pulpit/paradox/.

Psalm 137
"By the Rivers of Babylon"

[147] Some contemporary examples of the psalms' verses set to music: *On the Willows*, in the Stephen Schwartz Broadway musical *Godspell* (1971); inspiration for Leonard Cohen's "By the Rivers Dark" on his 2001 album *Ten New Songs*; verses 5-6 as the chorus of Matisyahu's single "Jerusalem" (2006).

[148] In fact, the Catholic Church, as part of the 1965 Second Vatican Council, decreed an exclusion of those last verses from Catholic liturgy as "incompatible with the Gospel's message." The Anglican Church of Canada would later do so as well. See Wikipedia, s.v. "Psalm 137," last modified September 5, 2022, https://en.wikipedia.org/wiki/Psalm_137.

[149] This structure analysis follows that of Rabbi Edward Feinstein of Encino, California, which he shared as part of my Zoom teaching of this psalm: www.youtube.com/watch?v=EOg7othYO7w. An alternative division of the psalm as suggested by Rabbi Benjamin Segal: vv. 1-4, nature of exile; vv. 5-6, the oath of memory; vv. 7-9, addresses God and the captors.

A great resource for the study of Psalm 137 is the material provided online by Sefaria: https://www.sefaria.org/Psalms.137.7?ven=Tanakh:_The_Holy_Scriptures,_published_by_JPS&vhe=Miqra_according_to_the_Masorah&lang=bi&with=Sheets&lang2=en.

[150] As for repeated sounds, note that in the first three verses, the suffix in Hebrew, *nu* (נו), meaning "we," appears nine times, emphasizing the collective nature of the longing and also suggestive of impatience — *nu, nu, nu*. In the first four verses, another repeated sound is *sh* from the Hebrew letter *shin* (ש), repeated ten times and suggestive of the middle sound and longing for *Yerushalayim*, meaning Jerusalem (which appears explicitly in three verses: 5, 6, 7). As for repeated words, in verses 1-4 the word *shir* (שיר), "song," appears five times: twice as a verb and three times as a noun. The word *al* (על), translated as "by," "upon," or "above" (depending on context), repeats in verses 1, 2, 4, and 6 and has the same sound as *olalei'ich* (עילליך), "babies," the third to last word. There is also the rhyme of *sham* (שם), "there," in verses 1 and 3 and *gam* (גם) "surely," in verse 1.

[151] As for a timeline, Babylonian Nebuchadnezzar sieged Jerusalem starting in 589 BCE, destroying the Temple in 586. The Persian Cyrus the Great would conquer Babylonia in 539 and issue a decree enabling exiles to return to Israel. Contemporary scholars estimate that about a third of the exiles took advantage of this opportunity of return; Babylonia was far more advanced economically.

[152] Ibn Ezra surmises that this is composed by a Temple singer now in exile.

[153] Position of Ibn Ezra and Bar Yosef, as if restrained from singing on foreign soil.

[154] The sound *tolalainu* in verse 3 repeats the sound of verse 2's *talenu*, meaning "we hung."

[155] Maimonides, *Mishneh Torah*, "Laws of Prayer and Priestly Blessings," chapter 14: The name was pronounced daily in the liturgy of the Temple in the priestly blessings of worshippers (Numbers 6:27), after the daily sacrifice. Other rabbis on Jewish law state that the tetragrammaton was pronounced only on Yom Kippur by the High Priest in the Holy of Holies when asking for forgiveness for the people.

[156] "The right" also appears in the victorious "Song of the Sea" (Exodus 15:6) in describing God's might: "Your right *Adonai* shattered the enemy." The King James Version fills in a gap: "Let my right hand forget her cunning."

[157] Noted in the comment by Ibn Ezra.

[158] This will endure as the Jewish "Remember the Alamo."

[159] Robert Alter will write, "Blood curdling curse pronounced on their captors, who, fortunately, do not understand the Hebrew in which it is pronounced."

[160] Genesis 36:1; Numbers 20:14-20.

[161] Jeremiah 9:24-25; Ezekiel 25:12ff; Obadiah 1:8ff. Also see the earlier prophet Amos 1:11.

[162] The word "destroy" in English is a translation of the Hebrew word *aru* (עָרוּ), which only appears in one other place in Psalms (141:8). There in context it means "to pour out" or "empty," as also in Genesis 24:20, when used to describe Rebecca pouring out her jar of water for Abraham's servant. The choice of a rare word in Psalm 137 points to the exceptional nature of the exhortation to pour out completely what is there!

[163] Later in Jewish history, John Hyrcanus (135-105 BCE) would forcibly convert the Edomites, the only such recorded case of forced conversions to Judaism. Herod was a descendant of such a family.

[164] The word translated "your babies" (עֹלָלַיִךְ) is also translated as "your sucklers," "infants," or "babes." Also see Isaiah 13:16.

[165] For eyewitness images of the brutality of the conquerors dashing to pieces mothers and their children, see Hosea 10:14 and Nahum 3:10. As for the brutality of ancient war, also see 2 Kings 8:12; 15:16; Isaiah 13:15-16; and Hosea 14:1. Medieval Spanish commentators Ibn Ezra and Radak see the concluding line as "measure for measure"; what had happened to the Jews will happen to the Babylonians. And indeed, when Cyrus conquers Babylonia, his troops will kill women and children; and a generation later, when Darius retakes Babylonia, his troops will kill women and children to save food (*Ancient Near Eastern Texts Relating to the Old Testament*, James B. Pritchard, ed. (Princeton: Princeton University Press, 1955), 314, cited by Benjamin Segal, *A New Psalm: The Psalms as Literature* (Jerusalem: Gefen Publishing, 2013), 647.

[166] Ashkenazim have the custom to recite this psalm on weekdays before each recitation of Grace after Meals, during the nine days of the month of Av and especially on Tisha B'Av. This is one of the ten psalms advised by Rabbi Nachman for "general repair" (*tikkun klali*).

[167] The Torah will quote God saying, "To me is revenge and payback" (Deuteronomy 32:35). After the Passover meal, the door is opened for Elijah the Prophet, who will announce the day of judgment and the coming of the Messiah. In that moment as an act of defiance, the Haggadah text then says, quoting Psalm 79:6, *Shafoch hamatcha*, "Pour out Your rage against those who do not know You . . ."

[168] Rabbi Adin Steinsaltz writes, "The psalmist does not say that he, personally, would be happy to carry out this act of vengeance, but rather wishes that someone else would do so." *The Steinsaltz Tehillim* (Jerusalem: Koren Publishers, 2015, 2018), 487.

[169] M. Berachot 5:2.

[170] Remah, *Orach Hayim* 360.

[171] Tosephta, *Sotah* 15:4-5, particularly common in the Yemenite custom.

[172] See, Penina Horowitz, "Trending: Temple Mount ashes for the huppa," *Jerusalem Post*, August 11, 2016: https://www.jpost.com/in-jerusalem/trending-temple-mount-

ashes-for-the-huppa-463880

[173] Words and melody by Rabbi Yitzchak Isaac Taub (1751-1821), the rabbi of Kalov, Hungary.

[174] See Tosephta of *Yoma* 9b:3; and related, BT *Gittin* 55a-56b, with the story of Bar Kamza and hatred among Jews prompting a Jew to incite the Romans against the Jews as disloyal, leading to destruction of the Temple.

Psalm 145
"Opening Your Hand and Satisfying Every Living Being"

[175] The previous verse was "Happy is the people whose lot is thus; Happy is the people for whom *Adonai* is their God" (Psalm 144:15), matching the opening of Psalm 1: "Happy is the person who has not walked in the counsel of the wicked." Psalm 144 comes full circle, focusing on happiness with an expansion from the individual to an entire people.

[176] Taking off the opening inscription (the first two words), Psalm 145 is composed of 150 words, suggestive for some of this psalm containing the essence of the 150 psalms.

[177] Reuven Kimelman's detailed analysis of Psalm 145 is twenty-eight pages long, with a close reading of the choice of words, the flow of the prayer, and its overall thought: https://www.researchgate.net/profile/Reuven-Kimelmn/publication/274107659_ Psalm_145_Theme_Structure_and_Impact/links/584d97c908ae4bc899330ac0/ Psalm-145-Theme-Structure-and-Impact.pdf.

[178] This is the last of the psalms explicitly linked to David. And I pause to bring another David to mind: Rabbi David Lieber, editor of the *Etz Hayim Torah and Commentary*, who once told me that this was his favorite psalm.

[179] Beginning with verse 4, the word "your doings" (מעשיך) will occur five times in the psalm (also vv. 9, 10, 17, and 19) and will refer to both physical creations and caregiving deeds.

[180] The phrase, traditionally called "the thirteen attributes of God, reappears in Numbers 14:19 as part of Moses's plea to God after the sin of succumbing to the report of ten spies and refusing to enter the Promised Land. Here, too, the word "truth" in God's initial quote is dropped. Likewise, in Nahum 1:3, the prophet who preached of Assyria's downfall of the seventh century BCE, paraphrases Exodus 34:6 while omitting the reference to truth.

[181] As stated by Radak and with many examples in rabbinic writings of *tzar ba'alei hayim*, the value of preventing cruelty to animals. In that light, Rabbi Moshe Isserles (Remah, *Yoreh De'ah* 82:2) will say that a ritual slaughterer does not recite the blessing for firsts (the *shehecheyanu*) when taking away life. In the Talmud (*Bava Metziah* 85a) is the account of Rabbi Yehudah HaNasi (the editor of the Mishnah), who was punished by heaven for thirteen years for his callousness when seeing the fear in the eyes of a calf bound for slaughter and saying, "For this you were created"; his bodily affliction only ended when he mercifully stopped his housecleaner from sweeping away a mice's nest.

[182] *Hasadecha* (חסדיך), "Your faithful of kindness" — the word *Hasid* means "faithful" or "follower" and may mean those who are kind. It is a word often identified with God's

relationship to the covenant. I combine the two meanings, faithful and kind, in the translation to convey both aspects of those highlighted in this interlude. The Talmud (*Yevamot* 64a) states that "the Holy One yearns for the prayers of the righteous."

[183] *Shulchan Arukh, Orach Hayim* 51:7

[184] *Olamim* may mean "worlds" or "times" and is the rare Aramaic word in Psalms. For other examples of Aramaic in scripture, see Daniel 3:33, 4:31.

[185] As to verse 20's expression "*Adonai* protects all those who love [God]," Radak (Rabbi David Kimche, France, 1160-1235) will say this verse shows that a relationship with God should be with love rather than with fear.

[186] Opening the hand palm upward began as a Sephardic custom (Mediterranean Jews) but is now broadly practiced in the Jewish community. The custom among Ashkenazic Jews (Germany/Eastern Europe) was to touch the hand tefillin when reciting the hand phrase and the head tefillin for the complementary clause.

[187] The concluding phrase of the psalm is "May all flesh bless [God's] holy name forever and ever." To which Rabbi Chaim Loew of sixteenth-century Germany commented, "I have but begun to praise."

[188] *Mishneh Torah, Berachot* 4b.

[189] The opening verses are "Happy are they who dwell in Your house; they shall praise You forever and ever" (Psalm 84:6) and "Happy is the people who are so favored; happy the people whose God is *Adonai* (Psalm 144:15). The first quote adds the context of communal worship and repeats the concluding phrase, "forever and ever." The second is the final line just before this psalm, conveying a summation of what came before as context to the praise that follows. Embedded in those two verses is the three-fold repetition of "happy," which is the basis for this prayer's name, the Ashrei. It is the same word that opens the book of Psalms. Praising God for the magnificence of God's works, especially ongoing caregiving, is now highlighted as an essential element of "happiness."

[At] the end of the psalm another verse was added, which will link Psalm 145 with the concluding psalms ahead: "We shall praise *Adonai* now and always. Halleluyah!" (Psalm 115:18). This closing quote moves the psalm to the communal "we" and culminates with the same word that will conclude the five psalms ahead. In the Babylonian Talmud, edited in Baghdad by 500 CE, the psalm is referred to by its first two Hebrew words, *Tehillah L'David*. The added verses and the subsequent naming as Ashrei only emerge with the first prayerbooks, composed by Sa'adya Gaon and Rav Amram Gaon in tenth-century Baghdad. These were two of the foremost leaders in the entire Jewish world and their emendations stuck.

[190] The Hatam Sofer [Moses Schreiber (Sofer)], (Frankfurt, 1762; Bratislava, 1839).

[191] There are many variations of this folk story, often attributed to the Ba'al Shem Tov as the featured rabbi. This telling is my own.

[192] *BT Berachot* 4b.

[193] Robert Alter, *The Book of Psalms: A Translation with Commentary* (New York: Norton, 2007), 500. An additional example of filling in the "nun" verse is found in an 18th/19th-century, Black Jews of Cochin, India manuscript of a text entitled *The Words of Gad the Seer*,

reading: "*Naflu*/All Your enemies fell down, O Lord, and all of their might was swallowed up." Scholars will differ regarding the dating of the content of this manuscript. See Meir Bar-Ilan, "The Date of the Words of Gad the Seer." *Journal of Biblical Literature* 109, no. 3 (1990): 475-492. https://doi.org/10.2307/3267053; Reuven Kimelman's lengthy essay on Psalm 145, "Ashrei — Psalm 145 and the Liturgy," https://www.researchgate.net/profile/Reuven-Kimelmn/publication/274107659_Psalm_145_Theme_Structure_and_Impact/links/584d97c908ae4bc899330ac0/Psalm-145-Theme-Structure-and-Impact.pdf (p.16); and note the Wikipedia essay on "Book of Gad the Seer" — https://en.wikipedia.org/wiki/Book_of_Gad_the_Seer.

[194] The Septuagint (second and third centuries, Greek), Vulgate (fourth century, Latin); Peshitta (fifth century, Aramaic).

[195] The verb form, perfect, also deviates from the psalm's consistent use of the imperfect.

[196] A letter is also missing from the acrostics of Psalms 25, 34, and 37. The nine acrostic psalms are 9, 10, 25, 34, 37, 111, 112, 119, and 145.

[197] This link is pointed out by Reuven Kimelman, "*Ashrei* — Psalm 145 and the Liturgy," https://www.researchgate.net/profile/Reuven-Kimelmn/publication/274107659_Psalm_145_Theme_Structure_and_Impact/links/584d97c908ae4bc899330ac0/Psalm-145-Theme-Structure-and-Impact.pdf, p. 24, citing fn. 129: *J. Ber.* 9:1, 12d, see *Midrash Rabbah* Psalms 16:8. *Siddur of R. Solomon ben Samson of Garmaise*, p. 57, suggests that the transition from direct to indirect speech of the benediction formulary derives from Psalm 145. The Talmud will counsel that a person should recite one hundred blessings a day (*Menachot 43b*), prompting with each an awareness of what might otherwise be overlooked. Maimonides will say, "Take care not to recite unnecessary blessings and make many necessary blessings as David said in Psalm 145:2." (*Mishneh Torah*, Hilchot Berachot 11:16).

[198] The Rabbis of the Talmud identified Psalm 145 as having a distinctive role in the Temple and placed it at the start of a group of psalms before the morning recitation of the Shema and as the sole psalm before the evening's chanting of the Shema. The Shema is a central prayer and focus of study as three paragraphs from the Torah that describe a covenantal relationship with God. The three blessing phrases of Psalm 145 also match up with the first six words of the Shema: Hear O Israel / Adonai our God / *Adonai* is one. As for the shifting from immanence to transcendence, Abraham Joshua Heschel wrote, "The dichotomy of transcendence and immanence is over simplification ... [for] God remains transcendent in His immanence, and related in His transcendence." Abraham J. Heschel, *The Prophets* (Philadelphia: Jewish Publication Society, 1962), 486.

[199] In its liturgical form, Psalm 145 begins with two psalm verses, 84:5 and 144:15.

[200] Taken from Psalm 115:18.

[201] This dot in the Hebrew letter *hey* is called a *mappiq*: a scribal notation to indicate that the final letter is to be pronounced as a consonant with the "hey" sound; in its absence the *hey* at the end of a word is silent.

[202] Rabbi Menachem Azaria Di-Fano (Mantua, Italy; 1548-1620), *Asaras Ma'amaros, Ma'mar Chikur Din* 4:11), cited in *The Kol Menachem Tehillim* (New York: Kol Menachem, 2013), 421.

Acknowledgements

Rabbi Elie Spitz

This book is the product of many steps, which began with my teaching each of the 150 psalms online during the height of the COVID quarantine. I want to thank my many students—some regulars and others occasional—who joined the class. Your presence motivated me to keep learning and teaching and deepened my love of psalms.

Many of the teachings included guests who joined me, whom I wish to thank: including Psalm 101 with Pulitzer Prize-winning composer David Lang, on his libretto and music commissioned by Lincoln Center; Psalm 137 with Rabbi Edward Feinstein on the honesty of psalms; and Psalm 150 with Jewish singer-composer Craig Taubman sharing an interfaith rendition. I also did summation interviews with two important writers on Psalms, Rabbis Benjamin Segal and Martin Cohen.

I want to thank Sue Riemer who suggested that her husband, Jack, and I should write this book together. And so, we began to write.

Among the readers who reacted to my unfolding essays were: Professor Julia Lupton, Cantor Shula Kalir Merton, Rabbi Alexis Pierce, Dr. Peter Pitzele, Rabbi Shalom Podwol, Joey Spitz, Dr. Linda Spitz, Erica Taylor, and Natalie Vishny.

Going from draft to manuscript was guided by my mentor Stuart Matlins, founding publisher of Jewish Lights Publishing, and content editor, Emily Wichland. Shira Dicker, publicist extraordinaire, helped in how to best present the manuscript.

We are so grateful to Larry Yudelson, publisher of Ben Yehuda Press, for his shepherding the manuscript into this book and to Laura Logan, for her skilled efforts as our copy editor.

Gratitude for contributions to the book's cover design to Dr. Peter Pitzele for the art of the lyre and for guidance to my graphic-artist nephew, Ethan Kaplan.

And I want to thank my *havrutah*, my partner, in the writing of this book: Rabbi Jack Riemer. Sharing this journey with you, Jack, has elevated and deepened my understandings. For decades I have admired your analysis of sacred text. Now, it is a great honor to have you as a friend and co-author on this writing that allows our voices to remain distinctive and to harmonize.

Together we thank Barbara Baim for her financial support of this project in memory of her husband, Joseph Baim. Joe, the son of a religious school director, was a successful lawyer who contributed generously to Jewish causes, particularly to advance Jewish education.

Rabbi Jack Riemer

I would also like to thank my teachers who have illuminated these psalms for me: Dr. Arthur Green, Rabbi Shai Held, Rabbi Abraham Joshua Heschel, Rabbi Joseph Schultz, Rabbi Benjamin Segal, Rabbi Meir Soloveichik.

About the Authors

Rabbi Jack Riemer is widely known as the "Rabbi's Rabbi of sermon-making" and in his mid-90s is still actively writing on the weekly Torah reading. He has taught sermon-seminars for rabbis across the country and composed prayers that appear in the prayer books of the Conservative, Reconstructionist, and Reform movements. He has published two collection of his favorite sermons: *Finding God in Unexpected Places: Wisdom for Everyone from the Jewish Tradition* and *The Day I Met My Father Isaac at the Supermarket: And Other Encounters with Biblical Tales* and three volumes of prayer introductions for High Holyday services. Among his other books are *Ethical Wills and How to Prepare Them: A Guide for Sharing Your Values from Generation to Generation* and *Wrestling with the Angel: Jewish Insights on Death and Mourning*.

Rabbi Elie Spitz served as the spiritual leader of Congregation B'nai Israel of Tustin, CA for over three decades and for two decades on the Conservative Movement's Committee of Jewish Law and Standard. He is the author of *Does the Soul Survive: A Jewish Journey to Belief in Afterlife, Past Lives*, and *Living with Purpose; Healing from Despair: Choosing Wholeness in a Broken World*; and *Increasing Wisdom and Guided Meditations to Strengthen and Calm Body, Heart, Mind and Spirit*. He has written many articles on Jewish spirituality and legal responsa on such topics as "Mamzerut: How to Respond to an Unconscionable Biblical Law" and "Computers and Privacy in the Workplace." His 30 minute video lessons on each of the 150 Psalms can be found at https://www.cbi18.org/a-psalm-a-day-archive/.

Reflections on the weekly Torah portion from *Ben Yehuda Press*

An Angel Called Truth and Other Tales from the Torah by Rabbi Jeremy Gordon and Emma Parlons. Funny, engaging micro-tales for each of the portions of the Torah and one for each of the Jewish festivals as well. These tales are told from the perspective of young people who feature in the Biblical narrative, young people who feature in classic Rabbinic commentary on our Biblical narratives and young people just made up for this book.

Torah & Company: The weekly portion of Torah, accompanied by generous helpings of Mishnah and Gemara, served with discussion questions to spice up your Sabbath Table by Rabbi Judith Z. Abrams. Serve up a rich feast of spiritual discussion from an age-old recipe: One part Torah. Two parts classic Jewish texts. Add conversation. Stir... and enjoy! "A valuable guide for the Shabbat table of every Jew."—Rabbi Burton L. Visotzky, author *Reading the Book*

Torah Journeys: The Inner Path to the Promised Land by Rabbi Shefa Gold shows us how to find blessing, challenge and the opportunity for spiritual transformation in each portion of Torah. An inspiring guide to exploring the landscape of Scripture... and recognizing that landscape as the story of your life. "Deep study and contemplation went into the writing of this work. Reading her Torah teachings one becomes attuned to the voice of the Shekhinah, the feminine aspect of God which brings needed healing to our wounded world." —Rabbib Zalman Schachter-Shalomi

American Torah Toons 2: Fifty-Four Illustrated Commentaries by Lawrence Bush. Deeply personal and provocative artworks responding to each weekly Torah portion. Each two-page spread includes a Torah passage, a paragraph of commentary from both traditional and modern Jewish sources, and a photo-collage that responds to the text with humor, ethical conscience, and both social and self awareness. "What a vexing, funny, offensive, insightful, infuriating, thought-provoking book." —Rabbi David Saperstein

The Comic Torah: Reimagining the Very Good Book. Stand-up comic Aaron Freeman and artist Sharon Rosenzweig reimagine the Torah with provocative humor and irreverent reverence in this hilarious, gorgeous, off-beat graphic version of the Bible's first five books! Each weekly portion gets a two-page spread. Like the original, the Comic Torah is not always suitable for children.

we who desire: poems and Torah riffs by Sue Swartz. From Genesis to Deuteronomy, from Bereshit to Zot Haberacha, from Eden to Gaza, from Eve to Emma Goldman, *we who desire* interweaves the mythic and the mundane as it follows the arc of the Torah with carefully chosen words, astute observations, and deep emotion. "Sue Swartz has used a brilliant, fortified, playful, serious, humanely furious moral imagination, and a poet's love of the music of language, to re-tell the saga of the Bible you thought you knew."
—Alicia Ostriker, author, *For the Love of God: The Bible as an Open Book*

Eternal Questions by Rabbi Josh Feigelson. These essays on the weekly Torah portion guide readers on a journey that weaves together Torah, Talmud, Hasidic masters, and a diverse array of writers, poets, musicians, and thinkers. Each essay includes questions for reflection and suggestions for practices to help turn study into more mindful, intentional living. "This is the wisdom that we always need—but maybe particularly now, more than ever, during these turbulent times." —Rabbi Danya Ruttenberg, author, *On Repentance and Repair*

Jewish spirituality and thought from *Ben Yehuda Press*

The Essential Writings of Abraham Isaac Kook. Translated and edited by Rabbi Ben Zion Bokser. This volume of letters, aphorisms and excerpts from essays and other writings provide a wide-ranging perspective on the thought and writing of Rav Kook. With most selections running two or three pages, readers gain a gentle introduction to one of the great Jewish thinkers of the modern era.

Ahron's Heart: Essential Prayers, Teachings and Letters of Ahrele Roth, a Hasidic Reformer. Translated and edited by by Rabbi Zalman Schachter-Shalomi and Rabbi Yair Hillel Goelman. For the first time, the writings of one of the 20th century's most important Hasidic thinkers are made available to a non-Hasidic English audience. Rabbi Ahron "Ahrele" Roth (1894-1944) has a great deal to say to sincere spiritual seekers far beyond his own community.

A Passionate Pacifist: Essential Writings of Aaron Samuel Tamares. Translated and edited by Rabbi Everett Gendler. Rabbi Aaron Samuel Tamares (1869-1931) addresses the timeless issues of ethics, morality, communal morale, and Judaism in relation to the world at large in these essays and sermons, written in Hebrew between 1904 and 1931. "For those who seek a Torah of compassion and pacifism, a Judaism not tied to 19th century political nationalism, and a vision of Jewish spirituality outside of political thinking this book will be essential." –Rabbi Dr. Alan Brill, author, *Thinking God: The Mysticism of Rabbi Zadok of Lublin*

Return to the Place: The Magic, Meditation, and Mystery of Sefer Yetzirah by Rabbi Jill Hammer. A translation of and commentary to an ancient Jewish mystical text that transforms it into a contemporary guide for meditative practice. "A tour de force—at once scholarly, whimsical, deeply poetic, and eminently accessible." —Rabbi Tirzah Firestone, author of *The Receiving: Reclaiming Jewish Women's Wisdom*

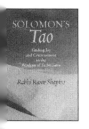

Enlightenment by Trial and Error: Ten Years on the Slippery Slopes of Jewish Mysticism, Postmodern Buddhist Meditation, and Heretical Flexidox Spirituality by Rabbi Jay Michaelson. A unique record of the 21st century spiritual search, from the perspective of someone who made plenty of mistakes along the way.

The Tao of Solomon: Finding Joy and Contentment in the Wisdom of Ecclesiastes by Rabbi Rami Shapiro. Rabbi Rami Shapiro unravels the golden philosophical threads of wisdom in the book of Ecclesiastes, reweaving the vibrant book of the Bible into a 21st century tapestry. Shapiro honors the roots of the ancient writing, explores the timeless truth that we are merely a drop in the endless river of time, and reveals a path to finding personal and spiritual fulfillment even as we embrace our impermanent place in the universe.

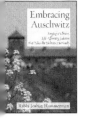

Embracing Auschwitz: Forging a Vibrant, Life-Affirming Judaism that Takes the Holocaust Seriously by Rabbi Joshua Hammerman.The Judaism of Sinai and the Judaism of Auschwitz are merging, resulting in new visions of Judaism that are only beginning to take shape. "Should be read by every Jew who cares about Judaism." — Rabbi Dr. Irving "Yitz" Greenberg

Recent books from *Ben Yehuda Press*

Judaism Disrupted: A Spiritual Manifesto for the 21st Century by Rabbi Michael Strassfeld. "I can't remember the last time I felt pulled to underline a book constantly as I was reading it, but *Judaism Disrupted* is exactly that intellectual, spiritual and personal adventure. You will find yourself nodding, wrestling, and hoping to hold on to so many of its ideas and challenges. Rabbi Strassfeld reframes a Torah that demands breakage, reimagination, and ownership." —Abigail Pogrebin, author, *My Jewish Year; 18 Holidays, One Wondering Jew*

The Way of Torah and the Path of Dharma: Intersections between Judaism and the Religions of India by Rabbi Daniel Polish. "A whirlwind religious tourist visit to the diversity of Indian religions: Sikh, Jain, Buddhist, and Hindu, led by an experienced congregational rabbi with much experience in interfaith and in teaching world religions." —Rabbi Alan Brill, author of *Rabbi on the Ganges: A Jewish Hindu-Encounter*

Liberating Your Passover Seder: An Anthology Beyond The Freedom Seder. Edited by Rabbi Arthur O. Waskow and Rabbi Phyllis O. Berman. This volume tells the history of the Freedom Seder and retells the origin of subsequent new haggadahs, including those focusing on Jewish-Palestinian reconciliation, environmental concerns, feminist and LGBT struggles, and the Covid-19 pandemic of 2020.

Duets on Psalms: Drawing New Meaning from Ancient Words by Rabbis Elie Spitz & Jack Riemer. "Two of Judaism's most inspirational teachers, offer a lifetime of insights on the Bible's most inspired book." — Rabbi Joseph Telushkin, author of *Jewish Literacy* "This illuminating work is a literary journey filled with faith, wisdom, hope, healing, meaning and inspiration." —Rabbi Naomi Levy, author of *Einstein and the Rabbi*

Weaving Prayer: An Analytical and Spiritual Commentary on the Jewish Prayer Book by Rabbi Jeffrey Hoffman. "This engaging and erudite volume transforms the prayer experience. Not only is it of considerable intellectual interest to learn the history of prayers—how, when, and why they were composed—but this new knowledge will significantly help a person pray with intention (kavvanah). I plan to keep this volume right next to my siddur." —Rabbi Judith Hauptman, author of *Rereading the Rabbis: A Woman's Voice*

Renew Our Hearts: A Siddur for Shabbat Day edited by Rabbi Rachel Barenblat. From the creator of *The Velveteen Rabbi's Haggadah*, a new siddur for the day of Shabbat. *Renew Our Hearts* balances tradition with innovation, featuring liturgy for morning (*Shacharit* and a renewing approach to *Musaf*), the afternoon (*Mincha*), and evening (*Ma'ariv* and *Havdalah*), along with curated works of poetry, art and new liturgies from across the breadth of Jewish spiritual life. Every word of Hebrew is paired with transliteration and with clear, pray-able English translation.

Forty Arguments for the Sake of Heaven: Why the Most Vital Controversies in Jewish Intellectual History Still Matter by Rabbi Shmuly Yanklowitz. Hillel vs. Shammai, Ayn Rand vs. Karl Marx, Tamar Ross vs. Judith Plaskow... but also Abraham vs. God, and God vs. the angels! Movements debate each other: Reform versus Orthodoxy, one- two- and zero-state solutions to the Israeli-Palestinian conflict, gun rights versus gun control in the United States. Rabbi Yanklowitz presents difficult and often heated disagreements with fairness and empathy, helping us consider our own truths in a pluralistic Jewish landscape.

Recent books from *Ben Yehuda Press*

Reaching for Comfort: What I Saw, What I Learned, and How I Blew it Training as a Pastoral Counselor by Sherri Mandell. In 2004, Sherri Mandell won the National Jewish Book award for *The Blessing of the Broken Heart*, which told of her grief and initial mourning after her 13-year-old son Koby was brutally murdered. Years later, with her pain still undiminished, Sherri trains to help others as a pioneering pastoral counselor in Israeli hospitals. "What a blessing to witness Mandell's and her patients' resilience!" —Rabbi Dayle Friedman, editor, *Jewish Pastoral Care: A Practical Guide from Traditional and Contemporary Sources*

Heroes with Chutzpah: 101 True Tales of Jewish Trailblazers, Changemakers & Rebels by Rabbi Deborah Bodin Cohen and Rabbi Kerry Olitzky. Readers ages 8 to 14 will meet Jewish changemakers from the recent past and present, who challenged the status quo in the arts, sciences, social justice, sports and politics, from David Ben-Gurion and Jonas Salk to Sarah Silverman and Douglas Emhoff. "Simply stunning. You would want this book on your coffee table, though the stories will take the express lane to your soul." —Rabbi Jeff Salkin

Just Jewish: How to Engage Millennials and Build a Vibrant Jewish Future by Rabbi Dan Horwitz. Drawing on his experience launching The Well, an inclusive Jewish community for young adults in Metro Detroit, Rabbi Horwitz shares proven techniques ready to be adopted by the Jewish world's myriad organizations, touching on everything from branding to fundraising to programmatic approaches to relationship development, and more. "This book will shape the conversation as to how we think about the Jewish future." —Rabbi Elliot Cosgrove, editor, *Jewish Theology in Our Time*.

Put Your Money Where Your Soul Is: Jewish Wisdom to Transform Your Investments for Good by Rabbi Jacob Siegel. "An intellectual delight. It offers a cornucopia of good ideas, institutions, and advisers. These can ease the transition for institutions and individuals from pure profit nature investing to deploying one's capital to repair the world, lift up the poor, and aid the needy and vulnerable. The sources alone – ranging from the Bible, Talmud, and codes to contemporary economics and sophisticated financial reporting – are worth the price of admission." – Rabbi Irving "Yitz" Greenberg

Why Israel (and its Future) Matters: Letters of a Liberal Rabbi to the Next Generation by Rabbi John Rosove. Presented in the form of a series of letters to his children, Rabbi Rosove makes the case for Israel — and for liberal American Jewish engagement with the Jewish statet. "A must-read!" —Isaac Herzog, President of Israel "This thoughtful and passionate book reminds us that commitment to Israel and to social justice are essential components of a healthy Jewish identity." —Yossi Klein Halevi, author, *Letters to My Palestinian Neighbor*

Other Covenants: Alternate Histories of the Jewish People by Rabbi Andrea D. Lobel & Mark Shainblum. In *Other Covenants*, you'll meet Israeli astronauts trying to save a doomed space shuttle, a Jewish community's faith challenged by the unstoppable return of their own undead, a Jewish science fiction writer in a world of Zeppelins and magic, an adult Anne Frank, an entire genre of Jewish martial arts movies, a Nazi dystopia where Judaism refuses to die, and many more. Nominated for two Sidewise Awards for Alternate History.

Made in United States
Troutdale, OR
12/07/2023

15453049R00144